SWIM
GINGER

One man's progress through changing times
1940 – 2005

Malcolm Deacon
Park Lane Publishing

First published in 2005 by
Park Lane Publishing
Wellstead Farm,
57, Green Street, Milton Malsor,
Northampton, NN7 3AT.

parklanepublishing.org
tel/fax (+44) 01604 858363

ISBN: 0-9523188-2-2

Printed in Great Britain by Antony Rowe Ltd., Chippenham, Wiltshire.

Acknowledgement is made to family members, and to Roger & Sonia Tame for
reading through the various drafts, proof reading, and making useful suggestions;
to Liquid Colour (Australia) for cover design idea and for SolveIT Computer
Solutions (UK) for technical assistance. Photographs p7 courtesy of John Douglas,
p34 Michael Tredgett, pp 79 & 86 Roger Tame and p199 Richard Jenks.

*To my family
and friends
past, present and to come,
and all those
who have helped to
nurture my mind and spirit.*

c1939. My father in holiday mood at Blackpool
not long before the outbreak of war.

CONTENTS

Preface

At one time I considered the writing of an autobiography an act of self-indulgent egotism, but as I have grown older realise that everyone has a story and needs to tell it. Over the years I have met many people who have had amazing adventures which remain untold; they pass away, their lives unrecorded; an immense loss to us all.

Perhaps I had something to tell, I thought, and was encouraged by family and friends. Once begun I found the task enlivening; looking back on the mistakes as well as the successes helps to get life into some perspective. Yet there was one overwhelming feeling that came from the exercise; I found it impossible to detach my experiences from the context of the times in which I have lived. Having been born at the beginning of the Second World War and deeply influenced by my parents and grandparents and others who had survived the First World War and the Great Depression I was struck by the profound changes that those of us who have lived into the 21st century have experienced. We are all caught up in the immense sweep of the human story and, whether we like it or not, our lives are influenced by events and developments mostly outside our control. Autobiography certainly has a role in the telling of social history from the personal point of view.

Early in my life I was thrown into a swimming pool and told to "s*wim, Ginger"*. It was a traumatic experience which with other "put downs" in my early life adversely affected my confidence. Thanks to the strength of a good home and the influence of gentle, caring Christian people I developed a determination to live life to the full and succeed against all difficulties. I did, eventually, learn to swim, so *Swim Ginger* is pre-eminently a motif for me of the humane side of life which, in spite of all the slings and arrows, remains cheerful and optimistic. This book is a dedication to all who have been encouragers to me. I hope it will make you reflect and also smile, and in so doing help you look at the present age of uncertainty with optimism and hope.

Malcolm Deacon   **Anno Domini 2005.**

1940, and the dark tides of war split many families.
My mother decamps with me to live with her in-laws.
My father goes off to war as the family home
is commandeered to accommodate
a family bombed out of Dover.

1940. My father leaves his wife, baby son, home
and job in the fight to preserve the nation.

Chapter One: War Baby.

During the sweltering summer of 1939 my parents to be, Bill and Betty, joined the heaving throngs on the pleasure beaches of Blackpool. Daily they claimed their deckchair spaces on the sands, slapped on sun oil and tried to forget the increasing alarm being felt as to the activities of Herr Hitler on the Continent. All these concerns seemed far away as they danced the foxtrot at the Tower Ballroom to the music of Reginald Dixon on the famous Wurlitzer organ. Arm in arm they returned to their modest hotel to find pleasure in each other.

It was during this holiday that I was conceived, and in the nine months or so following their Blackpool tryst much was to happen. Bill was to be conscripted into the army to fight in the war that had been declared on the 3rd September. Their newly purchased two-bedroom semi-detached house in Masefield Road in the Northamptonshire town of Kettering, was requisitioned for the use of an evacuee family from Dover. My pregnant mother had to decamp with her belongings to a Victorian terraced home a mile away. She philosophically surveyed the prospect of no husband to support her, the loss of her home, and life with her in-laws together with two evacuee boys from London.

I was thrust into the world on 9th April 1940, the day that the German armies were tramping over Denmark and invading Norway. My birth was long and difficult and, as I was in the wrong position for being born (technically a breach birth) my mother had a hard time of it. She later referred to the event in hushed tones declaring that the birth had been accompanied by instruments (forceps). For years I had the vague notion that some brass band had been present at this climactic event.

I first saw the light of day in the Newlyn Nursing Home, a large house being used as a maternity unit somewhere on the Rockingham Road. Mother soon returned with me to my grandparents' home in Wood Street and there we sheltered as best we could as the war intensified. It was a time of blackouts, tapes across the windows to prevent flying shards of glass, and the sound of sirens from time to time warning of the impending danger of bombing. Food was scarce and, although we did not realise it at the time, there was a period in the early years of the war when the U-boats were sinking so much allied shipping that the country had only three weeks supply of food left. I don't think I was a particularly robust child in my first year or so of life. When I was about five my mother was enraged at the suggestion by the clinic that I should wear irons on my legs to correct "knock knees"; she refused to co-operate thinking this a draconian measure and, I am glad to say, my legs grew normally.

My mother and me in 1940 at my grandparents' home.
In the background is an evacuee named Joey
who had escaped the bombing of London..

Wartime memories of an infant are necessarily vague but there are some which I vividly recall. One night, the familiar gut-wrenching sound of the siren had pulled us out of our sleep. We had retreated to the Anderson shelter in the garden, dug out by my father before he went off to join the Royal Artillery. We sat in the darkness as the dull sound of invisible enemy bombers growled overhead. After a while the all-clear sounded and we gladly hastened back to our beds. My grandfather carried me into the house but had to return in order to fetch several pillows and cushions from the shelter.

Stepping in he fell up to his neck in water for a main had burst somewhere along the street. We were lucky to get out when we did.

Such a story became part of family folk-lore as did the almost miraculous escape of Aunt Edith who had been bombed out of her house in Birmingham. Intrepid Aunt Edith had been blown clean through her front room window and into the street. She was fortunate enough to land in a bank of deep snow that broke her fall. Unhurt and undeterred she brushed herself down. Next day, when it was discovered that virtually every house, shop and church in the vicinity had been destroyed (apart from three public houses that were hardly scratched) she wryly commented that life was not that bad as one could still get a glass of stout.

On another occasion in these early years I lay listening to my own heartbeat in bed in the backroom of my grandparents' house. Suddenly a dark figure appeared at the window. The casement was slowly lifted and a soldier clambered through, scraping his boots on the sill and making enough noise to rouse the entire household. As I lay hardly daring to breathe candlelight flickered on the landing. It was my mother who had come to see what was happening. The soldier turned out to be my father who, reaching home on an un-expected forty-eight hour *pass*, had arrived in the dead of night. He had managed to get a lift on a lorry. He had no house key and, fearing to wake the neighbours, had borrowed the ladder kept in the communal entry between the houses. He had scaled the wall chancing upon my bedroom window.

This was the first time that I was conscious of knowing my father. It was a memorable occasion being cuddled by him in the middle of the night with my mother's excited face lit by a guttering candle. I smelled his uniform and felt its roughness, items which he would keep long after the war had finished and used until they were worn out. He would wear his army trousers with their wide white braces and his black army boots and thick khaki shirt when he sallied forth to tend his garden. They were to last him for more than forty years. A supreme example of spears turned into pruning hooks. During those dark war years my father's role in the Royal Artillery involved moving his ack ack unit from place to place. It was an attempt to fool the enemy into believing that Britain had more defences than in reality. He took part in defending Exeter and moved across the South coast and then to London to defend the capital during the Blitz. Although I was conscious of my father being far away and only seen a few times in my first five years I never doubted his love for my mother and myself. Every now and again the postman would bring a parcel which was a metal khaki painted rifle ammunition box wrapped in brown paper and tied with string. It was filled with straw and we scrabbled in it to find the bars of chocolate which he traded for his army cigarette ration. There were also seagull eggs lovingly packed and sent to supplement our meagre rations; the nearest to a fresh egg we could obtain was a sickly pale yellow powdered egg. The ammunition box travelled to and from the Pentland Firth and Scapa Flow where he was helping to defend this important part of the northern coastline. Also included were pieces of exquisite embroidery made by him during his off-duty hours. He also carved from driftwood models of contemporary British aircraft: the Lancaster and Halifax bombers, the Hurricane and Spitfire fighters. He sent a pack of playing cards that displayed allied and enemy aircraft, a device given to servicemen to assist aircraft recognition.

It was years later when I learned that he had been involved in the D Day landings riding the swell of the English Channel in a naval boat and guiding by radio the British and Commonwealth landing craft as they moved on Sword, Juno and Gold beaches. Towards this part of the war he had been assigned as a skilled radio operator to a joint army/naval group to provide vital wireless communication as the Allies made their move on the French coast. By 5 June 1944, the planned day of the attack, his ship had been in position for many hours awaiting in heavy seas the commencement of Operation Overlord. With a lightening of the weather on the 6th the order for the invasion was signalled. My father recalled the feeling of awe as the guns opened up with shells screaming overhead from the British fleet in the north and the answering German fire from the south. "We sat under this arc of fire coming from both directions", he said simply, "and just hoped we didn't get hit".

After the successful completion of the landings for the Battle of Normandy he returned to the army. In the following year my mother took me to Clacton in Essex where we stayed in a boarding house. I recall getting into an army truck with my mother and we sat alongside men in khaki who were in high good humour. We drove through the concrete tank traps and coils of barbed wire that blocked off every road from the seafront; the vehicle stopped in front of a battery of *ack ack* guns. There was my father who waved and came over to speak to us. Something was different; people were laughing and in excited mood. It was VE Day (8 May 1945) and upon the order to fire the guns blazed a crescendo of exultant flame and smoke into the sky and out to sea. The bystanders gasped and shouted as the brass shell cases came scorching from the gun breaches, too hot for the children to grab, as the black puffs of smoke over the North Sea signalled the end of the war. People's faces were lit with joyful triumph yet many wept with uncontrollable relief. The empty beaches with long coils of rusting barbed wire, the criss-cross of wooden defences against landing craft dug into the sand, and the concrete pillboxes with their tiny slits of windows are all part of that snapshot of childhood memory. Further down the coast, being broken up by the remorseless beat of the waves lay the wreck of a Junkers bomber, blown out of the sky, most likely I thought, by my Dad's guns. I wonder what happened to the crew.

It took a time for life to return to some sense of normality. War went on in the Far East until the dropping of the Atom bombs on Hiroshima and Nagasaki. In Europe there was the immediate clearing up of the mess, the freeing of the concentration camps and the rehabilitation of the millions of displaced people who had fled from the ravages of the conflict. How far a child knew at the time of the significance of events one cannot say but they are part of one's mental upbringing, and as the following years passed by the unfolding of the horrors of war were told in graphic and shocking detail.

My mother and I returned to my grandparents' home to await my father's homecoming. Grandfather gathered his information from the BBC *Home Service,* the *Daily Express,* the *News of the World* and the local *Evening Telegraph..* We kept a copy of a *Daily Mirror* front page, the headlines of which declared in capital letters: "Wanted Dead or Alive, Adolf Hitler, also known as Hidler, or Schnickelgruber." It told of his atrocities and the mass murder of millions. In a copy of the *News of the World* I remember being transfixed by the black and white photographs of the skeletal beings that had been incarcerated in the Nazi concentration camps. I learned for the first time about the plight of the Jews in Europe and wondered how anyone could hurt people like the pleasant Jewish family who ran a local corner shop.

In the outside toilet where we used torn squares of newspaper I considered it most appropriate to wipe my backside on a picture of Hitler whenever I could. He had taken away my father for the first five or six years of my life, but I was lucky as my father would be returning home. Several of my friends did not see their fathers again, and I was conscious in the following years of the emptiness that they felt. I had great empathy for one friend whose father had not returned from an RAF mission over Germany. He didn't talk about his loss but you could read it on his face, and in the obvious sorrow of his young widowed mother.

Such a social milieu had its effect upon me and everyone else. It dictated a way of thinking and behaving; our childhood games and activities reflected a militarised violent world. For years we would play war and lustily sing racist songs about the nation's erstwhile enemies. In hollow mockery of Walt Disney's *Snow White and the Seven Dwarfs* we heartily joined in the viciousness of:

> Heigh ho, heigh ho, it's off to war we go;
> To bomb the Japs, the dirty rats,
> Heigh ho, heigh ho, heigh ho.

In the early 1950's when my parents, very bravely, welcomed a German girl to our home to stay for a holiday I told my music teacher about our guest. Her face turned to a lurid purple, her eyes bulged and she let forth a tirade of invective against the Nazis. I found out later that it was suspected that her husband had been tortured and killed by the Gestapo. The pain of her loss was too hard to bear. She could not forgive. I was to learn many years later that the courageous German Christian pastor and theologian Dietrich Bonhoeffer, who had been involved in a plot to assassinate Hitler in an attempt to bring the war to an end, was hanged by the Gestapo on 9 April 1945; that was my fifth birthday.

Having had to spend his time by making himself useful in restoring a swimming pool in Colchester before he could be demobilised my father was suddenly home wearing his "civvy suit" and trilby hat. Like most men who had returned in one piece from the war he simply wanted to enjoy his own home and family, get back to his pre-war job and put behind him the wasted years.

It took several years to get access to our own house. When we were able to reoccupy it I recall the moment when the three of us unlocked the door and saw the shocking state the evacuee family had left it in. The wallpaper sagged from wall and ceiling, the kitchen was a filthy hovel and the garden had been used as a dumping ground for the ashes from the fire. My mother wept uncontrollably. However, they soon bustled about and worked hard at the restoration of their home. I recall helping to mix cement and laying out a new patio ready for the construction of a little conservatory. I was a bit too keen in tipping buckets of water into the mixture of sand and cement, but the sloppy screeding which resulted eventually hardened off. Dad was a very good decorator and soon had the place re-papered and painted.

I went with him to his decorator's shop where I turned the handle of the machine which trimmed off the edges of wallpaper rolls. The smell of size, paste, wallpaper and paint are all part of that rebirth of confidence following the dark, uncertain days of war. Paint was not in abundant supply in the late forties, and the range of colours was limited to black, grey, brown, green and *County cream*. There was a distinctive smelly distemper in various pallid pastel colours for painting the walls, and a chalky whitewash that I remember adorned the outside lavatory, and dark varnish which could be grained to enhance wood effects. Eventually, wallpapers became more colourful and by 1950 our house boasted walls adorned with luscious bunches of grapes, roses and even Elizabethan galleons in battle with the Spanish Armada. It was the age before the invention of brilliant white.

My home life was peaceful and loving. I was lucky. Some fathers had returned from the war to domestic life that proved far from paradise. Taught to kill or be killed and living in an environment of danger, coarseness and violence some men returned to find home life tame and trying. It was not uncommon for fathers to give their sons a beating with a belt for some misdemeanour; this was termed "giving some strap-oil", although happily the practice owed more to an earlier generation and was dying out. In fact, the war with its dividing of families had brought about a growing realisation of the value of children. Smaller families meant that instead of having to feed many hungry mouths parents could actually enjoy having fewer children and thus give them a better start in life.

Some men quickly discovered that their pre-war jobs were no longer theirs. In their absence others had stepped in to do the necessary work, notably women who had been liberated by the emergencies of the time. There was considerable feeling over some who had been exempted from military service because they were in "reserved occupations". It was a debateable issue when the sons of well-to-do manufacturers had continued making essential products for the nation, such as army boots, yet had increased their fortunes when the ordinary man had had to shoulder his kitbag and rifle and face an implacable enemy.

Some men returned to liberated wives who had "carried on" in their absence, particularly with the considerable numbers of American servicemen who, post Pearl Harbour, came to fight alongside us. It was common knowledge that one lady who lived along my grandparents' street "entertained" US servicemen. She had rather fetching silk underwear hanging on the washing line and she wore high-heeled shoes and black, seamed silk stockings; my mother spoke of her in caustic tones. When her husband returned in 1946 he found that she had decamped to Tennessee

In the immediate post-war years many US troops remained in the area. I remember contingents marching through the town, and roads that led from USAAF (United States Army Air Force) bases such as Molesworth and Chelveston were nicknamed "beer-can alleys" as the GI's habitually threw their empty beer cans into the hedges as they drove along. During the fifties many of them came to grief on the winding roads as their high-powered left-hand drive cars could not take the sharp and unexpected bends. One day, I was looking at a window display of model military tanks in a shop in Kettering High Street. "Hi Red," said a GI serviceman to me (referring to my ginger hair), "That's some tank there, the Sherman. That's a Yankie tank, Red, a Yankie tank. It won us the war". He proudly gave me some chewing gum, a rare treat, patted me on the head and swaggered off with his colleagues.

It was that casual bonhomie together with the smart uniforms made out of crease resistant material, the money, the access to luxuries such as chocolate and silk stockings that riled the ill-dressed, poorly paid British "Tommies" who saw them as great rivals for the girls. Local British girls had to resort to putting gravy browning on their legs to simulate stockings, drawing a seam using a black pencil. No wonder the adage became commonplace regarding the Americans that said: "They're over dressed, over sexed, overpaid and over here". Yet they were our comrades and without them the war would have had a different conclusion; they died in their thousands fighting with us

It was not just men coming home to wayward wives but husbands coming home to continue wartime habits that caused other tensions. I was conscious of several marital disputes (kids are very perceptive!) and one remarkable incident involved a neighbour. I listened to my parents' conversations and gathered that he had had quite a philandering war, and was evidently continuing it back in "civvy street". One night, sometime around midnight, he returned home and semi-inebriated crept noisily along the garden path thinking he was being discreet and quiet. His wife was waiting for him. We heard a loud clang as if he had been struck on the head by a frying pan or similar object, then a door slammed, and all went quiet. The next morning he was still lying semi-conscious on his doorstep. For a while we thought his wife had killed him, but he recovered and the whole matter was hushed up. I don't recall that he ever went "wenching" again.

17

In order to keep the country fed during the war years the population had been encouraged to "Dig for Victory". Gardens were turned over to the production of vegetables and fruit. Lawns were dug up and even the tops of Anderson shelters were covered with earth and used to grow tomatoes and the like. Many savoured the delights of allotments and kept them going long after the war had ended. My father had twenty poles of allotment and he took me with him on a little seat that he had bolted to the crossbar of his bicycle. I learned much about cabbages, onions, potatoes and Brussels sprouts, and the value of double digging and the necessity of bonfires.

All allotment holders had bonfires in those days, and my father was no exception. Ashes were always hot and ready to blaze up when the next lot of weeds were heaped upon them. Some time around 1950 he purchased a large piece of land which he bought at the pre-war price of £400. Situated close to his house this little empire superseded his allotment and became his pride and joy. It contained an orchard, a well and plenty of ground in which to grow enough vegetables to feed half the street. On this land he rejoiced in keeping a bonfire going day in and out. In the evening he would stoke it up so that it smouldered sullenly for hours until in the midst of the night it would burst forth with crackling flame so that neighbours would leap from their beds thinking an incendiary bomb had fallen.

Some had kept hens, ducks and geese to help the war effort. Several neighbours and friends clubbed together to keep a pig, feed it and share in the meat when it was slaughtered. The keeping of pigs fell foul of government regulations; to keep a pig one had to declare it to the Food Office and when it was slaughtered such honesty deprived the family of their bacon ration. I knew of several people who kept clandestine porkers. My aunt, for example, was a farmer's daughter and fed half a dozen pigs in a secret sty several fields away from the farmhouse. She would trudge across the fields with an old-fashioned yoke on her shoulders from which dangled two buckets of swill each balancing the other. She never grew more than five feet tall and always maintained that the chore of feeding the pigs and carrying such heavy loads had stunted her growth.

Gradually the realisation dawned that war was over, although for some it did not cease. One old friend, a Grenadier Guardsman who had been imprisoned by the Germans for most of the war would have, for the following fifty years, the same recurring nightmare: he was in a field full of human excrement and he could not find any way to escape.

It took time for general reconstruction and rehabilitation to come about, and for the easing of restrictions. Bread had been rationed towards the latter part of the war and was the first to be put off-ration in July 1948 followed by jam in the following December. The system of Points Coupons had been introduced in 1941 and all commodities ranging from food to fuel were strictly controlled; it was to take until May 1950 for this system to end. In 1948 the weekly allowance per person came to 13 ounces of meat, 1½ ounces of cheese, 6 ounces of butter or margarine, an ounce of cooking fat, 2 pints of milk, 8 ounces of sugar and one egg. A restaurant meal could consist of a maximum of three courses and did not have to cost more than five shillings. Few working people could afford such a luxury, although the more affluent found ways round this restriction. Likewise with rationed clothing the wealthier were able to provide a bit of extra colour. Tea was taken off–ration in October 1952 followed by cream in April 1953. My mother, however, kept her old ration book in a drawer just in case hard times returned.

Recycling is not a new idea as this was a practical necessity and was done in our own homes. Nothing was ever thrown away. Items like rubber bands, string, glass and wood were hoarded and used again and again long after their original use was forgotten. This led to a great deal of accumulated detritus being stored in drawers, boxes, attics and even under the bed. Not once did I ever catch my mother out when asked for any special item; she would search diligently for hours until she emerged triumphantly saying "I knew I had one somewhere". This affected the whole mentality of a generation and when my parents died I found stores of wartime blankets and other items tucked away in their house.

The big news for all children came in February 1953 when sweets were taken off-ration. There was a mad rush to get to the shops, endless queues and much disappointment when the first batches of sweets were rapidly sold out. A few years before this I tasted my first ice cream; it cost three pence, and it was a Walls vanilla. My grandmother, mother and I shared it on a blue saucer each taking a turn to have a spoonful; I had the privilege of licking every scrap off the wrapping paper. My mother queued for hours at the corner greengrocer's shop to buy the first bananas to reach us after the end of the war. She brought one home triumphantly and I, ashamed to say, spat it out as I didn't like it!

Children's birthdays were always held in the home and reflected the general austerity of the period. Food became a little more plentiful; if there were trifles and jellies served at the table everyone first had to partially fill themselves up with slices of bread and butter. Usually one had a single present given, and the party proceeded with organised games such as musical chairs and pass the parcel. For such events everyone had to change into plimsolls and wear their best clothes, girls wearing dresses and the boys little suits and ties. It was a far cry from the ease and comfort of more modern clothes such as trainers, jeans and T shirts.

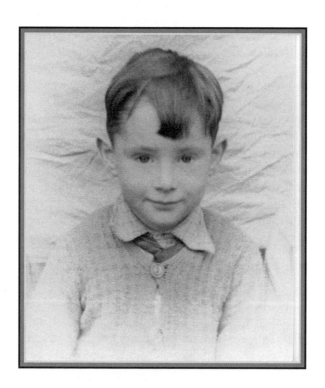

Chapter Two: Diverging Pathways.

At the age of five and a half in the September of 1945 my mother took me to the local Park Road Infant School. She recalled that after the first day at this late-Victorian red-brick establishment I said: "I am a big boy now and I would like to go to school on my own". I do not recall her taking me there after that. At least the school was at the end of the street and there was neither much traffic nor any fear of being molested by anyone. Mother would see me off at the front door and I would join the troupe of children making their way to the educational delights that awaited us.

I cannot remember much about the Infant School The headmistress was a formidable lady who insisted that we little ones should have a sleep on raffia mats on the floor of the hall every afternoon. She was typical of many female teachers in those days in remaining single as prior to the 1944 Education Act all women teachers who became married were forced to resign. It was not surprising, therefore, that all my primary school teachers were single women. The few men teachers we had were "Emergency Trained" coming from the armed services to fill the many vacancies following the war. Class sizes were well over forty. In 1946 equal pay with men was recommended for women teachers although it took until 1953 to be implemented.

Of course, I knew nothing of all these things at the time. I was more concerned with survival in the environment of the playground which has always been the great sorting place of childhood. There we learned who were the shy ones, the bullies and those who would play with you pleasantly. One afternoon, sometime in 1946, we children had something special to do, namely, to take forward the jar or tin that our mothers had given us to receive a present. Into each receptacle was spooned out chocolate powder, a gift from the people of Canada to all the children in the United Kingdom. We were told neither to lick it nor dip our fingers in it but to take it straight home to mother. I did so with great solemnity and enjoyed for the very first time a drink of hot chocolate.

At the age of seven I passed from the Infant School into the Junior School; although on the same site these two establishments existed in parallel universes. Once in the junior school we were

21

subjected to a regime that prepared us for the decisive *eleven-plus* examination. I can't say that I was a shiningly outstanding pupil and soon incurred the wrath of one teacher. I forget the misdemeanour but I was sent to stand in front of the headmaster who after lunch always sat at a desk in the school hall. As school reassembled for the afternoon session I stood politely in front of the headmaster. He was clearly intent upon reading some papers and after ten minutes had not moved a muscle. He was asleep. I stood for an hour and when the bell rang for playtime he gave a snort, opened his bloodshot eyes and told me to go away. I did as I was told and truthfully replied in the affirmative to my teacher's question as to whether the headmaster had seen me. In later years I learned that he used to enjoy a liquid lunch at a local hostelry and would sleep it off in the first hour of the afternoon pretending to be working at his desk.

Some of my teachers were lovely people. I fell in love with my first Junior School teacher and would have risked life and limb for her. Another was very kind man who picked me up from the cloakroom floor when I had had my nose bloodied. I never forgot him and was privileged to work as his deputy in later years. His name was Jack Ward: he had been a Major in the Kings Own Africa Rifles and had come into teaching. One day, he said, he was having a bath out in the African bush when his "boy" shouted to him to run. He leaped out of his canvas bath just in time as an army of giant soldier ants descended on the camp eating everything in its way, including the bath.

The Junior School headmaster was clearly worn out, and soon retired. He was followed by a younger man who seemed interested in the welfare of children. I quite liked him, and after thirty years in teaching myself can look back upon this period with an experienced eye. He clearly had his work cut out with some of the formidable figures who made up his staff, some ill-disposed to change, and to children. He had the task of implementing the ground-breaking 1944 Education Act. It could have been a year or so after I had left the Junior School when one evening as I was walking home I was joined by the headmaster. He spoke to me with great kindness and wistfulness. He lived near the school and I wished him goodnight as we parted at his gate. News percolated through the next morning that he had not appeared at school, and it was announced later that he was dead. He had committed suicide that

22

night. I had been possibly the last person outside his family to speak to him. I was stunned, and have often wondered whether it was the job or other reasons that had led him to such an awesome decision.

Children, however, do not dwell on the mysteries of the adult world for too long. Life is for the taking and there is much to get on with. There are games to play and in the local park after school huge crowds of children would congregate. I always wondered why so many boys gathered around the swings until I realised that they were all admiring the white knickers of a girl who, knowingly or not, did a daily cabaret for them as she swung to and fro.

Wartime memories were everywhere. In the street outside my grandparents' house stood a brick air-raid shelter that was eventually demolished. Nearby, during the war years, galvanised iron bins had been placed to take any food scraps which were then fed to the pigs. It was part of the "war effort". One of my friends took me into his father's study and opened the drawer of his desk. In it there was his father's service revolver, and it was loaded. For a money box I had a former Mills bomb, hand grenade, which had been hollowed out and a slit cut into its side. One elderly neighbour would knock his pipe out on an artillery shell which he kept in the fireplace until it was realised that it was still live.

All the iron railings around the park had been cut down to provide metal for "munition" manufacture. There remained for a time a static water tank that had been built as a resource in case of incendiary fires. Nearby were the air-raid shelters whose interiors were approached down a brick ramp. I recall seeing one of my friends doubled up with pain at the mouth of one of these evil smelling, underground bunkers. He had had to relieve himself and in the faeces that he left were numerous white threadworms. Poor food, the results of wartime shortages and post-war austerity, had its effect on many children. Many were very thin, and one boy had had a tape worm over thirty inches long taken out of him. For a time I suffered from boils and had a tooth extracted one Christmas Eve to release the huge abscess that had formed underneath it. After my doctor injected me with penicillin my health improved.

Back in school all was rigid and unyielding. Classes of nearly fifty children would sit in rows of twin-seated iron framed desks arranged on tiered flooring so that the brightest sat close to the teacher and the dimmest furthest away. One morning my friend

"Wagger" had been to the corner sweet shop and had bought several frozen lollies wrapped in metal foil. The bell had rung before he could eat them so he brought them into school and stowed them away in his desk. Over the next hour or so they dripped steadily onto the floor. He was quite a popular character for his family was the first in the area to obtain a television set. I remember seeing my first television pictures, in black and white, of Jack Hulbert with Cecily Courtnedge trying on hats in a milliner's shop. There must have been twenty children packed into his parents' front room. This would have been about 1950. At that time the BBC only provided television for a couple of hours in the afternoons for housewives. There was no television in the mornings or when children came home from school as that was considered the time to do homework and for mothers to cook the family meal. This was called the Toddlers Truce. Evening programmes began around seven-thirty, the announcers both men and women wearing evening dress. At the conclusion of the programmes at eleven o'clock the picture of the clock face of Big Ben was shown as a time check prior to the playing of the National Anthem and close down.

There was always the radio to listen to. Much of the music of the era was carefully aimed at children, a practice which declined after the sixties; sadly, modern children have to listen to music that is basically composed for adults. There were many musical gems broadcast on Saturday mornings by Derek McCulloch (Uncle Mac) such as *The Runaway Train, Sparky's Magic Piano,* Arthur Askey's *Bee Song* and the *Three Little Fishes* that "swam and swam right over the dam". Uncle Mac's Children's Hour on the BBC Home Service during the week attracted a large children's audience. There were the stories of *Larry the Lamb,* of *Norman and Henry Bones the Boy Detectives,* Noel Streatfield's evocative *Ballet Shoes* that told how poor yet talented children achieved their ambitions, and the exploits of *Jennings and Derbyshire* at their middle class public school. In the evenings there was *Dick Barton, Special Agent* which was discontinued in favour of a new everyday story of country folk called *The Archers.* I originally hoped that this would be stories about Robin Hood.

As I came to the end of my Junior School years I began to realise that life in school was far from fair. The school was segregated on academic lines with streams of A, B and C classes.

24

Although reasonably bright I was ascribed to a "B" class and managing to remain at the top of that class, nevertheless, missed out on the extras which only the A stream enjoyed. They had the opportunity to sing in the school choir, act in plays, take part in sports and do a number of things denied the rest of the school. The sheer injustice of this came home to me when I realised that I had taken the eleven-plus examination without knowing it whereas the "A" class had been mercilessly crammed for the previous year.

Back in 1943 the Norwood Report had been published as an attempt to put social theory into educational practice. The Education Act of the following year, a great landmark in educational development, owed much to Norwood's ideas that there were three types of mind. Firstly, there was the child who was "interested in learning for its own sake", secondly, a technical child who had "an uncanny insight into the intricacies of mechanism" and finally, the child who could "deal more easily with concrete things rather than ideas". The educational system was built up on this tripartite assumption: the minority brightest would go to the Grammar Schools and bulk of the population, the hewers of wood and drawers of water, would go to the Secondary Modern Schools. As I had passed the eleven-plus examination but was considered a borderline candidate for the grammar school I fell between the two extremes so was considered to have "an uncanny insight into the intricacies of mechanism" so was sent to one of the specially established Central Schools.

What a vivid memory I have of those last days of junior school when we parted company from those who had been our school mates for up to seven years. There was a sense in which we were all going our different ways, to different social strata, to different opportunities and different lives. We were part of a society that divided its children at a tender age and we were set upon paths not of our choosing. One classmate who had failed the eleven-plus bitterly remarked that we would not meet again on friendly terms. His gloom and sense of failure contrasted with the cocky celebration of those who had succeeded and who saw life in a rosier prospect. Our subsequent school uniforms would demarcate our differences. Many years later I met up with an old classmate who had struggled to learn to read. He was wearing a smart suit and sitting in an expensive car; in spite of never being a good reader he had started his own business and had succeeded. He was a pillar of his community and a lovely family man. We shook hands warmly and I went home greatly cheered.

Together with one girl from my Junior School class I was the only other person from my school to go to the Central School. I duly reported there in the September of 1951 complete with new leather satchel, pencil box and crisp new uniform which included a cap. I didn't return home in the same tidy condition as new boys' caps seemed to end up being thrown onto roofs or used for football practice. There were very big boys in that school and some were prefects who told you what to do. Nevertheless, unlike the monastic seclusion of all the other secondary schools there were girls to grow up with, although they had their own playground.

Within the school there were vocational courses such as carpentry, plumbing and brickwork for the boys, and shorthand and typing for the girls. There was some interchange and I remember having some typing lessons as well as one lesson in making cakes. During the lunch breaks volunteers were recruited from time to time to unload a lorry of bricks. As several bricks at a time were hurled from hand to hand from lorry to stack you had to be careful not to bend down to pick up a dropped catch as the next load would smack you on the head.

Here we met the world of work with some of the teachers being skilled tradesmen themselves. It was of no use any boy asking to be excused to go to the toilet during a lesson as the reply would be to "tie a knot in it". One enthusiastic plumbing teacher gave lessons on how to wipe a lead joint with real moleskin. Whilst I studied the main academic curriculum I was fascinated by the school's vocational side and opted in to a number of practical lessons. At the age of eleven we were afflicted by a carpentry teacher who was a terrifying personage. If you were a fraction of an inch out in your work he would ceremoniously chop up your wood with a silver axe. My first project was made out of a delightful pinkish timber called Parana Pine. What a pity it was a pipe rack given lovingly to my father who never smoked in his life. It ended up in the garden shed and for years was home to a set of screwdrivers until it was commandeered by a family of robins who successfully hatched out several broods of fledglings.

The science laboratories were approached with a certain amount of trepidation as here dwelt the fearsome science master. A tiny man physically he held everyone in awe. He was a brilliant teacher who certainly knew his subject and encouraged me to enter the National Bird and Tree Competition which involved observing and recording the life of one bird and one tree over the period of a year. I won a medal for my efforts. His method of inculcating discipline with the unruly and lazy was to administer a whack on a boy's backside with the wooden side of a blackboard rubber. It was also rumoured that he might put you in the fume cupboard where a Kipp's apparatus bubbled away making noxious smells. On one occasion the sheer force of his right arm sent a boy powering across the laboratory in a cloud of chalk dust right into the stomach of the headmaster who had just entered the room. Both ended up in a heap on the floor. It was undoubtedly a matter of some pride to have weathered the blackboard rubber and lived to tell the tale.

In that first year of secondary education my class teacher was a young history graduate who awakened my interest in the past by presenting lessons on the Glastonbury Lake Village. She suggested we might make a model village using sticks and clay. Being something of a wanderer I knew where we could get some clay in one of the ironstone quarries on the edge of the town. So after school at 4pm one sunny late September afternoon several of us lads set off on our bikes with our teacher. In those days we would think nothing of cycling many miles. Our poor "Miss" struggled to keep up with us on the ten mile round trip. We hadn't warned her that the clay was situated at the bottom of a thirty-foot cliff and that we had to approach the quarry across fields, hedges, barbed wire and be on the look-out as we were trespassing. She must have regretted her rashness in coming with us, but we returned with saddlebags full of thick grey clay and subsequently made a superb model.

Ever grateful to my teacher, at the end of that first year, I thought I would send her a present. I thought an appropriate gift would be a pair of pigeon's wings as she had sparked an interest in many things. In those times pigeon, rabbit and pheasant were delicacies often enjoyed by my family. Although we lived in town we were close to the rural scene. On one occasion I had shared a hedgehog stew with a friendly Romany gypsy who regularly parked his traditional caravan along a local lane. So I thought that a pair of

27

beautiful pigeon wings showing nature's grace and complexity was a touching gift to a wonderful teacher. I duly packed them in a box and posted them off to her home address that I had inveigled out of the school secretary. When the next academic year started after the school holidays my former teacher took me aside to thank me for the present. Unfortunately, she had been away from home for the duration of the summer and I had not sufficiently salted the wing joints. When she opened the parcel it was full of maggots which she had given to a local fisherman friend. However, she said she appreciated the gesture.

It was during this time that the school introduced us to the municipal baths in an attempt to teach us to swim. After a walk across town we entered the cold, bleak environment of the Baths. On either side of the water was a row of changing cubicles, one side for the girls, the other for the boys. Above were the galleries for spectators and at the nearest end to the door, the deep end, were the diving boards. At the far end was a slipper bath flanked by the toilets whose sopping wet floors mingled with the cold clammy tiles of the bath surrounds. The whole building was a chlorine smelling, echoing cavern and became for me a place of dread. An instructor virtually threw me into the water, laid hold of me and put a rough belt around my middle and hauled me through the water urging me to "swim, Ginger".

I was terrified, and the fear lasted until I was nineteen when with other friends who had been similarly put-off swimming we decided to go to the baths together every day until we could swim. We succeeded. *Swim Ginger* became for me a motif for a personal determination to battle against the arrogant and insensitive. In an almost identical replication of the incident when I was a young teacher one of my pupils was thrown into a swimming pool by a domineering instructor; the child promptly had an epileptic fit and I had to jump in to save him. Needless to say I made very strong representations on the matter.

When universal education was made compulsory in 1870 many parents protested that they would lose the vital income which their children brought in. Over the years leeway was given for children particularly in rural areas to have some days off to help bring in the harvest. There were other needs as in the 1914-18 war when children picked blackberries for the making of jam for the army and navy. There was a vestige of this tradition in my childhood and children could spend days picking rose hips.

I was twelve years old when the opportunity came to help bring in the potato harvest as there was a shortage of agricultural labour. We were given a week off school so a number of us reported for work early in the morning at a farm near Rothwell. It was a blissful September morning with mist evaporating as the sun rose in a cloudless sky. We were each given a bucket to collect the potatoes flung by the horse-drawn machinery from the rows. We were to be paid by the bucketful. The first sight of two beautiful heavy horses pulling *the spinner* up the slope evoked a time-honoured idyll of rural life. As the horses drew alongside us they broke wind in time with their hoof beats creating a smell that made our eyes water. The farmer hooted with laughter at our discomfiture. After this experience we were sure to steer clear when the horses came up the slope on their first morning run, as horses are creatures of regularity.

In December 1952 London experienced the Great Smog. For five days the air was filled with particles of soot and sulphur dioxide, the result of the burning of coal as well as atmospheric conditions at the time. Four thousand people died from respiratory failure. Similar problems were experienced in other towns and cities, and it was about this time that a terrible "pea souper" descended upon Kettering. We were in class when our Mathematics master nearly choked to death on the evil yellowish smog that enveloped the town. It was not possible to see your own hand in front of your face. The school was situated half way down a slope and, as we were sent home at lunchtime, I recall walking uphill and out of the choking cloud into brilliant sunlight. Looking back I could see houses, shops and the school appearing to be sinking in a swirling sea of thick yellow ooze into which smoke from many chimneys poured their effluence. In 1956 the government brought in the first *Clean Air Act* although pollution-induced smogs were still a feature until the early sixties.

c 1915
My paternal great grand-parents sit in their back garden surrounded by their ten children.
My grandmother is extreme left, middle row.
Many families took the opportunity of being photographed together especially during
the First World War as there was a high chance that the sons would be killed.

Chapter Three: Freedom to Roam.

During my childhood contemporary children's fictional characters such as Richmal Crompton's *William Brown* and Enid Blyton's *Famous Five* together with *Rupert*, the creation of the *Daily Express,* shared a freedom to roam wherever they liked. Rupert, for example, could go off to the North Pole with a snowman for sundry adventures; his mother did not turn a hair as long as he returned home in time for tea. The Famous Five would trot off with a horse and a caravan across the countryside, unaccompanied by adults and lacking any sense of danger, solving mysteries and catching unsavoury criminals. William Brown lived a very full anarchic life outside his home and away from his family who neither cared nor understood him and were only too pleased to see him in bed or out of sight.

Children of my generation identified with such freedom, and the sense of security once the war had finished led parents into a relaxed view of children's play and explorations. From a young age I was free to roam, to go to the park or play in the local woods and fields that lay on the edge of town. The rules were simple and demanded that you came home on time and reasonably clean. I was always on time for my meals but often returned looking, as my mother often remarked, "as if you have been drawn through a hedge backwards".

I wonder how far parents realised the escapades that such freedom led us into. There was one occasion when a dozen or so of our gang decided to split into two groups, one going off to the local disused quarry in order to ambush the others who would follow fifteen minutes later. According to plan the two groups set off at differing times and, sure enough, a vigorous hand-to-hand battle was fought out amidst the trees, hills and hollows of the quarry side until it spilled out into the quarry floor nicknamed "the Valley of the Yellow River". Across the rocks and boulders we scrambled until a cry was heard from one of our friends. He had gone up to his middle in heaving yellow mud and was being steadily sucked under. Immediately war was suspended as branches were thrown for him to grasp. One of the lads ran off to get help and returned with two men and a ladder; they pulled the boy out by his hair, just in time as the mud had reached his chin.

Such dangers were seen as part of growing up, and the more dangerous the better it appeared to some of us. In and around the local area were various railway tracks and furnaces all connected with the ironstone industry. There was a local blast furnace whose two tall chimneys belched forth grey smoke. Around it lay heaps of slag and there was a narrow gauge railway on which were placed light trucks used for moving ore or pig iron. This scenario was a great fascination to boys who would sledge down the slag heaps using railway sleepers or ride on the trucks until their clanking warned the foreman there were children messing about.

Of immense danger was the actual moment when the quarrymen would set off dynamite to blast the ironstone substratum that had been exposed by the huge mechanical excavators. Once blasted, smaller excavators would load the iron ore into trucks to be transported to the great Stewarts & Lloyds steelworks at Corby. At night great glows of orange flame could be seen in the sky as the furnaces were charged. Day and night waste gas from the processing was burned off from the famous *Corby Candle*. We boys would approach the quarry edge under cover of the wood through which the pit had been gouged. We would watch the preparations for blasting from the quarry edge. Men would drill the ironstone stratum at regular intervals, fill the holes with explosives then after the sound of a siren and the waving of a red flag the whole earth would shake in a series of smoky rumbling convulsions. Stones would rattle around us, but what a thrill!

Across the central and south-east part of England during the early years of the war some five hundred airfields had been constructed. Within cycling distance from my home were a number of former wartime airfields; wonderful places to explore. One such was Harrington from whence, as I learned in later life, a major undercover operation was launched by the American Office of Strategic Services and the British Special Operations Executive in 1944 -5. Part of the Bedford Triangle of secret bases Harrington saw many B24 Liberator bombers take off to parachute teams of Carpetbagger agents into enemy occupied Europe.

Around 1949 as adventurous boys a group of us cycled across the deserted airfield to the control tower. My friends and I clambered up the outside iron steps to the control room, eerily empty with the floor littered with papers. The chalk board on the wall still denoted the last flights that had been made from the airfield which had been quickly abandoned once the war had finished. I picked up a microphone from the remnants of a pilot's helmet which lay in the dust. I did not know then that from this very base on 4 February 1945 the British Prime Minister, Winston Churchill, set off in a Liberator for the historic Yalta Conference in which he, American President Franklin D. Roosevelt and Marshal Stalin shaped the post-war world. Along the main runway in later years my father was to give me my first lessons in driving his car.

My life in these years was balanced between town and country. Most Saturday afternoons, whilst my father went to a football match or tended his garden, my mother took me to see my other grandmother in the village of Walgrave six miles away. She was not able to drive in those days so we would travel by green United Counties bus. The village was another world, rural and quiet, where I met my grandmother, cousins and other relatives. Mother had been one of a family of eight and, as with many families, one child, a brother, had died in infancy. My maternal grandfather had been a skilled hand-sewn cobbler but through necessity became a labourer working on the ironstone quarries at Scaldwell. He would cycle to work each way to do a hard shift, wheel-barrowing ironstone across rough wooden trestles that spanned the quarry. The quarry was the starting point of a unique overhead cable system which took ironstone across the Northamptonshire fields. Grandfather clearly helped in feeding one of the many bucket chains which silently whisked tons of ore to local railheads en route to various steel works. After work he would return home and then, in season, tend his garden and allotment in order to feed the family. He always started the day at four o'clock in the morning.

Grandfather also kept a pig in a sty at the bottom of the garden. When the time was right for it to be slaughtered he would slit its throat; the animal would wander the garden until it dropped, the blood providing fertiliser for the ground. I recall the sides of bacon hanging from hooks in the kitchen, the taste of home-cured gammon, the crispy crackling and the smell of chitterlings frying on the stove. The family diet was supplemented by wild rabbit which grandmother would skin and gut in the kitchen. The occasional pheasant or even wood pigeon found their way into her stew pot.

33

My maternal grandfather Edgar Walden tends his onions.

Grandmother made potato whisky in a large bowl in the washroom. When I was nine or ten my cousin and I had a cupful of this deadly beverage one Saturday afternoon. We were just recovered enough to return to school the following Monday, although my legs felt like jelly for the rest of the week. Grandfather Walden died suddenly, having walked with the side of a pig on his shoulder to a relative's house; he collapsed and died of a heart attack on the doorstep. My mother did her best to support grandmother after this tragedy, especially as grandmother still looked after a disabled grown-up son. I remember him, my Uncle Arthur, sitting in his chair, smoking a pipe, waiting for the football results to start on the wireless. In the gloom of a late winter afternoon with his pipe smoke wreathed round his head by the sole feeble light of the wireless he would mark his Vernons Pools coupon and dream of a better life freed from the restrictions of a paralysed body.

It was all very sad, especially as his paralysis had come about following an accident; some say he had fallen out of a tree, others that he had been kicked by a horse. He had been taken to hospital where he had been immersed in a bath of cold water, a favoured treatment at that time. Arthritis had set in followed by paralysis from the waist downwards. After my grandmother's death

Uncle Arthur went into a Cheshire Home where he was happily settled. He would come to our house for holidays, driving along the roads in a blue invalid carriage powered by a sputtering two-stroke engine; he often went missing sometimes ending up in the ditch.

Those Saturday afternoons nourished my sense of freedom and exploration. Together with my cousin Michael, who lived next door to my grandmother, and other friends we roamed far and wide, climbed the elm trees at the edge of the village and thought we could outsmart the village constable who was sharp-eyed and cleverer than we thought. Haystacks were wonderful places to play. Our constable would make a show of riding out of the village on his bicycle evidently intent on seeing that his other villages were law-abiding and tranquil. Thinking that the coast was clear we boys would continue playing on the stacks but were surprised when our policeman reappeared, tweaked our ears and sent us packing. It was good humoured yet effective. We went and played elsewhere.

Playing elsewhere had its traumas. I remember playing the autumn game of "whooming". It must be called by other names in different places but whooming is the art of piercing a fallen apple from the orchard on a stick and flicking it so that the apple whooms away at great speed. Apples nearing a state of rottenness would make exquisite squelching sounds when they landed. There are obvious hazards to such a game. Little did we imagine one day that whooming was to get so complicated. I let fly a particularly fine Codling apple that transcribed a spectacular trajectory across my grandmother's garden straight into her neighbour's. It was unfortunate that the apple had taken the stick with it and that both had landed amongst the neighbour's washing.

Of great consternation was that the stick had lodged itself in the leg of a pair of large ladies' long-legged directoire knickers that fluttered in the breeze on the clothes line. Waiting for darkness to fall my cousin and I crept cautiously to the washing line and proceeded to try to release the lodged missile. Our poking with a stick only made matters worse, creating muddy marks and holes and succeeding in lodging the obstruction ever more firmly. We abandoned all attempts and I was relieved to escape on the bus leaving my cousin to face the music. Yet nothing was said. Perhaps the neighbour didn't notice.

My cousin's dog, Peter, was a remarkable creature. He was an ABC dog, "All Bits Combined", having a strong touch of Airedale in him. His instinct proved infallible; he knew if my mother and I were coming on the bus, or not. My relatives would watch his behaviour for just before two o'clock when the bus was due to arrive he would saunter to the bus stop and wait. If we were not on board he knew not to bother. It was uncanny.

In those days of the late 1940's and early fifties the street lights in the village were still lit by gas. I recall darkening afternoons with the light gradually coming on as the lamp man did his rounds ensuring the mantles were lit. The village nourished in me a sense of family origins as both my parents' families came from the same place. There were the stories of village characters: the farmers, the owners of the shoe factory, the leaders of church and chapel, and the schoolmaster. There were the family stories, intrigues and scandals that gave rise to the local phrase which made reference to some loose or mysterious relationship as "our cat ran up your entry". One such story I was able to investigate more than fifty years later. A relative had mysteriously died whilst coming back from a dance in another local village. It was during the war and she was walking home during the blackout. A cyclist had run into her and she had been left fatally injured. Her brother, my uncle Fred, had been away on active service at the time and for years had the suspicion that she had been assaulted and murdered. I was able to approach the police who opened up the files and we were assured that it had been an accident.

Economic necessity led many to leave the village. My paternal grandparents moved to the nearest town, Kettering, to find employment. Moving six miles was a long way to them, and they would return frequently to the village usually on foot to see relatives or have a holiday. My grandmother had originated from Thorpe Malsor, a village close by, yet in those days anyone from beyond the village confines was like a foreigner. My own parents would stay all their adult lives in Kettering whilst I gravitated to the county town twenty miles away. When my wife and I moved house to Northampton in 1972 my mother thought we had gone to another planet. She did not live to see our son living on the other side of the world in Australia. This epitomises the widening of experience and global awareness which came about during the latter half of the twentieth century.

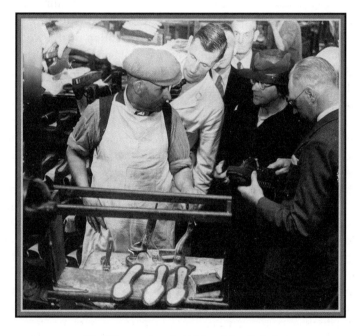

"Pop" Deacon at work at his bench in a Kettering
shoe factory with the foreman and some VIPs.

My paternal grandfather, "Pop", was born in the village of Walgrave in 1889 and received an elementary education in the National School. Leaving at the age of twelve he entered the local trade of shoemaking and learned the art of hand-sewing. At that time much hand-sewn work was done in the sheds, or "shops", at the bottom of cottage gardens; the finished work was then taken to the factory for finishing. Village life had a vigorous social side centred upon church and chapel and public house. Boys from church or chapel created rival gangs who wrestled each other on the village green. When there was no work a pint or two in the public house and a sprawl on the grass was the usual way to relax. It was during this period of his teens that grandfather met with an accident. Whilst stitching a shoe "upper" his needle-like awl slipped and penetrated his eye. It took several hours by horse and cart to get him to Northampton General Hospital. By the time he had arrived the sight of his eye was lost, yet strangely it was almost certainly to save his life.

With the outbreak of war there was great pressure for men to enlist. Many saw it as a way of seeing something of the world; the first time to leave the confines of the village. The government's poster campaign with General Kitchener declaiming "Your Country Needs You" led to a recruiting surge. My grandfather duly reported to the enlisting office but was told that having no right eye made him incapable of sighting a rifle. He was of no use to the army but could produce boots instead. More than four decades later, in 1958, I drove him back to the village where he soberly pointed out the war memorial on which are inscribed the names of all his friends who perished in the Great War. He was the only one who survived.

Grandfather's glass eye played quite a significant part in my early childhood. In the years when my mother and I lived with my grandparents in Kettering as he washed himself at the kitchen sink his glass eye would sit on the windowsill balefully looking at me. "I've got my eye on you", he would remark; I believed him. Even when he went to sleep in his chair by the fireside his right eye was still open so there was no way of telling whether he was awake or not.

Next door to my grandparents' terraced house lived an elderly couple whose spinster daughter cared for them. She spent all her working life in the shoe factory earning sufficient to keep the family going. She was one of many thousands who had lost brothers, husbands or sweethearts in the slaughter of the Great War. Her fiancé had been killed in the Battle of the Somme and she never recovered from her loss. Many women of that generation did not marry as so many young men had been wiped out. In many a family there was an unmarried daughter or maiden aunt reflecting the social devastation that war had brought.

1940 and the outbreak of another war.
My father and grandfather pose with me in the arms of
my great grandmother in New Row, Walgrave

Relieving the daily round and common task of life were the summer holidays. There would be the annual Factory Fortnight when most places of employment closed and the masses looked forward to sunshine and fresh air. In a time before widespread use of the motor car many would use the railways to get to the seaside. My father was unusual in that he had owned a car before the war and had kept it in "mothballs" until petrol became available again. It was a black Morris 8 which boasted chromium rimmed headlights and black rubber running boards. As part of the increased confidence of the late forties he traded it in for a Morris 10; this was upwardly mobile in social terms as few people owned a car in that part of town.

During the fifties we drove out on Sunday afternoons taking the grandparents for a ride in the country before coming home for tea. There was the annual autumnal trip to see farming cousins in Bedfordshire, spending a day on the farm amidst the cattle, sheep and poultry and the score of cats which swarmed about the yard and farmhouse. We would often return home in the growing dusk witnessing the wholesale straw burning in the fields that signalled the end of harvest and the coming of winter. The changing seasons and the tasks of the countryside were an important part of our heritage. Beautiful sunsets, changing cloud formations, the immense beauty of the stars all spoke of man's place in a cyclical and ordered universe.

Part of the regular cycle of events to which children looked forward was Bonfire Night on November 5th. From about 1950 my father allowed all my friends to build a massive bonfire in our large garden. There were always plenty of branches to burn. Dad would insist that he lit the fire, usually with a can of paraffin or even petrol, and as the flames and sparks rushed upwards into the dark sky we felt part of an age-old ritual that went back long before Guy Fawkes or the burning of bones in the Middle Ages, but to rituals of the ancient peoples who marked the disappearance of the sun and the coming of the winter solstice. Fireworks such as Roman Candles, Jumping Jacks, Catherine Wheels and bangers were very popular. The whole event finished indoors away from the damp coldness with hot drinks, baked potatoes and sausages.

Coal fires produced huge quantities of soot, and a regular visitor was the chimney sweep who would ask children to go outside the house to see if his brush was sticking out of the chimney pot. One day, on our next door neighbour's house some workmen were repairing the roof. At the same time the chimney sweep was at work inside. When his brush emerged from the chimney pot they quickly unscrewed it and hid it for a time behind the chimney stack. Much puzzled the sweep scanned the rooftop for the missing brush. The workmen had hidden themselves. After a while of much puzzlement the sweep re-emerged from the house to find the brush head mysteriously returned.

One of the hazards of coal fires was the frequency of the chimneys themselves catching fire. This happened one early evening in my home when a great fall of burning soot engulfed the carpet, setting it ablaze. I was only about eight years old at the time and was so terrified that I ran all the way to my grandparents' house. By the time they brought me home the fire brigade had been and doused the flames. Mats in front of the fire were often pitted with black burn marks where sparks had fallen from the fire. In a shoe making town a common fuel was the old shoe "lasts" which were used to mould the leather when the shoe was being made. They each contained a central metal spring which when burnt through by the fire would frequently explode onto the mat. One of the smells from that era was the pungent stench of burning leather as many who worked in the shoe factories brought cuttings home for fuel. Grandma always boiled her kettle on a hob by the fire, made toast on a toasting fork and complained when granddad spat into the flames and missed. When kettles boiled in front of the fire one had to be quick with a cloth to pick them up or else there would be a hissing of steam as the water boiled over into the embers. It was lovely sitting by a glowing fire as the darkness of evening came on; putting on the lights would break the magic. No wonder the generations who endured war sang about keeping "the home fires burning". The hearth was the focus of the home; since time immemorial humans have gathered round its warmth to find security, fellowship and peace.

Winters during the war years (1940-42) had been particularly severe but no-one who experienced the winter of 1947 will ever forget the coldest and harshest spell of weather for over half a century. It was, without doubt, the snowiest period of the 20th century with drifts reaching as high as fifteen feet in places. From late January through to mid March almost Arctic conditions prevailed with frequent power cuts, dislocated transport and shortages of the main fuel, coal, which was badly needed at the power stations. Entire roads and hedges disappeared in a sea of snow. I woke one morning to a strange whiteness. Looking out of the window, having melted the ice on the pane with my breath, I saw a glistening white blanket that reached above the lintels of the doors. Everything had disappeared; only the tops of line posts protruded strangely by a few feet. Going downstairs and opening the back door we were met by a wall of snow. We dug a tunnel through it using the coal shovel in order to get to the outside lavatory. That was frequently frozen in winter, and kettles of hot water had to be

41

carefully used to free the ice. Out in the streets nothing moved. The silence was palpable. As people emerged into this eerie landscape shovelling began but it was a mammoth task. As the days passed the roads became lined with snow, piled as high as a man on either side of the street. Some traffic managed to get through but horses fell on the compacted ice and shops ran out of vital commodities. Schools were closed for a time and many adults could not get to work.

We children thought it was wonderful, but after a few weeks of soaking gloves and chapped faces and hands decided it was not so glorious. I recall coming home from school through a biting wind that fanned stinging particles of ice into my eyes; night-time was drawing near, the blood-red sun sinking out of sight and the thought of another night of biting frost made me hurry to the comfort of the fireside. Ice on the garden pond reached at least ten inches thick and it could not be smashed with a sledge hammer. At night there was a strange silence that contained within it an almost audible creaking as the frost bit ever harder. The worst was not over, however, for with the thaw came many burst water pipes, and flooding. It was a miserable winter that hit us all hard as most people were in reduced circumstances trying to recover from the war.

Yet there were other aspects of the winter period to which all looked forward, particularly Christmas. Many servicemen had come home to families they had not seen for years. Christmas was special, and parents did their best to save up for something special for their children. I recall in the early years receiving brown paper parcels tied with string and fixed with a blob of red sealing wax. They contained second-hand *Rupert* books, kindly passed on by an older friend's mum. There were painted lead toy soldiers, a mouth organ, coloured pencils, roller skates, sweets and useful things like new socks, scarves and pullovers. Father Christmas managed to get a bicycle into my bedroom one year.

Christmas Day was a magical time with everyone bustling about, especially my mother whose great enterprise was to provide the best meal she could. We only ate chicken or turkey at Christmas, and bottles of wine, whisky or sherry rarely appeared at any other time. There was always a pork pie for breakfast on Christmas morning, and precious tinned fruit (especially sliced peaches) was used to make a trifle for tea. On Boxing Day it was customary to get some fresh air by going for a brisk walk before returning to yet more indulgence. Families would usually visit one another at this time and would walk together along the empty cold streets to and from their destinations. We played card games and for once in the year I was allowed to gamble for pennies which were then all handed back at the end of the game. The living room and front room were decorated with long paper garlands, my father fixing thin wire through the centres in case they fell down and caught aflame in the fire. Christmas was quickly gone, however, for my father soon returned to work to do his stock taking.   There were dances to go to on New Year's Eve when at midnight folk listened to the emotive sound of Big Ben from London, an audible symbol of the strength and unity of the Nation and the Empire.   As the chimes ceased the hooters on factories and railway locomotives heralded another year.

As soon as the war ended there was an immediate rush to catch up with lost leisure time.   Holidays at the seaside came back into vogue. My parents spent the year looking forward to their annual holiday; Blackpool, Bournemouth, Clacton, Eastbourne, Llandudno and Torquay were favoured spots.   There was no thought of ever going abroad. My parents seemed a bit better off than many and didn't favour another form of holiday experience then very popular with families, that of the holiday camp.

It was apparent to the casual observer when we were going on holiday.   The car would have a vigorous clean both inside and out and it would be stacked with luggage as we set forth on the highway. Mother would always take a roll of toilet paper with her just in case, and there was always a sense of adventure as it was most possible that the engine would boil over, or worse.   On one occasion the car broke down at traffic lights in the middle of Wigan.   Father was a member of the Royal Automobile Club and I liked to return the salute of RAC motorcycle patrols as we passed them on the road.   On one occasion, when the fan-belt broke, mother surrendered one of her stockings in order to see us safely to our destination. My parents' routine was always the same and included a full fortnight in a good hotel with three solid meals each day. They would decamp to the beach for as much time as possible and I was allowed to wander wherever I wanted, on pier and beach, slot machine arcade or funfair. It was a freedom which in the light of subsequent social changes seems almost irresponsible, yet there was no sense of fear of child abuse or abduction.

Father could never stay away too long as his garden needed constant attention. Near the well was a *Victoria* plum tree that annually gave a bumper crop of juicy orangey pink fruit. All children practised the art of "scrumping", and it was an accepted part of childhood as long as one did no damage and only took a few pieces of fruit. Many a scrumper went down with subsequent tummy-ache. However, there was a man who lived close by who regularly stole my father's plums. One evening, towards dusk, there came a terrified shout and then a faint splash. Going out with torches we discovered the thief had fallen through the wooden well lid and had dropped into the water. My father threw a rope to him and hauled him out much shaken and soaked. Thinking that was the end of the matter, and parting on reasonably good terms, my father was enraged at being summoned to go to court to answer the charge that he had failed to keep a secure well lid. I sat with my mother in the court to hear the case, which was dismissed. My father had the last word, however, assuring the magistrate that if the thief repeated his descent into his well he would leave the ****** down there. The magistrate could hardly hide his amusement as the case ended in laughter. The scrumper did not return!

As the fifties unfolded there was a feeling of progress in the air. Many of the former wartime airbases in the area were being demolished and given back to agricultural use. Old runways were being ploughed up and Nissen huts demolished. From the USAAF base at Molesworth Dad bought some second-hand timber to build a garage. Harold Macmillan as Minister of Housing and Local Government had presided, much to Winston Churchill's delight, over a successful programme of building 300,000 houses per annum. In 1959 as Prime Minister, MacMillan was to declare that the nation had "never had it so good". This was reflected in a greater variety of food in the shops and domestic improvements. House conversions were being made with indoor toilets and bathrooms making a huge improvement to living standards. Being a practical man my father did such things himself and got me to give a hand. Meantime, the large garden had to be tended and kept in cultivation as one never knew when hard times would return; fresh vegetables and fruit were needed to keep us healthy. So for my fifteenth birthday I received from Dad a new garden spade!

44

Chapter Four: Street Life 1946 – 1956

Children of my generation and background lived on the street far more than our modern counterparts. There was less to do in the home with relatively few books, little distracting television and no computers or telephones. Once any homework was done come rain or shine most children congregated in the local park or in the street. With traffic fairly light children could play reasonably safely and games of rounders, cricket or football would only be interrupted by an occasional shout of "car"; the game would be temporarily postponed then immediately resumed.

Coal, milk, bread and other goods were still delivered by horse and cart. My grandmother watched out for the horses as they passed her front window. She was ever ready with a coal shovel to scoop up manure in the street to put on her back garden. She often could be seen bringing a steaming heap of dung perched on her shovel through the entire house to be deposited on her choice rose bush.

One day, after lunch, on my way back to school I was passing the Co-op milkman's stationary horse when it took a liking to the shoulder pad of my school blazer. With a deft lunge it bit a chunk out of my blazer and proceeded to munch contentedly at this unexpected delicacy. I arrived at school with one sleeve missing and was the object of much merriment; no-one believed me when I told them a horse had eaten it. My mother made vigorous representations to the Co-op who graciously gave me a new blazer from their clothing department.

Clothing was particularly colourless, dull and uncomfortable for most children. The post-war austerities affected every aspect of life and many families could ill-afford school uniform. The transfer to secondary school at the age of eleven was a very expensive time for parents. My mother was a skilled seamstress and made most of my clothes for me. They were never made to fit exactly as it was assumed that an over-large pair of trousers would soon be filled by a boy's growing backside. Long trousers were more expensive than short ones, and as trouser knees tended to wear out quickly so mothers were reluctant to cover their sons' legs prematurely. Girls' skirts and dresses were deliberately given huge tucks and large hems so that as they grew their clothes could be adjusted accordingly.

Most girls had at least one dress or skirt with a deeply coloured band of material circling it. Having been hemmed up the material had not faded as had the rest of the garment; when let down it glowed with pristine brightness. Even shoes that had become too small had their toes cut away to make sandals for the following summer. My grandfather being a shoemaker always made sure I was well shod. The eldest children in a family would wear any new clothes which were then handed down to younger siblings. Many of the latter complained that they had never ever had new clothes. What good clothes we possessed were reserved for Sundays, holidays and other special occasions. It was no wonder that children were allowed out to play with the stricture of not getting clothes dirty or torn for there was little else to wear.

Skirts and short trousers worn whilst having to walk or cycle everywhere brought many sore and chapped legs in winter weather. Winters were definitely colder and I remember huge icicles hanging from house gutters. We would throw ice or snowballs at them to make them crash to the pavement. Having played outside then trying to thaw out in front of a fire, developing hot-ache and chilblains, certainly had long-term effects on rheumatic and arthritic conditions in later life.

Few houses had central heating and families would gather so close to the coal or wood fire that the soles of the shoes began to singe whilst the rest of the house was freezing. Ice that made fantastically beautiful patterns on the inside of single glazed windows had to be scraped off in the mornings. The next day's clothes were put under the eiderdown whilst one slept so that they would be warm to put on the next morning. Whilst dressing, one's breath hung like mist in the air. It was no joke cleaning out the ash from the previous day's fire early on a winter's morning, laying the newspaper, then the sticks (usually damp) and the coal trying to start a fire. Many children had to help by chopping sticks or cleaning out the grates. Once a week the dustmen came, tipping the rubbish into tin bath-like containers which they then shouldered to the dustcart tipping much of it along the path. At Christmas they almost demanded a substantial tip. It was a filthy job.

Many women still practised the duty of scrubbing and whitening their front steps, and sweeping or washing the pavement outside their homes. Dog dirt and spit were the hazards of walking on town pavements. A campaign to educate the public to refrain from spitting because it spread the dreaded tuberculosis bacillus went on throughout my childhood years. Frequent visits of mobile clinics with X Ray equipment, particularly to local shoe factories where leather dust was a hazard, attempted to stem the incidence of the disease.

Street games were often enlivened by mischief that was neither malicious nor deliberately damaging. One shoe factory near my grandmother's house had a metal letterbox with a mirror-like shiny interior. We could not resist putting a notice beside it which read "A monkey lives in here". From across the street we would have hilarious fun watching the succession of people of all ages peering intently at their own reflections. One favourite trick was to tie the knockers of two houses that faced each other on opposite sides of the street. The best thing to use was thin string. After carefully tying the knockers in the up position all one had to do was to await a vehicle which in passing would break the string. Both knockers would fall and both householders would open their doors to peer up and down the street eyeing the other suspiciously as the only possible culprit.

A popular children's activity was to construct one's own trolley out of a set of old pram wheels and some pieces of wood. A great deal of effort and ingenuity went into some of these magnificent creations; some had seats and even brakes. Ideally, one required a slope in order to skim down the streets at breakneck speeds. As traffic increased it became more dangerous and a number of children of my acquaintance ended up in hospital having broken bones. One of my friends who broke his arm was actually wheeled on a home-made trolley all the way to the hospital. Children's trolleys mirrored an adult preoccupation with trucks and handcarts. Three youngish men, who lived nearby, all brothers, could be seen striding daily with a handcart to and from their family allotment. Trolleys were useful in an age when there were few cars and only bicycles. In the post-war years collecting salvage was an attractive way of making a few shillings. Children looked out for empty beer and lemonade bottles that had deposits of a few pence payable on each. One shopkeeper soon realised that the proliferation of bottles being brought to his shop came from his own bottle store at the rear of his premises. He soon nailed up the fence.

One great money-spinner was waste paper, and I put my trolley to great use with many a stack of paper being trundled to the local waste merchant who would weigh them on giant scales and grudgingly hand out a few precious coins. One paper run netted me twelve shillings which was a considerable sum, as a man's wage in the local factories was only about £4 per week. Metals such as lead, copper and iron also provided a useful source of pocket money.

It was on the night of 31 January 1953 that huge storms devastated the East Coast. Hurricane-force winds produced a massive tidal surge and places like Canvey Island, Felixstowe, Southwold and Lowestoft were overwhelmed by the North Sea which ran eight feet above normal. 307 people died, hundreds of homes were destroyed and livestock perished. The reaction was instant and united, and children in the streets around where I lived immediately began to raise funds for East Coast Flood Relief. Trolleys that had lain unused in garden sheds were re-commissioned and a major effort began to collect salvage and set up sales of toys and home-made cakes and sweets. Hundreds of pounds were raised in a corporate effort of human solidarity. It evoked in the young the wartime spirit of our parents.

Only three days before the terrible floods on the East Coast another event had taken place which riveted the nation's attention. Two young men had been convicted of the murder of police constable Sidney Miles during a bungled burglary. The youngest defendant, Christopher Craig, was only aged sixteen at the time and his accomplice, Derek Bentley, was a mentally defective nineteen year old. In spite of Craig being the one with the gun it was Bentley who was hanged on the basis of conspiracy. Forty-six years later in July 1998 after continuous efforts by Bentley's family to clear his name he was given a posthumous pardon. I recall the intense interest of everyone at the time and the shock when Bentley was put to death. The trial was manifestly unfair and led to moves for the abolition of capital punishment. It was the Labour Government under Harold Wilson with Roy Jenkins as Home Secretary that enacted the eventual legislation that came into effect in November 1965. The last hangings in Britain took place in August 1964.

My paternal grandmother was one of a family of ten children who had all been brought up in a small terraced house only two streets away from where she lived for her married life. Indeed, most

48

of her brothers and sisters resided within a few miles of their childhood home, finding employment in the town. Some worked in the shoe factories; one was a butcher, another a grocer and one worked for the Electricity Board. This extended family had its own solidarity. My great grandparents celebrated their Diamond Wedding Anniversary and I remember the whole family gathering for a special party. I was very young and spent the time dashing about the hall hired for the occasion.

Over the garden wall.

Next door to my grandmother lived her youngest sister Vera. They would spend time from their household duties chatting over the garden wall. Upon great grandfather's death Vera took her mother in to live with her. One evening my father informed me that great grandmother had died. He took me next door to see her laid out in state in the front room. Neighbours and friends as well as family came to pay their respects. It was the first time I had seen a dead person. Great grandmother rested there with an insouciant smile on her face. My father told me that after having her customary supper of pork pie, pickled onions and a glass of Guinness she had let out one almighty belch and had passed away to glory. It was a great way to go! When the funeral procession left the house some days later all the neighbours stood in the street as a mark of respect. It was a common sight for people to stand still as funeral corteges passed by, with men touching or doffing their hats.

The laying out of the dead was often done by local people who specialised in the craft. Two ladies in the street did this useful public service and were called upon frequently to exercise their skills. On one occasion an elderly male neighbour passed away and the two ladies arrived to do their duty. They cleaned, dressed and made the body ready putting in a set of false teeth that they noticed in a glass in the kitchen. After a while the widow came down stairs complaining that she could not find her dentures. Realising their error, the two ladies made frantic efforts to exchange the teeth before rigor mortis set in. One diverted the attention of the widow whilst the other swilled the teeth under the tap and returned them to their rightful owner.

The British chip shop is an amazing institution and we post-war children took great delight in entering such hallowed halls. Condensation streaming down the plate glass windows and the smells and sounds of frying drew us through the door where a motley assortment of humanity waited patiently and hungrily for the next batch. After the war better potatoes, the use of beef dripping and a more plentiful supply of fish began to tempt all palates. For three pence (soon steadily to rise to sixpence) one could obtain a good helping of chips and we would liberally dose them with salt and vinegar. If you were cheeky enough to ask, the proprietor might give you free of charge a greaseproof bag full of batter bits scraped from the bottom of the fryer. Triumphantly we would carry off our newspaper-wrapped spoils to consume on the steps of a nearby ball-bearing factory.

Life revolved around the corner shops. It was an age before the advent of the supermarket. There were numerous shops catering for all kinds of needs: greengrocers, confectioners, tobacconists, clothiers, general stores, bakeries, newsagents and off licences. One such was a particular local off-licence that sold not only tobacco products and sweets but also an array of wines, spirits, beers and ciders. It had a little red neon sign that flashed on and off.

A considerable cross section of people gravitated to this little corner shop. Near to my grandparents' house lived one of the street's characters whom we nicknamed "The Beer Bottle, Jug and Jitty Man". A life-long bachelor, our friend was a man of punctilious habit. He worked in a local shoe factory and wore a pair of brown boots that he kept gleaming with polish. He had tacked on to the soles of his boots metal studs known as *Blakeys* to prolong wear. He clattered and sparked as he marched vigorously to and from work and home. His boss considered him the best worker in the factory and protected this simple soul from any banter, for factory life could be strident and coarse.

Our friend would arrive home to his widowed mother and spinster sister for his tea, punctual to the minute. Later in the evening we children observed him proceeding to the off-licence to obtain his daily quota of beer. He clutched a large porcelain jug that may have held a quart. After entering the shop to purchase a jug-full of draught ale he then sidled into the alley, or jitty, at the back of the shop to swig it all down. Re-entering the shop to have the jug refilled he took it home dutifully to his family. I don't think that they were fooled by this simple artifice but his daily routine was amazing. Sometimes, especially on a Saturday night, he might have several sessions in the jitty with his jug. He would then roll home spilling some of the contents on the pavement. He had quite a penchant for collecting the numerous cigarette ends that littered the pavements and gutters which he re-rolled to make his own smokes.

He was but one of many characters who inhabited the town's streets and who were well-known and considered harmless. They were certainly tolerated and respected and helped. They did their best to survive in a society that made little official provision for those who had some mental difficulties. What we would term special needs at the turn of the 21st century had a variety of official terminologies in those days such as "idiot", "moron", "imbecile" or "sub normal". In villages there were always those who had been the product of close intermarriage. A great deal of truth lies in the saying that the invention of the bicycle led to the decline of the village idiot. There was still a fear in an older generation of the workhouse and the lunatic asylum. My grandfather would sing a song entitled *Christmas Day in the Workhouse*. It evoked its own pathos and inherent fear of institutionalisation that recalled the evils that Dickens had described in his novels.

51

In my youth it was clear that society included those who were socially, physically or mentally handicapped; they had their place in town or village life, finding what work they could and being cared for by family and friends as long as they were able or had the means. The sad fact was that when elderly parents died or became incapable of looking after their offspring the latter had to go into an institution or struggle to survive with few state handouts. The National Health Service had only come into being in 1948, and schools were only just coming to terms with the profound changes demanded of the landmark Education Act of 1944.

One vivid character I remember from the Kettering of the fifties was a man nicknamed Puffing Billy who would shunt himself like a railway locomotive up and down the aisles of the Woolworth's store. Another well-known personage had the amusing habit of keeping his money in his socks. He would go to a shop to buy an item and then go through the ritual of removing a sock to hand a sweaty coin to the bewildered shop assistant. There were other personalities, one such being a former fireman who, it was said, had had his nerve endings damaged by fighting so many fires. How true this was no-one could tell but in the bitterest of weather he would be seen walking around the town wearing above waist only a thin string vest. One man, a blind piano tuner, had fallen headlong down a cellar entrance which someone had left open; he evoked great sympathy as he tried to recover from appalling injuries to keep on working.

Being out and about on the streets and along the country lanes meant that we met some of the characters who came and went. There were the Romany ladies who would come with their wicker baskets from door to door selling wooden clothes pegs, bunches of "lucky" heather and lace. There were "the gentlemen of the road", the tramps, who would sleep in empty barns and under hedges and beg a crust of bread and a drink of water. We children looked for the secret signs they were supposed to leave at gates and doorways telling other travellers whether the owners were helpful or hostile. One tramp, well spoken and courteous, always wore a battered bowler hat; I found him one day sitting on a grassy bank eating bread and cheese with a red and white spotted napkin on his knees. A regular visitor was the knife grinder. Children would gather round as he set up his apparatus, his cycle propped up so that he could use the pedals to whirl round his grindstone. The sparks flew from the kitchen knives local housewives had given him to sharpen. Often the knives would be blunter and much worn and gouged after he had been around.

Another focal point of street life was the nearby bakery. When bread came off ration in 1948 there was a welcome return to white bread. The wartime National Loaf had been restricted in size and weight and had an unappetising greyish tinge. One day my mother sent me off to the bakery to get a sixpenny loaf. I brought it back still warm; it had a delicious golden crust and the smell was enticing. I thought that it wouldn't hurt to just take a small piece of bread from the underside. Mother wouldn't notice. The bread was magnificent: white, warm, and fluffy in texture. I sat with a friend on the steps of a boot factory and we took it in turns to burrow into the loaf's inviting interior. When I eventually returned home it looked perfectly fine as long as one did not turn it upside down. Mother put it on the breadboard at teatime and proceeded to slice it, whereupon it collapsed like a deflating balloon.

The bakery was a busy place on Sunday mornings. Dozens of families relied upon the heat from the Saturday baking still being sufficient to cook their Sunday roast dinners. Virtually everyone ate roast beef or lamb with Yorkshire pudding (Northamptonshire style with the meat in the middle), potatoes and vegetables. Late on Saturday night or early on the Sunday morning a steady stream of people would bring their dinners to the bakery for slow cooking. Lunchtime saw a queue waiting to collect their meals and, if they managed to get the right one without argument they would scuttle back to their homes where hungry mouths waited to be fed. The Sunday roast had to last at least for a cold meat meal on Monday so it could not all be eaten. One treat for a Sunday night was to have a piece of cold Yorkshire pudding salvaged from the midday meal. My mother always prided herself that her Yorkshire pudding contained "two good eggs"! We were doing well!

When my parents and I moved back to our semi-detached house a mile from the terraced streets where we had spent the war years we went into comparative luxury; the house had a spare room which my father converted into a bathroom. In 1951 only a third of all houses had a bath. In my grandparents' terraced house folk generally had a bath once a week, and as a young child I was bathed in front of the fire in a large galvanised tub which usually hung on the wall outside. Buckets of warm water would be brought from the copper in the kitchen, a slow and laborious process. Once, I remember painfully sitting on a sharp metal bottle top that I had been playing with and had let slip into the water. My grandfather said that the mark it produced on my buttock resembled a crimped mince pie.

The adults of the family bathed when I was in bed, I suppose, although my grandmother thought nothing of stripping down to her waist, exposing her ample bosom, to wash in the kitchen sink. In the community of those days anyone might walk in at any moment, and grandma didn't turn a hair. Many people availed themselves of the local public baths and would make a visit to scrub off the weekly grime in the municipal slipper baths; at least the water was hot.

On the outskirts of the town there stood a building known as the "Fever Hospital". Children didn't venture near it as it was believed that somehow it would contaminate you. My father had spent a time there in his younger days recovering from smallpox which in the early decades of the century still produced epidemics. Fear of illness was whipped up by the local press which always highlighted any cases of poliomyelitis that usually occurred during summer months. Polio was a dreaded disease and lurid descriptions of people having to spend months in iron lungs in order to breathe produced much panic. Whenever there was an outbreak the swimming pools and other places where the public gathered were avoided like the plague. It was of some comfort to learn in 1952 that the Salk vaccine had been developed. This was the year before the discovery of DNA.

Fear of infection, however, did not seem to affect attendance at the special Saturday morning picture shows at local cinemas. Five of these served the town, and it was a matter of kudos to belong to one of the children's cinema clubs. I was a proud member of the Odeon Club; we thought ourselves much superior to those who went to the Granada or the Savoy. For sixpence children would gather to enjoy a noisy session that approached near riot when the projector broke down, as it often did. On members' birthdays they each would receive a free admission card for the following week.

Every Saturday we would sing lustily a song that was tantamount to a national anthem:

We come along on Saturday morning
Greeting everybody with a smile.
We come along on Saturday morning
Knowing it's all worth while.
As members of the Odeon Club
We all intend to be
Good citizens when we grow up
And champions of The Free.
We come along on Saturday morning
Greeting everybody with a smile, smile, smile;
Greeting everybody with a smile.

Children's cinema was an on-going experience that helped to produce a social bonding and togetherness that, in spite of its apparent chaos, was both comforting and exhilarating. Here we met the world of cowboy and Indian, of detectives and crime, of science fiction and daring adventure. The lives of fictional superheroes like Tarzan and Superman together with the characters portrayed on the wireless, *Dick Barton Special Agent* and the like, were acted out in play in the streets. Play was the great outlet of emotion and wish-fulfilment, a means to experience the world and a way of coming to terms with it.

Left: awaiting results in piano and elocution at a local eisteddfod c 1950.
Right: Roger Tame and myself in rehearsal. c 1955.

My parents had aspirations for me and sent me to piano and elocution lessons. My teacher despaired of my regional accent saying that I spoke beautifully when in her drawing room but like the rest of the town when outside. Such experiences brought me into touch with another segment of society, with those who entered eisteddfods and took music examinations, of poetry and drama. My parents also hired a private tutor who helped me with basic language and arithmetic. I have always appreciated the things they sacrificed for my future as there was precious little encouragement for the arts in my junior school situation unless you were in the "A" stream.

Enthusiasm for things musical led to various adventures in my teen years with a variety of instruments, including a French horn, a guitar, a piano accordian and a banjo. In the age when skiffle groups began to be popular the ability to keep time on a washboard, a one-string base or even be able to strum a guitar or banjo was deemed a great asset. I took part in several skiffle, folk and jazz groups. My great friend Roger Tame and I did quite a dashing duet on piano and piano accordion, entertaining mostly in church halls, often rehearsing in my front room. I was only fourteen when in a moment of rashness I bought for five shillings a Victorian pedal harmonium. It had come from an old cinema. Several friends and I borrowed a handcart to transport this musical treasure home, a matter of several miles. On the way we stopped two or three times to render a few tunes to amused audiences in the streets. Not having told my parents of my purchase they flatly refused to let it in the house. There was no room for it in the shed or garage. Eventually, my grandmother had pity and let me lodge it in her front room on a temporary basis. Needless to say, it stayed there for several years until I finally sold it for ten shillings, much to her relief.

The need to earn some cash became overwhelming as there was sheet music and records to buy. The culture of the teenager was beginning and if you had a girlfriend you needed to treat her to the cinema. Thus I obtained my first part-time job as a delivery boy for the *Home and Colonial Stores* in the town's High Street. It involved an eight hour week (an hour after school at 4.30pm every weekday except Thursdays and four hours on a Saturday morning starting at 9am). The pay came out at ten shillings and sixpence a week (a half guinea). The glory of this job was that I was given my own green delivery cycle complete with a large pannier at the front. After school I would report to the shop to be given various deliveries over the town. What an eye-opener this was, meeting people of all types some with the most bizarre feeding habits. One family it seemed ate nothing but bread and tinned tomatoes. Coming back from a delivery was a great joy as you could put your feet up on the pannier and rocket back downhill into town.

Once deliveries were finished there were jobs such as flattening out the cardboard cartons for salvage down in the damp cellar. On Saturday mornings there were other duties such as boning the bacon. When taking out the ribs from a side of bacon we often found numerous maggots. One of my older second-cousins worked in the store and we would flick fat maggots at each other with our boning knives. In an age of greater hygiene we might shudder at some of the standards that were commonplace. I recall rolling the cheeses along the floor through a wet patch that was the result of a leaking toilet. The customers said they enjoyed the rich mature flavour of our cheese.

My father let me work with him from time to time and here was an opening into the intriguing world of the building trade. Dad managed a wallpaper and paint section of a busy builder's merchants. I used to help serve behind the counter or do jobs in the store. Decorators, builders, glaziers, plumbers and plasterers came in to banter and joke and tell tall stories of recent triumphs or disasters. One of my friends who had become apprenticed as a plumber was sent one day to find his mate who beckoned to him to come up to the upstairs of a terraced house. My friend dutifully obeyed but entered the wrong house only to find himself in the bedroom of a lady sitting up in bed. All he could think of saying was "Is my mate here?" The woman's reply is unprintable. Such amusing tales would set all along the shop counter a roar with laughter.

Social class consciousness was never far away and the distinctions of rank in the armed services spilled over into civilian life. My father, who was proud of being an ordinary bombardier, always saw red when military ranks were retained long after people had left the services. One such general manager arrived at the shop and gloried in the title of "Captain". He had his name and rank emblazoned on his office door. One evening my father hosted a promotional evening at a local hotel for the Shand Kydd range of wallpapers. It was a prestigious evening with free drinks and food and I was allowed to attend.

The Captain approached my father and started talking about the War, and in the hearing of many spoke to him in condescending terms: "And what sort of war did you have, Deacon?" he asked in a loud patronising voice. The room went quiet. My father paused, looked him coolly in the eye and very quietly replied: "When you have spent days and nights picking up bits of children's bodies and putting them into body bags during the blitz on Brixton you don't like to crow about the War, Captain". This last word was uttered with such contempt that the Captain gulped and changed the subject. It was very noticeable that he never again referred to himself by his former military title. It is a fact that I have observed over many years that the men and women who have seen the realities of action in war rarely if ever want to speak about them!

Meantime, out in the streets, life was going on and things were not as innocent as one might think. As I grew up I became aware of the thugs and bullies who were about. Children and young people were very much involved in gangs, usually those who lived in the same street but from the teen years those who went to the same secondary school or interest group. There was one boy in particular who struck terror in other children; he ended up in Borstal. The very word had a ring of fear and the film *Borstal Boy* reinforced the image of this ruthless individual. We kept well out of his way.

One day, when I was about twelve, another boy in my secondary school class decided to beat me up. He had been picking on me for weeks and during one lunchtime as I cycled home chased me along a back alley; it was a dead end. He came at me with a viciousness that terrified me, but realising that it was either him or me, I smacked him hard with my fist on his nose. To my amazement he burst into tears and fled. After lunch his mother brought him to school and accused me of being the bully. The headmaster, to his credit, defended me and I am sure that this bully learned a lesson. He left me alone from that day forward.

Such an event stood me in good stead for a period of growing street violence. It was the era of the Teddy Boys, named after the fashion of wearing Edwardian style long draped jackets with velvet collars and cuffs. Complete with their crepe soled shoes, drainpipe trousers, and bootlace ties the Teddy Boys dominated the town's streets on Saturday evenings and other times. There was something captivating and individualistic about their attire. I recall having an argument with my mother about whether I could wear fourteen inch bottoms on my trousers. My father tartly remarked that thin trousers made us look spider-legged. I was allowed sixteen inch bottoms and no narrower. We all copied the fashion of having Tony Curtis quiffs and the "DA" cut at the back of the head. We grew our hair into sideburns. I remember clearly reading in *The Daily Express* about a new singing phenomenon in the United States who was Greek godlike in appearance. His name was Elvis Presley and his pelvic gyrations caused a sensation. In 1956/7 hits like *Hound Dog, Don't be cruel, Love me tender, All shook up* and *Jailhouse Rock* captivated youth on both sides of the Atlantic. Rock n' Roll had arrived. I played my 78rpm record *Rock Around the Clock* by Bill Haley and his Comets on my gramophone until the needles wore out.

Not all Teddy Boys were violent but rival gangs from out of town came deliberately to pick a fight. Some vicious incidents occurred which involved the use of bike chains and flick knives. Wise young people kept clear but when the cinemas, dance halls and public houses all disgorged their clientele at the same time on a Friday or Saturday night the proverbial fire and gunpowder did mix with explosive force. Extra police were drafted in at these times. It was an age for gangs; even young children would roam the streets in large groups. I learned the valuable lesson of being on good terms with all and sundry and, whilst maintaining a personal independence, was considered an honorary member of no less than three local gangs. It was a survival technique.

On Christmas Eve 1956 I saw a girlfriend off at the bus stop as she lived out of town. We said goodbye and as I walked home a drunken youth lunged at me with a broken bottle. The only move that I had learned in attending a Ju Jitsu class was to step back, catch your adversary off balance then leg him up. This I did, but he managed to knock himself out on the pavement. For a moment I thought I had killed him. A police constable happened to see it all and was soon on the scene. He asked me if I was all right, told me to go home and have a happy Christmas. Meantime, he said, my assailant could sober up in the cells over night. I heard no more of the incident, but it was a salutary reminder that all was not sweetness and light on the streets.

Young people always like to get together away from adults. Sunday evenings were particularly special as most of my friends went to church for the evening service then later gathered at someone's house. One particular friend, Derek Neal, whose early life had been marred by tragedy as his parents had died went to live with an elderly uncle who himself became blind. It was to his house that we often went to watch *Sunday Night at the London Palladium* whilst drinking coffee. His uncle could put up with us. The latest jokes from the *Goon Show* were often worked over and the week ahead started with much adolescent bonhomie. Derek was Kettering's first Youth Mayor, an initiative in civic responsibility far ahead of its time. When I was a student in London I visited him when he had to go into The Middlesex Hospital for major surgery; a more cheerful, optimistic and positive man I have yet to meet.

Being a pupil at a co-educational school had its advantages and the school gallantly promoted dances. We attended ballroom dancing lessons to learn how to waltz, tango, quickstep or foxtrot. Jiving was in its infancy. I found that an ability to dance and not trample your partner's feet went down well with the girls. It was the time when *The King and I* hit the cinema screen and my first girlfriend and I walked home after a school dance hand in hand, and like the lovers in the film "kissed in the shadow afraid to be heard". We won the raffle at one dance and ate a complete box of chocolates in the interval, only to be violently sick afterwards. To impress girls one had to have a bicycle with special handlebars that resembled a pair of cow horns. Boys would zoom past the local girls' school just as they were coming out at the end of the day. Our black slim jeans and quiffed haircuts stiff with lacquer made us feel invincible. We enjoyed going to the annual fairs which occurred in the neighbourhood. Kettering and Rothwell Feasts were part of the summer ritual. I recall walking home with a friend late at night from Rothwell Fair. I was the worse for wear having imbibed a quantity of *Woodpecker* cider. The roads were empty of traffic yet knowing we were very late decided to take a short-cut over the fields. I fell over a recumbent cow, which rose up menacingly in the darkness, and returned home plastered in mud. My father was none too pleased with me!

A sense of mischief seemed to possess us in our teens. Never knowingly did we do any damage apart from the occasional broken window due to footballing in the street. Long before the days of spray paints and marker pens there was no notion of scrawling graffiti on every wall. I recall that several of us acquired one of the old street lamp cowls which the local council were replacing. This large metal object shaped like a pointed Chinaman's hat resided in the loft of a friend's house. From time to time it would mysteriously appear sitting on top of the local pillar box, much to the amusement of passers by. Then, just as mysteriously, it would disappear only to re-emerge again some time later. It became the object of much public speculation; when and where would it appear next? We kept the game going for quite a time. As far as I know the cowl still resides in that house loft.

Sex education as such was virtually non-existent at school, and my parents never spoke about it. Mothers whispered about women's matters and parents made little mention of anything that was remotely carnal. As a result, wild stories of people's blood drying up if one masturbated or the catching of some dreadful disease coloured young people's views of sexuality. It was known that certain newsagents would sell rude magazines from under the counter, but in the light of the modern explosion of pornography it was tame stuff indeed. Although it was an era before AIDS a large number of young people of my generation did not practise full sexual relationships until they were engaged or married. Parental control was much to the fore and I came to grief several times with fathers, having brought their precious daughters home late. It is interesting to see how many of my contemporaries who started going out together in their teen years stayed together for long marriages. Quite a number of them have never been out with anyone other than their spouse.

There were no free handouts of condoms and the thought of asking for them in the chemist shop was a daunting prospect. Asking for such things was like going to a hotel and signing in as Mr & Mrs Smith; there was a whole social reticence that controlled behaviour at many levels. This had its good as well as bad effects but overall provided a framework of protection; if a girl did get pregnant the vast majority of young men accepted their duty to provide for her and the child, and most married. The general expectation from our parents was that one became engaged then married in one's early twenties, waited a few years to start a family and then settled down. Yet all this was about to change with the so-called Swinging Sixties that brought about a revolution in attitudes; in so-doing the result was a new range of problems as well as freedoms.

Chapter Five: Widening Horizons.

One of the presents I received for my tenth birthday was the first edition of a new comic for boys, named by the editor's wife as *Eagle*. From April 1950 and for the best part of the following decade, *Eagle* (with its sister comics, *Swift*, *Robin* and *Girl*) fascinated a young readership at a time when the wireless, books and the cinema were the major means of entertainment. Every Thursday lunchtime, dead on midday, I would rush to my grandparents' house to devour my weekly meat pudding and potatoes as well as the latest activities of Dan Dare. The inspiration for *Eagle* came from the Rev Marcus Morris who, concerned with the amount of violent and horror comics flooding the country from the United States, wanted to bring a more positive and wholesome message to the 8-14 age range of boys in Great Britain. Together with Frank Hampson as chief artist (and later Frank Bellamy, who had been born in Kettering) *Eagle* had spectacular success over the next decade.

The fifties were a time when heroes flourished. In 1954 a twenty-five year old student, Roger Bannister, became the first man to run a mile in under four minutes. Real-life wartime heroes like Guy Gibson, Leonard Cheshire and Douglas Bader were the inspiration for Dan Dare who was claimed to be "the pilot of the future". There was a great deal of ideology within the comic strip, which was colourful, brilliantly drawn and exciting. The story began with attempts to reach Venus in order to provide food for a starving Earth. This had great resonance with the realities of rationing. Dan Dare represented a world finding its unity under the United Nations, itself a major hope for a world recovering from a global conflict.

Other characters and stories, both fact and fiction, made up the *Eagle's* contents, notably Harris Tweed Special Agent, Luck of the Legion and Jeff Arnold. There was much stunning artwork and themes such as cutaway drawings of famous ships and detailed lives of men of courage like Saint Paul and Jesus Christ. Yet it was to the emergence of science fiction as a genre that *Eagle* contributed its most lasting memorial. The BBC's *Journey into Space,* films such as *The Day the Earth Stood Still,* and the writings of John Wyndham and Arthur C. Clarke appeared in the following years. Dare Dare was very much a role model and I, and many others, was thrilled by his adventures. The original creators of *Eagle* were gifted visionaries who presented a new world of progress and invention.

Part of this excitement was finding out how things worked. One particular friend had a great interest in radio. We all had a go at making old-fashioned crystal sets, but this was the age of valves and condensers; it was quite easy to make a simple wireless. One day in his dad's barn we set up a direction rod in the roof and connected it up to an ex US army dinghy radio transmitter. The equipment crackled and hissed and we had a fine time until the GPO arrived to close us down; we had interfered with a number of important wave bands. Another great friend was Graham Rigby who shared in my passion for astronomy. We would frequently compare notes and observations and were particularly fascinated by the planet Mars, probably because of the radio adaptation of H. G. Wells *The War of the Worlds* which gripped our attention at that time.

Chemistry held a similar fascination. The average chemistry set which parents bought you for Christmas was a pretty poor thing and contained only a few bangs and smells. With a little ingenuity it was possible to buy potassium nitrate (saltpetre) and sulphur from the local chemist; these with home-made charcoal made credible gunpowder. String soaked in saltpetre solution, once dried, became a useful fuse. Other chemicals such as barium and strontium nitrates could give home-made fireworks bright green and red colours. Magnesium ribbon, used in photography, would give a brilliant white light, and potassium chlorate (available in pill form for the treatment of angina) was a powerful explosive; one acquaintance pock-marked his face and blew a finger off whilst mixing this chemical with others. I once blew a dustbin lid in the air some thirty feet. Home-made rockets would go much higher if sent up an old drainpipe as a launcher. It is amazing that I survived my youthful years with all this experimentation. I still have cold sweats when I think that I would count my shop-bought fireworks ready for Bonfire Night setting them out on the mat in front of the sitting room fire!

At a national level science and invention came to the fore in the Festival of Britain in 1951. Based mainly on the South Bank in London the Festival organisers were adventurous in sending touring exhibitions across the country. King George VI opened the new Royal Festival Hall, designed by Robert Matthew, at the commencement of the Festival which lasted from May to September.

It was during this time that I had a thrilling ride with a neighbour known as Uncle Frank. He was a van driver and often travelled to the London Docks to collect bales of cloth for the local clothing factories in Kettering. It was exciting being his "mate" for the day, and it happened to be at the time of the Festival. We set off and duly arrived at the docks where we picked up a consignment of cloth from a warehouse. I remember my grandparents telling me that the glow from the fires of the warehouses along the Thames set alight by enemy bombing during the war could be seen from as far away as Kettering. We were suddenly amongst the still ruined riverside with much work going on to demolish and rebuild.

The Festival provided an opportunity to build new river walls and walkways, reclaim land, restore derelict wharves and open up new vistas of St Paul's Cathedral, the Houses of Parliament and the City. Sir Hugh Casson's design for the whole site of the Festival embodied the architectural concept of the unity of buildings and spaces. The Festival aimed to recreate something of the spirit of the Great Exhibition of 1851 which presented the ingenuity of the British Empire to the world. The Festival of Britain in 1951, likewise, wanted to espouse the quality of British industry, arts and science.

From our van we saw the crowds milling around the South Bank Exhibition and the Festival Pleasure Gardens at Battersea. There was the world's first purpose-built Telecinema which screened large-scale film and television including experimental films using 3D effects. Most memorable visual landmarks were the Dome of Discovery, then the largest dome ever constructed, and the needle-shaped construction of steel and aluminium known as the Skylon. On the way home we stopped at a Transport Café and Uncle Frank treated me to fish and chips, bread and butter, apple pie and custard and a large cup of well-sugared tea. It cost half-a-crown (twelve and a half new pence).

Not long after this, on 6 February 1952 the death of George VI was announced from Sandringham. He had succumbed to lung cancer. He had been thrust into being the monarch following the abdication of his brother Edward VIII. Unlike his brother, George was much admired especially for the way in which, with his wife Queen Elizabeth, he had stayed put in Buckingham Palace at the height of the Blitz on London. They had toured factories, visited troops and had gone to see for themselves the devastation of the ordinary little homes of England that had been destroyed. I remember the solemn announcement of his death and the subsequent state funeral on 15th February and burial at Windsor Castle.

There was a growing enthusiasm for the new monarch, George's eldest daughter Princess Elizabeth, who was proclaimed Queen whilst staying at Treetops Game Lodge in Kenya. She and her husband, the Duke of Edinburgh, returned to London. On 2 June 1953 the Coronation took place at Westminster Abbey and the whole nation and Commonwealth was agog with excitement. Across the land there were street parties and folk gathered around the few black and white television sets that were available. My father patriotically hung bunting across the front of the house with Union flags fluttering from the window ledges.

On Coronation Day itself my parents and I were travelling home from a short holiday at Clacton. Our Morris 10 purred us back home on a rainy day along roads utterly deserted of traffic or pedestrians. Children were given commemorative books and mugs from their schools. Greatly popular from toy shops were models of the Coronation Coach complete with horses and grooms in bright livery. On the day itself it was announced that Mount Everest had been conquered by Sir Edmund Hilary and Tenzing Norgay. The news had been deliberately held back so that it would coincide with the Coronation; the summit had been reached on 28 May. These were yet more heroes; along with a young queen there was a deep sense that a new Elizabethan age had begun. The old Empire was in decline but a new Commonwealth was emerging and Elizabeth became a key figure in the transformation from subservience to fraternity. In those days there was great interest in Royalty, and many local people would often try to catch a glimpse of the Royal Family when they stayed at places like Boughton House, the home of the Duke of Buccleuch. Several times have I been to the church at Weekley and seen the Royals coming home from worship, with then only a minimal police and security presence.

During the fifties few people travelled overseas. My school gave me the opportunity to go to Belgium for a week. My parents were keen to support this, and so a party of us went to Bruges where we stayed in *The Hotel Venice du Nord*. The boys actually slept in the upstairs of a working bakery. During the night we could hear a rumble of machinery and white clad figures could be seen mixing dough. In the morning the smell of fresh bread was delightful. The war had only been finished eight years and, as in England, much reconstruction was proceeding apace. We travelled into France and saw a number of burnt out houses along the coast near Dunkirk. Some beaches were still out of bounds, yet to be cleared of mines.

We spent a day on Walcheren Island in Holland and were overwhelmed by the welcome given us by the local people. In 1944 the Allies, especially Royal Marines and Canadian forces, attacked the island which had become a major Nazi defence of the River Scheldt and the approaches to Antwerp. The population fled their homes as the whole area had to be deliberately flooded. The battle cost 8000 Allied lives. I recall the great old windmills in Flushing with their sails still intact and the joyful Dutch people who embarrassed us with their hugs and kisses.

Schools continental tour. August 1956

I went to Belgium a second time several years later, and in this cockpit of European history saw again the results of human conflict. Miles of neat rows of white gravestones mark where so many young men died in the wars of the twentieth century. At the Menin Gate at Ypres we stood as *The Last Post* was sounded and international flags were lowered, a daily routine that continues to the present. On the Menin Gate are thousands of names of men who were killed, a potent symbol of the futility of war.

I don't know how much these solemn thoughts bothered us as young people, but there was one consideration that came closer and closer as the years passed. At the age of eighteen all boys had to join the armed services for their two years National Service. I didn't particularly worry about this prospect and wondered which service to aim for. Again, my school came to my assistance and, under the leadership of Joe the Geography master, a number of us went to Chatham Naval Dockyard for a week's stay. Joe was a wonderful man who with only one arm could beat anyone at tennis, conduct choirs and deliver swift retribution to any recalcitrant.

The Chatham experience has lasted a life-time for me. We stayed in the barracks, were roused from our beds at six every morning, and carved off slices of marmalade for our toast and enjoyed bacon and eggs in the ratings mess. We went to gunnery school, visited some of the "D Class" destroyers that were in dock and, surreptitiously smoked *RN* cigarettes. This gave me serious thoughts about a career in the Royal Navy and I went back for a more extensive stay to further explore the possibilities.

It was at this time that a large black submarine glided into the Chatham dockyard. It had the number 571 painted on its conning tower. It was the *USS Nautilus,* the world's first nuclear-powered submarine. In 1954 it had been commissioned and in January 1955 it had made history with the signal "under way on nuclear power". With several others I went aboard. In the following years *Nautilus* made the first submerged crossing from the Pacific to the Atlantic Ocean being the first to reach the geographic North Pole. Crew members joked that the submarine resurfaced every four years so that the crew could re-enlist. It was the prospect of signing on for many years that made me waver and I decided to put off a naval career, particularly as it was rumoured that conscription might be phased out. It was finished officially in 1960; I missed it by about a year.

Even international music idols such as Elvis Presley had to do their military service; he served from 1958-60 with the American 3rd Armoured Corps in Germany. Several of my friends who were a little older were called up for National Service. One of them joined the army, and after a few months found himself being parachuted into Egypt. President Nasser, angry at the refusal of America and Britain to finance the building of the Aswan Dam declared martial law in the Canal Zone and took control of the Suez Canal Company. Fearful of the cutting off of vital oil supplies Britain together with France and Israel attacked Egypt on 26 July 1956. The episode was a disaster and ended with the UN evacuating British and French troops in the following December. I was glad that my friend came home in one piece and having a sun tan. Yet it was a time when discerning folk could see that British influence as a colonial power was waning and that fear of the Soviet Union was driving political thinking. We were living through the Cold War which was yet to reach its peak in the sixties. It was during these years that Ian Fleming created his fictional James Bond and I remember reading *From Russia With Love* when it was first published in 1957.

From the beginning of July 1957 through to the end of December 1958 the scientific community acknowledged the International Geophysical year. Solar activity during this period was going to be at its highest and it was hoped to launch an artificial satellite to help map the Earth's surface. On 4 October 1957 the Soviet Union unexpectedly launched Sputnik I, the world's first artificial satellite. It orbited the planet on an elliptical path taking 98 minutes for one full circuit. We were all agog for it was clear that a moment of history was in the making. We all tried to locate it in the sky as it passed overhead. Sputnik I ushered in a new age that had serious military, political, scientific and technological repercussions for us all. The Space Age had begun, and the US and the USSR entered neck and neck in the subsequent Space Race.

In the following years I became friendly with Geoff Perry, Senior Physics Master at Kettering Grammar School as he was one of our neighbours. Steff and I got to know him when a rocket from one of our firework parties came down with a thump on the caravan in his front garden where he happened to be working. Geoff was a pioneer in the telemetry of spacecraft. He became very excited when he and his Kettering Group monitored shortwave signals of the Russian Kosmos 57 spacecraft. He was to achieve well-deserved fame in the following year when he discovered that a satellite had been launched from a hitherto unknown cosmodrome at Plesetsk in Northern Russia. His research excelled that of the CIA, much to their embarrassment. He received no less than four honorary doctorates for his work. His wife told me that he was so dedicated to his task that he kept monitoring instruments by his bed so that he wouldn't miss anything!

The developing Space Race was one aspect of the Cold War. Rivalry between the Communist Bloc, predominantly the Soviet Union, and the West, notably the United States of America gradually intensified as the fifties unfolded. There was great apprehension amongst ordinary folk as to the likely outcome of such hostility. The image of an atomic mushroom cloud hung over the common consciousness. It was really believed that the world could end within a few minutes, with missiles from the Communist East raining down on us all. At the former wartime RAF airfield at Harrington new work was proceeding apace with the construction of silos for Thor missiles. One only had to drive along a particular stretch of the A1 to see dozens of missiles pointed towards the east.

In 1952 Britain exploded its first test atomic bomb thus becoming the third nation alongside America and Russia to possess a nuclear weapon. British physicists gained many Nobel Prizes for their work during this period. I recall going to church and, instead of a sermon, seeing a *Fact and Faith* film entitled *God of the Atom*. Such films were part of an evangelical response to the fearful world we had entered since Hiroshima. Indeed, religious teaching had been a strong element in my life and the Christian understanding of life and death was a great strength and comfort at a time when there was growing uncertainty as to the nature of the post-war brave new world.

A large number of children reported every Sunday morning and afternoon to one of the many Sunday Schools in the town. Parents were glad to have the time to themselves; mine went to bed in the afternoon. Sundays were quiet times and it was expected that little work should be done. Shops were closed apart from some newsagents who opened for a few hours. One did not consider going to the cinema or getting a bag of chips on a Sunday! It was a day for visiting the family and for quiet reflection, even if you didn't go to a place of worship. The Sabbath tradition was a long one and stemmed from the religious observance of the past. Many, but not all, went to church or chapel. It was considered unseemly by some to play loud music, do the washing or (as one neighbour bitterly complained) have the wireless on especially if one listened to modern, lighthearted programmes such as *Life with the Lyons,* or *the Billy Cotton Band Show.* A few strict people refused to read newspapers on the Sabbath. There were quite a few who were total abstainers from alcohol and did their best to keep the young away from the demon drink. Some had good cause, for many men had spent their wages by Friday evening and wives had to make do in order to keep families together and fed.

There was a gradual easing of Sabbath observance, the legacy of the Victorian period. The war with its restrictions had given impetus to a desire to go out, get away from the humdrum and meet with other people. The local pleasure park became a centre of social togetherness. In the summer months concerts were given on Sunday afternoons and evenings from the wrought iron bandstand whilst folk listened from the comfort of wooden chairs, walked across the park, played bowls, putting or giant draughts. Families gathered, and whilst the adults chatted the children ran around and played on the grass. Fond memories include a particular evening concert with a brass band playing as the sun cast an orange glow in the deepening purple of the sky. Shadows lengthened, cast by the park's avenue of lime trees. People, smartly dressed for Sunday, stood or sat entranced as a lovely peaceful summer evening closed and families returned home to prepare for the week ahead. This was what the war had been fought for; peace!

From the age of five or six I attended a Sunday School at Carey Baptist Church, a late-nineteenth century structure of brick with extensive halls and ancillary buildings. Crowds of children congregated at two o'clock on Sunday afternoons. A variety of willing cheerful volunteers endeavoured to instil some order and teach Christian truths to a motley assemblage. Sunday School was a positive influence as it brought to our attention the needs of others in the world, made us look at ourselves and sowed seeds of responsibility.

Like many Nonconformist Churches my church was named not after a traditional saint but in memory of one of its modern heroes. I became imbued with the life of William Carey who had been born into a humble family in Paulerspury, Northamptonshire in 1761. He had become a Christian in early life, worked as a cobbler (like my grandfather), became a schoolmaster, and minister in Moulton and Leicester. By his own determined effort he taught

70

himself foreign languages, succeeding against much opposition in founding the Baptist Missionary Society in Kettering in 1792. This was the first of its kind, and inspired a global missionary movement which involved most Christian denominations.

Carey volunteered to be the Society's first missionary and spent the rest of his life in India. Here he had translated the Old and New Testaments into many Indian languages, especially Bengali, Urdu and Sanskrit, established schools and the Serampore College, Asia's first university. He was a noted botanist and his own private garden became the foundation for the Botanic Gardens of India. He died in Serampore in 1834, a great benefactor to the subcontinent and much revered. His great motto "Expect great things from God. Attempt great things for God" is carved on the stone memorial at the gates of the Mission House in Kettering as well as on the lectern placed in his memory in Westminster Abbey.

Such a figure could not but impress my growing awareness of the global challenge of the Christian Gospel. Men like Andrew Fuller of Kettering had spent a lifetime in supporting Carey's efforts in India. Fuller, like a man supporting a friend descending into a dark well, dedicated himself to being "a holder of the rope". His rugged faith and determination was matched by another Kettering Baptist missionary, William Knibb, whose fearless and courageous stand against slavery did much to change views in Britain and helped its abolition in Jamaica.

Such men were part of a powerful ethos which saw the world as a mission ground upon which the love of Christ had to be shown by practical and committed effort. Missionaries coming back home "on furlough" gave illustrated talks to the Sunday School. They showed pictures of the people they served and befriended and brought interesting artefacts such as carvings, weaving and jewellery from exotic places. We were told that children in the Tropics kept their teeth white and clean by using fibrous material like bamboo. Greatly impressed, I attended valedictory services that bade "God speed" to missionaries going out to "The Mission Field" in places like the West Indies, Pakistan or the Chittagong Hill Tracks of Bangladesh.

May 1955 saw the visit to London of the American Southern Baptist evangelist Billy Graham. Thousands flocked to hear him and, for several weeks, daily packed Wembley Stadium. I recall

71

coach loads of people going from Northamptonshire to his London Crusade, many returning inspired and changed by his powerful oratory. I travelled with others to Wembley and was caught up in the fervour of the event.

I was baptised that year by total immersion. Fourteen young people were baptised that Sunday. In the chapel the floorboards of the platform in front of the pulpit were taken up revealing the white tiled baptistery entered by several sets of steps. The minister, the Reverend Donald Black, baptised us dipping each one under the surface. It was an amazing experience coming up from the water and starting a new life *in Christ*. This led to me becoming a Church member being able to vote and take office. I joined a fellowship that contained many superb characters who were loving, generous, kind and very human. From that time I began to develop a wider outlook on life, seeing myself as part of the world Baptist family but developing as the years have passed to an ecumenical and global vision of the Christian Church.

There was a lot of fun and fellowship within the churches of my youth. We met young people from other churches at school, at dances and in the town. Kettering in those days had only one set of traffic lights, at the corner of Gold Street and Silver Street, so it was not difficult for anyone to say: "Meet me at the traffic lights". We came across many other young people in activities organised by the County Youth Service going on residential weekends at Grendon Hall. Those were the days when Harry Whittaker began the Northamptonshire Association of Youth Clubs. Whittaker was an enthusiastic pioneer whose lasting legacy of the NAYC still does valiant work for young people. Organisations such as the Boys' and Girls' Brigades, the Scouts and Guides held young people in interesting activities, supported them in their growing up and gave structure and guidance in an age of some uncertainty. It was a time when organisations such as Moral Rearmament and other ideological groups were active. Many young people like me joined the United Nations Association inspired by the ideal of a global community at peace with itself.

I ventured into youth leadership, starting a youth club at Carey Baptist Church and being delighted at its numerical success. Keen on Rock n' Roll we booked up a band from Corby called *The Invaders* and billed it as *A Hot Dog Stomp.* For three shillings young people would have a live band and a free hotdog. We planned to cater for a hundred. We did our publicity too well as over three hundred turned up on the night. There was plenty of stomping even though the hotdogs ran out. Yet I ran into trouble for my efforts, not from anyone from my own church, but from someone of a more puritanical persuasion who declared that dancing was evil and quoted Salome dancing before Herod. I countered this criticism by quoting back King David dancing before the Lord in the Temple.

Meantime, school days were coming to an end and GCE examinations at O Level were looming. Young people could leave school at fifteen if they were not taking examinations at sixteen. Many started work going into apprenticeships. Staying on I took my examinations in the quietness of another Baptist Church near the school and hired for the occasion. It was very pleasing to pass eight O levels. Choosing a career was an intense experience. Reluctantly, I had decided that the Royal Navy was not for me. The Careers Service interviewed me and amongst the questions I was asked was "Do you like the smell of oil"? Upon my confirmation that oil did smell fine it was suggested that I might try an apprenticeship with British Thompson Houston at Rugby. The apprenticeship in electrical engineering would last seven years and my parents would have to fork out quite a bit of money as the pay was very poor. This left me distinctly unimpressed so I applied for the post of trainee draughtsman in the Borough Council. I was told that I was one of two applicants and that subject to examination results and all being equal the Grammar School boy would get preference over me. The job was eventually offered to me but by that time I had decided upon the teaching profession as a career. I opted to stay on at school and help pioneer the school's first Sixth Form, study for some A Levels and apply for Teacher Training College.

The inspiration for this sudden decision had been growing in me for some years, and I thank the Church for this. At the age of fifteen I was asked if I would like to teach in the primary department of the Sunday School. Several other young people like my friend Roger Tame did the same. I loved it, enjoying the freshness and vitality of little children who put their trust in you. There was the outstanding influence of two single women, Maisie Langley and Anne Gilby, who ran their departments with such love and dedication that one had to be impressed. Every Sunday morning and afternoon Anne, for example, held a large body of Juniors spellbound by her stories about Christian heroes from the Bible and the everyday world. In the week she taught shorthand and typing to the journalists at the *Evening Telegraph,* but on Sundays she poured out her love for the children. She was a gifted story teller. Many were influenced by her. Likewise with Maisie, and many others, who attended the Sunday School week after week in all weathers giving their time and enthusiasm so willingly and freely. Society is a poorer place without its network of Sunday Schools which have sadly declined since the sixties.

Chapter Six: Finding a Career (1956-60)

Consciousness of social class has been a predominant factor in British life for generations. I recall when quite young playing at a friend's house and some visiting relative of his speaking very disparagingly about my local accent as being "common". When I returned to school at sixteen to be part of a small innovative sixth-form I met up with an acquaintance who, likewise, was staying on to study a GCE Advanced Level course. He had been at my Junior School and was one of the few who had gone to the Grammar School. "What are you going to do with those oddments?" he had asked, referring to my GCE O level passes. My "oddments" were virtually the same as his, yet he clearly considered anything that I achieved or did would be of inferior quality to anything he accomplished. I reflected then that he was an academic snob; his father was a factory worker yet mine was a departmental manager; he lived in a terraced house and we lived in a semi-detached. What was it then, I asked, that divided us? Clearly, aspirations inbred by the educational system had something to do with it, apart from the personality of my acquaintance, as many other friends were Grammar School boys and did not have the same attitude.

Another aspect of snobbishness reared its head when I asked a girl to accompany me to the theatre. It was going to be a matinee performance of a Shakespearian play in Northampton. We would go on the bus, have a meal then come home. What could be simpler? Her father was a well-to-do manufacturer; her mother had come from a working class background and money had really gone to her head. I was not considered the right sort of friend, and so mummy and daddy took us to the theatre in their large Jaguar car and brought us back to their home for afternoon tea. It was mummy who dismissed me from the front door with a finality which hinted, "Don't come back". The poor girl had no say in the matter. Such chaperoning had more to do with a previous century but was still practised in the fifties. Expensive foreign finishing school education for one's daughter could not be wasted!

During my college days I met with a different kind of social elitism, albeit of a regional kind. Being asked away for a weekend with friends was quite an eye-opener. My hosts lived in the new Forest and took me to rather an elegant ball on the pier at

Southampton. The talk of the evening included yachts and horses, and the usual gossip about human peccadilloes. Somewhere in the conversation I was asked where I came from. I told them Northamptonshire. A glazed look came over the eyes. "Oh that's where Robin Hood came from", came one reply." No, you fool", said someone else. "It's a place near Edinburgh". Coming from the East Midlands I have become used to people thinking that Northamptonshire and its adjacent counties are somewhere in the cyberspace between London and Scotland. In the late fifties with the road system undeveloped by motorways it was common to find people grossly ignorant of other parts of the country. People living south of the Thames certainly thought that civilisation ended at Potter's Bar. In my own experience many lived, worked, got married, had families and died in their own locations, travelling little and consequently being ignorant of so much of the world around them.

On 2 November 1959 the first motorway, the M1, was opened by the Minister of Transport Ernest Marples. The motorway then only stretched from St Albans to Birmingham and covered 72 miles. With some friends I soon sampled the novelty of this major road which Marples had declared would open up a new, exciting form of travel in the scientific age. There were no lights, no central reservations, no crash barriers and no speed limit. In the early days there were few vehicles on the motorway, especially at night, but traffic volume soon reached 13,000 a day, but nowhere near the day and night pounding of about seven times that amount in the early 21st century. On that first trip on the M1, sometime in spring 1960, we zoomed southwards in a friend's Humber Super Snipe to live it up with a coffee and a bun at the new service station at Newport Pagnell. As we travelled along, a car moving north shed a wheel which rolled across the entire road to bounce on the opposite grass bank; the car continued for a minute or so before it slewed onto the hard shoulder. No-one was hurt.

Most people, if asked, would have easily placed themselves in the social class hierarchy ranging through working class, lower-middle, middle, upper middle, to upper class; beyond this was the notion of aristocracy and then royalty. Most people hoped for betterment of life but the snob, always aspiring to a level or two above reality, in effect despised his own background. Yet social life was changing with a blurring of distinctions. The war had had an effect upon the class structure and the relationships between classes. The working class had strengthened its hand, and in the post war reconstruction with a shortage of workers and skills, wages had dramatically risen. Taxation policy by the post war Labour government hit the upper-middle class hardest thus smoothing out some of the financial barriers between them and the working classes.

Within social groupings there were numerous gradations; many working class folk considered themselves "respectable" in contradistinction to those who were deemed "rough". "Oh yes, my dear", my mother (a seamstress) would say, referring to one of the buttonhole specialists who did work for her, "Mrs Smith is a very respectable lady. She always does a good neat job". Where you lived had its pecking order, too. My parents gravitated from terrace house to semi-detached. It mattered socially if you were an owner-occupier or a council-house tenant. It was the height of achievement to own a detached place with a large garden and a drive at the front upon which to park a car. My mother was employed over the years as a companion to several elderly well-to-do ladies who lived in substantial detached residences. She always remembered her humble rural background and that she had "gone into service" for a doctor's family when she left school at thirteen. Doctors walked two inches above the ground to my parents who never questioned their advice or treatment and had total faith in their professionalism. If you were "under the doctor" who knew all about you and your needs then that was sufficient. Our family general practitioner had treated three generations of us and was a great friend.

Life in the school Sixth Form was very pleasant. Going back to school and being given the task of prefect, and having free periods in which to study was a new experience. The small group who comprised the Sixth Form dedicated themselves to getting their noses down to work. We owed it to ourselves and to the staff who did their best for us with few resources. I decided to study 19th Century British and European political history, English Literature and Art. I threw myself into the work with a degree of relish.

Conscious that my parents were supporting me I determined to get another part-time job in order to earn my keep and obtained a job as a messenger boy for the Shoe and Allied Trades Research Association at SATRA House in Kettering. Here was a new experience which involved me going for a two hour stint after school every day. My job was to visit all the offices and laboratories to pick up the outgoing correspondence, take it to the Director, collect it after signing, then in the main office see that it was enveloped, franked and, most importantly, get the mail to the General Post Office in Kettering before 6pm. It was a mile and half ride on my bicycle and I often arrived by the skin of my teeth as the mail was being cleared from the box. I enjoyed that job very much and learned how easy it is for anyone anywhere to walk around with a piece of paper in hand looking busy and get access to the most restricted of places.

Towards the end of my Sixth Form days and, with examinations out of the way, I volunteered to undertake some observation in Avondale Junior School. It turned out to be some full teaching experience as the school teacher I was placed with was more than happy for me to take the class for quite a few lessons. Teachers, nearing the end of a tiring year, were always ready to let a student come in. I loved the job and spent five great weeks with a class of over forty ten year olds. It was a revelation, but one that convinced me that I was doing the right thing in aspiring for the teaching profession. Children in those days sat in neat rows. Class lessons were straight "talk and chalk" with the teacher delivering some information, answering questions then letting the children get on with some expression work such as writing or illustration. I enjoyed learning to write and draw on the blackboard, techniques which were to generally fall out of favour in later years but ones which did serve as good demonstrations of how to present work and how to draw.

It was quite a daunting prospect, choosing a teacher training college. There were many, especially in London, and I was relieved to be offered an interview at the first of my choices. My father accompanied me to the Borough Road College in Isleworth, Middlesex one day in November 1957; he waited for me while I went in for interview. It was dark when I emerged from the building; the lights from the college's neo-gothic windows twinkled, and across the playing fields the evening rush of traffic could be seen on The Great West Road. This place would soon become very familiar to me. A letter eventually arrived confirming a place at the college subject to satisfactory examination results.

Meantime, the summer holiday had arrived and there was need to get a full-time job. In the fifties employment was relatively easy to acquire. The post-war boom in employment had not subsided, and there were plenty of jobs for students. I obtained work at Wicksteed Park. The park had been gifted by Charles Wicksteed, a local philanthropist, to the people of Kettering. My first day there was spent picking up litter from the previous weekend, but greater things lay in store.

There was a vacancy at the Pets Corner, and I quickly found myself in charge of a llama named Guy, some penguins, some coati mundi, a chimpanzee and a host of rabbits and guinea pigs that were busy reproducing as fast as they could. In addition to this there were goats and, in an adjoining field, a number of sheep whose hooves needed cutting and disinfecting with iodine. This last job, which was undertaken with the local RSPCA inspector, taught me that sheep, when scared, can jump over a person in order to escape; one did that to me when I tried to catch it. The experience of looking after animals confined in such a small space as a Pets Corner convinced me that it was not a humane thing to do. The developments over later decades to provide animals in captivity with appropriate living conditions, especially in wildlife parks, are a much welcomed change.

My father's Morris 10 was well used once I had learned to drive.
The roads were relatively empty of traffic.
Left: outside Roger Tame's house in Kingsley Avenue, Kettering.
Right: fooling about with Tony Briggs, Geoffrey Martin
and my young cousin Roger Turnell. 1959

Towards the end of the summer of 1958 I took my driving test. My father had sat me at the wheel of his Morris 8 some years before, propped up on cushions, and allowed me to drive down the old runway at Harrington. He had provided me with useful tuition, allowing me to drive us on holiday, and paying for some professional lessons as the test loomed ever nearer. My driving tutor told me that in the town the examiner would take me on one of several routes, and we had driven them all, so I was ready for the emergency stop when it came; I stood the car on end, almost catapulting the examiner into the windscreen. In 1958 there were very few cars on the roads and I remember at the end of the test easily parking the car outside the testing station, switching off the engine and waiting for the verdict. Amazingly, I passed!

That September I found myself in London. Suddenly, everything had changed and I was to take lodgings several miles away from the college for the first year. My fellow lodger was my elder by several years and, fresh from national service in the RAF, must have considered me a bit green round the gills. He would disappear for the weekends to see his girlfriend in Enfield. We lodged with a delightful couple whose son had emigrated to Canada. They had spare space in their semi-detached house in Heston so did good business with the college in letting out a bedroom and the downstairs sitting room to us.

Heston was still semi-rural with fields, yet to the north was Southall and to the south was Hounslow, bourgeoning centres of population. Heston airfield had been part of the origins of Heathrow International Airport; already in the late fifties aircraft activity was increasing. The first night I spent in my lodgings terrified me as the sound of an aircraft was so loud and close that I jumped out of bed, but soon got used to the aircraft coming in over the house at regular intervals of every few minutes. I obtained a part-time job at Heathrow for a short time, cycling there to work on Saturdays in the catering section of British Overseas Air Corporation somewhere near the present Alcock and Brown Memorial statue. However, I didn't work there for long as there were plenty of other things to do.

Finding your feet in college life is not always easy. The first week was the longest I had ever spent in my life. I actually caught the train home being rather home-sick one weekend only to find that my girlfriend who had sworn undying affection was going out with her local milkman. It was a kindness to us both, and we parted company with good grace. Returning to London with a lightness of step I felt free to meet whatever challenges there were. Yet coming home on another weekend I was shocked to see how ill my father was. Being concerned with my own future, with examinations and getting a college place and working throughout the summer of 1958 I did not notice how sick he had become. He was diagnosed with tuberculosis and had to spend time at a sanatorium in Rushden before he could resume normal life. My mother gave him every attention and cared for him with touching devotion.

It was exciting catching the train; the slamming of doors, the hiss of steam and the acrid smell of smoke, the shrill whistle of the guard as the train pulled southward to London arriving in the echoing cavern of St Pancras station. A quick race through the labyrinthine tunnels that connected with the underground, and out westward along the Piccadilly Line to Osterley was my usual route. At Osterley one met the Great West Road on which I rode the familiar red London buses. Within a few weeks I had my bicycle delivered to my lodgings and travelled freely along the cycle tracks to and from college.

Borough Road College originated in the school founded by Joseph Lancaster in 1798 in Southwark, London. Lancaster was a pioneer in educating the many destitute children of the capital. In 1804 his school moved to the Borough Road in Southwark and then fifty years later to Isleworth in west London. The college is now part of Brunel University and is called its Osterley Campus. When I was there it was much different, being a men's college of only several hundred students training specifically for teaching. The college comprised a long Victorian building with additional annexes built on the playing fields during the war for the use of the Admiralty and known to all as "the Ship". The toilets which featured large at the end of the main corridor were colloquially referred to as "the White City".

After my first year in "digs" I came in to reside in college for the second and final year of training. We were allocated bedrooms high up on the top floor of the building. Laying in bed on the first night I became aware of a rumbling sound which appeared to be getting louder and closer. It was one of the customs of the place for cannon balls to be rolled from one end of the attic to the other. A ball would rumble overhead then, ten minutes later, it would rumble back. All good fun, as were the fire drills. The whole college would be evacuated once a term, usually late at night. It was amazing that upon the sound of the siren the college jazz band would appear in order to entertain the rest of the college as they mustered on the playing fields.

There was an annual summer Rag Week in which students collected for various charities. I played my piano accordion standing on the bar of a pub in Hounslow High Street and collecting almost a bucket full of small change. One year there was a spectacular Physical Education display put on in Hounslow High Street by the PE department. When the students carried away the wooden horse upon which they had been cavorting it was discovered that a complete toilet had been firmly fixed to make a traffic island in the road.

We were not long in college when the first of our teaching practices were announced. I was to go to a Junior School in Brentford along with another student who happened to own a two-stroke motorbike. We decided to travel together and duly rode into Brentford, past the Gillette razor factory and arrived at the school. As we entered the gates it was clear that something sensational had just occurred; the children were agog with excitement and told us that there had been an armed robbery at a bank nearby. It turned out to be the first of its kind in which a weapon had been used and fired in London; the shape of things to come.

There were other teaching practices throughout the course. One was at Strand-on-the-Green in Chiswick, close to Kew Gardens. It was a delightful spot and in the lunch hour we would sit at the riverside tables of one of the local pubs with a pint and eating our sandwiches. My colleague for that occasion had been preparing some lessons on King Charles I. We were encouraged to put life into our lessons and my friend asked me to get his class ready for his dramatic entrance. All the children were sitting quietly when the skylight above their heads opened, a rope ladder descended and the fully costumed figure of King Charles began to descend, as it were from the famous oak tree. Unfortunately, my friend's leg got caught in the rope and he found himself dangling upside down above the heads of his class. There was a near riot. He decided after that to make the beginnings of his lessons less spectacular.

I joined the college Country Dance Band which comprised drum, violins, piano and me on piano accordion. We played at most of the London training colleges and, as we were a men-only college, it was good to get to meet women from their colleges. We were very modern as we recorded from tape a 78rpm long playing record of our repertoire. Nothing, however, could have prepared us for the visit of a famous personage. The Principal had announced that as it was the centenary of the college we were to receive a visit from a VIP. We were to go about our daily routines as usual.

We were having a practise in "The Ship" one morning when the doors of the hall swung open and a bevy of official-looking people entered. We were in the middle of playing a lively Irish jig. There stood the Principal, several senior staff and other dignitaries, but in the centre was none other than Elizabeth, the Queen Mother. She advanced on us with a smile and beamed up to me with the comment: "Oh, I do love the sound of a squeeze box". "Yes ma'am", I stammered, "but I'm no Jimmy Shand" (A very popular Scottish dance band leader at that time). At this she laughed and went on to say that she enjoyed sounds like accordions but particularly enjoyed the bagpipes. "I'm rather partial to the bagpipes, you know". After a few more minutes of conversation she wished us goodbye with a wave of the hand and sallied out followed by her gaggle of officials. The doors shut, and we were left in a state of bewilderment.

Like many students of the time we considered it appropriate to dress in a particular style. The camel coloured duffle coat, the long striped coloured college scarf wound round the neck and casually thrown across the shoulder, a Tyrolean hat stuck jauntily on the head were all part of the with-it student. It helped to smoke a pipe, preferably a curved one, and puff contentedly on evil-smelling tobacco. A black blazer with college badge and bright red waistcoat with gold buttons completed my sartorial perfection. I thought that a smart briefcase made of leather would impress when riding on the underground and travelling on the train. The colloquial expression for travelling into London was "going up the Smoke". Never once did I feel London to be unsafe, although it always paid to be careful.

Members of Borough Road College Christian Union 1959-60
The fellow on the back row extreme left still has a quiff!

Coming home for the Christmas vacation was always enjoyable and I worked on two occasions for the General Post Office. Students were welcome to help with the Christmas post. It meant an early start, sorting and then going on the rounds delivering before daybreak. There were special extra deliveries at various times of the day, and I enjoyed taking a little red van to the railway station to await the early post from London.

Staying in London over the weekend was quite an experience. Friday lunchtime would come and I would make tracks for the underground and spend some time in the West End. There was a good jazz club in Soho called *The Half Moon Dive* and you could get a cheap meal at one of a number of Forte restaurants. 1958-60 was a time of some excitement in the world of entertainment. I was present at the London opening night of a musical which had been a sensation in New York in the previous year. Written by Jerome Robbins, Leonard Bernstein and Arthur Laurents, *West Side Story* was to become one of the greatest theatrical hits of all time. I had been attending lectures in the University of London by Professor

A.C.Bradley on Shakespearian Tragedy. *West Side Story* was a modern interpretation of *Romeo and Juliet,* so I wanted to see it. I found the choreography, the colour and movement, the gritty social realism, its tenderness and pathos and sheer energy totally captivating. In 1961 the film version, starring Natalie Wood and Richard Beymer brought it to a wider audience.

Also in London there were other theatrical attractions. At Puddle Dock in the City, Bernard Miles was building the new Mermaid Theatre. Henry Fielding's play *Lock up your daughters* was one of the racy new musicals that the Mermaid had to offer. Friends would come up to London to stay with me for the weekend and we became regulars at the Whitehall Theatre where Brian Rix's famous farces were running. Leo Franklin, the actor, recognised us one evening sitting in our usual place on the front row and with a classic line "Let us (s)pray" -he was playing the part of a vicar armed with a soda water siphon- gave us a good soaking. We had a laugh with him after the show.

There was more meaty theatrical material to see. At the Round House in Camden we went to see plays such as Bertolt Brecht's *Caucasian Chalk Circle*. The Irish playwright Brendan Behan, influenced by Brecht, was active at this time in espousing the IRA cause; I recall the night when his greatest drama *The Hostage* was first staged in London; I was sitting close to him when he caused uproar by drunkenly heckling the actors from the stalls. Apartheid in South Africa was a major issue, and I found myself swept up in the student demonstrations that focussed indignation on South Africa House at the corner of the Strand, filling nearby Trafalgar Square.

Suddenly, college life came to an end. The time had passed rapidly; final examinations and teaching practices were all done and dusted. There was the Leavers' Ball and farewells. I took a last look at the main hall where we had taken our meals remembering particularly the occasions when huge salvers of fried eggs and chips and jugs of milk had been the standard Wednesday supper following the usual football or rugby matches. There had been huge rivalry between colleges and one annual tussle was the match with St Mary's Roman Catholic College in Twickenham. That was always a lively affair. I said goodbye to my study which was situated on the ground floor, and recalled the times that my window had been used by fellow students coming in late at night and circumventing the locked front doors. There were the debates in the Common Room, and the late night reading in the inner library when I read through one by one all the novels of Thomas Hardy. Strangely echoing, the emptying corridors reminded me that we were scattering to take up careers in many parts of the country. One door was closing yet another was opening. It was time to go.

Land's End 1961. A journey to the West Country in Roger Tame's Ford *Prefect* was something of an adventure especially when the car could conk out at any time.

Chapter Seven: A Class of Fifty-nine.

I returned to my parents' home in the summer of 1960, glad to support my mother who had continued to care for my father. He had been cured of tuberculosis yet the aftermath was a debility which took time and new developments in drugs to cure. Dad had been an able footballer in his young days, playing for the noteworthy Walgrave Amber FC which produced numerous professional footballers. Dad himself had played some trial games for Birmingham City FC, and had turned out for the Kettering Poppies FC at various times. It was good to see him getting back to some of his old vim and vigour in later years and kicking a ball about in the garden with me and his grandson Julian.

In the summer of 1960 I was employed by the Co-operative Bakery in Kettering as a driver and rounds man covering staff vacancies in the holiday period. Every summer for the next four years I worked for the Co-op; the wages were a very useful supplement to a young teacher's salary. With average wages at this time at £16 per week my initial salary of £10 per week needed some supplementation. Duties at the bakery started early in the morning, and one had to arrive promptly in order to take the bread from the ovens to fill up the van ready for the day's deliveries. Lateness meant that most of the bread had gone so customers would not be amused.

I drove a red Ford 30cwt van and often had to rattle along the road to Corby delivering bread and cakes to the Co-operative shops before they opened. At other times I worked the machine that sliced and wrapped the bread. Wrapped bread was an innovation and was seen by some as a good way to get rid of the previous day's leftovers. Going out into the rural hinterland was a delight and I soon got to know many people who lived on the outlying farms and smallholdings and in the hamlets and villages of the Nene Valley.

Every week I would deliver a specially ordered tray of stale bread to an elderly countrywoman who lived in a semi-derelict thatched cottage. She would greet me at the door with a toothless chortle, pay me and take her bread. One day she called to me to go inside the cottage. It was a hot afternoon and the flies buzzed in the windows of the dim room and stuck ingloriously on the yellow flypapers hanging from the dark beams. The place was filthy, and the smell was almost unbearable. My customer sat on a sofa with a large pig resting its head in her lap. She was a wonderful character and told me that she had been widowed for some years. Her late husband had been, in his prime, "the strongest man in Northamptonshire" and a noted wrestler. She liked nothing more than a glass of beer and some stale bread which she shared with her pet sow. Never before or since have I met anyone with such a contented outlook on life.

One day I didn't close the van's rear doors properly and stalled the engine on a hill shooting out several trays of bread into the middle of a village street. My deliveries covered a range of people: one was a smallholder who insisted on giving me bantam eggs to take home, and there were cottagers, pub landlords, farmers and townsfolk. A distinguished gentleman lived in a house near Woodford at the end of a very long leafy track. He was the author, artist, naturalist and countryman Denys Watkins-Pitchford known as "BB" (named after a type of lead shot). I met him as I was delivering a loaf of bread and his milk and spoke to him often conversing on a range of subjects. I learned of his early life in Lamport, his career as a schoolmaster at Rugby and his fears of the way in which the countryside was being despoiled by contemporary farming methods. It was a period when hedges were being grubbed up to make way for large scale prairie type fields. He was eloquent in his criticism of the use of agro-chemicals which he declared was responsible for the destruction of wildlife. A decade later his wife died of an inexplicable illness which he adamantly believed was caused by pesticides sprayed on adjacent fields near to their next home, the Round House at Sudborough.

One particular summer I worked with one of the regular rounds men; together we had to cover the whole of Thrapston as well as adjacent villages. My colleague knew everyone, especially in one particular road in which he always spent some time. He would send me ahead and ask me to wait for him when I had finished my deliveries. He was usually gone an hour so I took the opportunity to have my morning sandwiches. He would eventually return to the van somewhat dishevelled and a little breathless. He had several lady friends in that road, and he would visit them each in turn for a breakfast-time tryst. He admitted that he was getting a bit jaded by the routine.

In July 1960 I attended the Kettering Divisional Education Office for interview. There was a huge teacher shortage so any anxiety about getting a job soon evaporated as the education officer showed me a list of a dozen vacancies and invited me to make a choice. Being advised not to work initially in the town where I had latterly been at school I chose Corby, easily accessible by bus. Following a quick telephone call to the head teacher it was agreed that I go for interview that very afternoon. I duly arrived at what had been the old village school, expanded to accommodate about eight hundred children, and reflecting the expansion of Corby as a major steel making town. My interview was successful and the head teacher of the Rowlett Junior School said he would be glad to see me when term started in September.

The day duly arrived and I reported for duty bright and early. I found that my classroom was located in a row of wooden sheds that reminded me of prisoner of war camp billets. Upon the ringing of the school bell children lined up and after the command went to their classrooms. Up the wooden steps to my classroom trouped no less than fifty-nine children all aged seven or eight (second year juniors). They shoved and squeezed into the iron framed desks that were set in serried rows. There was hardly any room to walk between them. Apart from the teacher's high wooden desk, a blackboard perched precariously on an easel and a cupboard, there was no other furniture in the room. I faced a mass of little faces each one of which was weighing me up. Several did not speak English. Yet they were a grand lot of children and in spite of the difficulties we established a good working relationship. After a term another teacher was found for the school and my class was reduced to forty-eight.

One of my fellow teachers in the row of sheds was an ex-naval man who had trained for teaching. He had been brought out of retirement by the needs of the staffing shortage. He was well over seventy, a smart powerful figure whose moustache bristled as he spoke. I had only been at the school for a short while when I was accosted in the playground by a mother who was charging her pram like a gun carriage across the playground. On this equipage rode several infants of various ages. Her manner was anything but pleasant. She was clearly after my colleague's blood and thought I was he. I speedily pointed out where his classroom was located. There ensued a lively exchange in which the woman threatened my colleague with the steel-shod boots of her husband who was intent on making mincemeat of him. "Madam", he exclaimed flicking the wrists of his immaculate blazer with his fingers, "I will accommodate your husband when the shift finishes tomorrow afternoon. Kindly convey that to him".

The staffroom was agog; the woman's husband had a notorious reputation and had fists as big as dinner plates. Undaunted, my colleague left school the next afternoon promptly at the four o'clock bell. He made his way to the main gates of the steelworks where he waited for the shift to clock-off. Several of us followed at a discreet distance. Soon the exodus of workers began, and all was rush and bustle as pedestrians and cyclists pushed past our friend who stood immobile and poised for action in the middle of the roadway. It was like a scene from the film *High Noon.* Suddenly, his adversary came out of the gates, saw him, stopped, and then hurriedly ran back into the steelworks. The duel was over. With a smile on his lips our friend went home to his tea. No more was said.

I tried very hard to enliven my lessons and make a rather dull and sombre classroom a little more attractive. The lack of space, however, militated against anything ambitious, and the major thrust of the curriculum remained an emphasis on the 3R's (Arithmetic, Writing and Reading) plus the fourth R (Religion) which in law was the only compulsory part of the curriculum. We had to follow the Agreed Syllabus which had been hammered out by the various denominations to provide an acceptable outline of Christian faith and history. Some history, geography, literature, art and singing were attempted as well as games and PE.

Young teachers like me soon learned that to survive in the blackboard jungle one had to have sound discipline. Once you had established yourself you could relax and enjoy the vibrant life of the children. There were many nationalities represented in the class which comprised about equal numbers of boys and girls. I rather enjoyed teaching Physical Education and in the school hall one day was confronted by an austere lady who announced that she was the PE Inspector. That particular lesson was based upon an idea I had developed during a teaching practice in one of the London schools. Taking a sheet of manila card I had affixed a coloured circle with a split pin in the centre. On the circle were the names of the four teams (red, blue, yellow and green) and by moving the circle the team names would rest against an activity (beans bags, climbing frame, footballs, ropes etc). Before the lesson the children would know what to do when I said "Team Activities".

This evidently impressed the inspector who, after the lesson, expressed satisfaction with my work. She then asked if she could borrow my chart promising me that it would be returned straight away. Several years later when I was working in another school the same inspector appeared and proceeded to castigate me for my lesson. "You should be better organised", she said and produced from a roll of visual aids the very same chart, now much dog-eared, that she had borrowed from me. "I would recommend that you plan your lessons on these lines", she haughtily advised. By this time I had lost my timidity and expressed pleasure that she had remembered to give me back my chart and pointing out that it had my name and college written on the back. She blustered somewhat before withdrawing. The head master congratulated me as he had been "trying to get rid of that old trout for years".

Back in Corby the life of school went on with many a comical episode. Teachers never relished the thought of dinner duty when one had to keep an eye on hundreds of ravenous children as they packed into the school hall. The smell of cabbage and mashed potatoes permeated the hall for the rest of the afternoon. As a sop to the staff, anyone doing a dinner duty could have a free meal, which had to be taken alongside the children. The cook did well considering the resources she was given, but never did get the hang of meat balls. The meat ball issue was a hot topic in the staffroom, and one day a rebellion broke out when the entire staff doing dinner duty sent back their meat balls topped by white flags of surrender made from match sticks and paper. Custard was another bone of contention, it being so solid that several declared they had bent spoons trying to lever it out of the jugs.

Staff also had to take their turns at playground duty when the energies of myriad little souls burst forth in a confined tarmac area. No wonder there was a constant stream of grazed knees and cut heads. During one boisterous morning the teacher on duty did not notice that two older boys had slipped quietly out of the wooden gates and into the street. They quickly returned with the spoils of their expedition, namely a huge bunch of bananas which they had purloined from the open cart of a greengrocer making deliveries in

91

the street. Everywhere children were munching bananas, and even members of staff on playground duty were being offered the illicit fruit when the police arrived. It was an embarrassing moment.

Most of the children in the school came from other parts of the town and had to be transported to and fro. Another duty for staff on a regular basis was to supervise children on to the double decked buses that queued up in front of the school at the end of the day. As many as a hundred children would swarm on to each bus, and I often rode shotgun up to the Town Centre where the children were disgorged to go their homeward way. Now and again the duties of dinner, playground and bus would coincide making a long hard day.

Educationalists in the early sixties were suggesting visionary ideas for buildings in which to nurture the child population. Freedom, light and space were keys to an enlightened education. My classroom with its creaking wooden floor and metal windows looked out upon a farmyard on one side. During the summer, windows would be tightly shut to keep out the flies and the smell of a mighty dung heap. If the wind shifted to another quarter there was the smell from the Smith's Crisps factory. From another direction the choking acrid fumes of the Stewart's and Lloyd's steelworks would waft on the breeze. It was all very salubrious.

Poverty was still evident, and I recall two brothers who never appeared at school on the same day. The simple reason for this was they only had one pair of shoes between them. A kind staff member, once we knew what the issue was, gave their mother some shoes. In my next school I met twin girls from a circus family who were forbidden to do PE in the winter months. They were sewn into thick newspaper underskirts for the winter and would not remove them until the spring. Things were good for families when there was plenty of work, but when strikes or layoffs occurred there was little money to tide families over. My fiancée, Steff, worked for the Inland Revenue in the Kettering office and had to go over to Corby to open a one-day-a-week tax office there. Whenever there was short-time working the place became lively in the extreme; so violent did things get that all the furniture in the reception area had to be firmly screwed to the floor otherwise it had the habit of being used as weaponry. Meantime all the furniture and goods being bought on hire purchase were being returned to the shops.

In the main, health had greatly improved by the sixties and childhood illnesses were of the usual kind. Being a teacher had its fascinations especially when parents sent notes explaining their offspring's absences. One mother wrote: "Dear Mister, Ronald was off with the diarear (crossed out) diahoyer (crossed out), the runs. I have put a spare pair of pants in his pocket with a paper bag in case he shits himself again". Another wrote that her child had not attended school the previous day because his clothes had been soaked as he had broken his "akweryhum". The entire school staff puzzled at this unusual word, thinking that he had had some terrible rupture. The child himself explained that his gold fish tank (aquarium) had broken. Not having much heat in the house and no spare clothes he had had to wait until they were dried out. It was of considerable amusement when parents signed off their letters in what was then a commonplace way, "And oblige, Mrs Smith". Often the comma would be left out!

After two seminal years in Corby I moved to the same Junior School in Kettering where I had had my pre-college experiences. The head teacher was into the pre-retirement mode and didn't really want any fancy innovative teaching. He wanted a quiet life and after lunch would repair to his study to do his "administration". His snores could be heard from the adjacent classroom where a class of lively children, and an equally lively teacher, endeavoured to make as much noise as possible. Class sizes numbered about forty, and in those days if one did an art lesson every child did the same thing. The head teacher controlled the stock and one had to ask him for the requisite number of pieces of paper. Naturally, children being children, someone spilled water or paint so down to the head's study flowed a stream of children asking for paper, pencils, exercise books and glue. The staff would wait until the afternoon to do activity lessons so that he frequently missed his beauty sleep.

On my very first day I unwittingly caused a rebellion. At playtime I went timidly to the staffroom to meet my new colleagues. I was asked if I wanted a drink. "Yes please", I replied innocently, "I'll have a cup of tea, please". There was a perceptible gasp. "We don't drink tea or coffee here", said the head master pompously, "we have cocoa. It is very good for you". He handed me a cup of steaming cocoa with a crinkly skin already forming on its surface. "I don't like cocoa", I said. At this the entire staffroom erupted. They, too, did not like cocoa and had been forced to consume it for years! It was disgusting stuff made from the children's milk leftovers (children still were given a third of a pint of milk daily) and they wanted a change! What was wrong with tea or coffee, they demanded. And whilst they were about it, why couldn't women teachers wear slacks and not skirts especially as they were fashionable and warmer in cold weather? The head teacher withered under the onslaught while I stood bemused. The bell rang for school to restart. I never did get my drink, but by the end of the week tea and coffee were on the staffroom table and slacks could be worn in suitable weather. Mind you, the head teacher had a quiet word with me as he didn't like me starting to grow a beard. "You will never advance in this profession", he muttered, "if you have whiskers. Shave it off"!

It was a strange experience working alongside one of my former teachers. We became good friends. Yet it was clear that old ways took a time to recede. My memories of the rigidity of my Junior School years returned when I saw the children segregated into two streams. Streaming had been a major educational device for decades, but the streaming that I now encountered contained all the hallmarks of social division. The children were segregated into S and R streams; I never did find out what those letters stood for, although when the children went into the school hall for assembly the S streams sat on (S)eats and the R streams sat on....the floor! All my sense of injustice flooded back to me and I vowed to work against such a system which treated half the children with contempt.

Every year there were necessary tests in the basic subjects yet the results were put up on large sheets in the foyer so that all could see. The weakest children academically were always at the bottom, and even at their tender age you could see the growth of a resigned "couldn't care less" mentality. A new head teacher soon began to change the ethos, bringing in lively assemblies, drama, music and a more relaxed and humane attitude to children who were struggling. I was heartily glad to see the change. He was a great character who enjoyed dressing up as the dame in local pantomimes. One morning in assembly I think he was much flushed with the success of the previous evening when he dismissed the school with "I thank you folks!" and a suitable theatrical gesture. The old head had retired to look after his smallholding on which he kept pigs. It is said that his wife used to point him out to visitors as "the one wearing the hat". On his last day boys who were leaving the school pelted his office windows with unripe pears. I watched them do it from my classroom window, and didn't interfere. He deserved it.

It was during these years of the early sixties that I met Steff Loasby at a party at a friend's house. Although she was "going out" with someone else I found out who she was, where she worked, bombarded her with tokens of my affection, and we became engaged. The first time I took her out I thought that I would impress, so I borrowed dad's car and arrived in style at her house. The wretched vehicle refused to start so my future father-in-law ended up giving us a push along the street.

During these years from 1960-64 the Cold War moved on with the building of the Berlin Wall in 1961. The USSR stole a march on the Americans with the launch of Vostok 1 which completed one orbit of the planet. In it was the first man in space, the cosmonaut Yuri Gagarin. Matters became serious in 1962 with the Cuban Missile Crisis when President John F. Kennedy demanded that the USSR remove its missiles from Cuba. It was a knife edge of fear for everyone. We all thought that the Third World War was about to start. The crisis passed and the world let out a collective sigh of relief.

Yet news from the United States became even more riveting. In that same year Marilyn Monroe, the great film icon, was found dead. More dire news struck the world on 22 November 1963 when President J. F. Kennedy was assassinated. I remember that day as did everyone else alive at that time. Kennedy was gunned down whilst riding in a motorcade in the city of Dallas, Texas. It was early evening in Kettering when I was walking to Steff's parents' house. The overcast clouds were dark and threatening. There seemed a terrible oppressive feeling in the atmosphere. Entering the house I saw the television news being broadcast. The black and white pictures told the awful and stunning truth. Other major issues such as the rights of black people were very much to the fore in the United States. Back in 1955 the issue of civil rights had flared when a black woman named Rosa Parks refused to give up her seat on a bus to a white person. The Civil Rights Movement commenced in earnest, and in 1963 the Rev. Dr. Martin Luther King Jnr. uttered his famous

95

"I have a dream" speech which resonated around the world. Five years later he, too, was assassinated.

House prices had begun a steady upward movement. We found a pre-war three bedroom semi-detached house in Kettering and paid £2450 for it. Before the war a new house would have cost about a fifth of that amount. My salary came to some £14 per week. We took out a mortgage for £1800 which was a fortune to us. Interest rates were at a post-war high of 6% having moved upward inexorably from the pre-war 4%. Within twenty years variable mortgages would reach a peak of over 13%. Luckily, we were both working and spent several years saving hard to pay the deposit.

My father kindly came to wallpaper several rooms for us. I tried my hand at carpentry and made a saucepan rack that resembled a cyclone disaster area; nothing was straight or square, and it collapsed when I loaded it with utensils. DIY was very much in its infancy during these years, but necessity being the mother of invention led me into a steep learning curve and I improved. After work we would cycle to the house and work long into the evening decorating and preparing our new home. We invited friends round for a *stripping party.* When they arrived they were given wallpaper stripping knives and had to do a bit of work before they could get their supper.

The background to my life has always been the happiness and appreciation I feel for the wonderful friends I have. Although I have been blessed with so many folk who have offered me unquestioning loyalty one couple in particular, Roger and Sonia Tame, have been there always for me. Roger, from my early childhood shared many a hilarious escapade such as the trip we made to the West Country in his old Ford car. When he met Sonia, who had so many interests such as gardening that Steff and I also shared, the friendship gelled even more. Roger was the natural choice as my best man when Steff and I married. I reciprocated by being his best man. We have enjoyed a natural and easy companionship over the years and consider them as part of the family.

The sixties were a time when most heterosexual couples got married. The living-together phenomenon was yet to commence in any large-scale way, as was the movement for homosexuals to "come out of the closet". 1963-4 was something of a watershed in British social life, however. The media centred their attention on the pop scene in "swinging London" with idols such as Marianne Faithful, Mick Jagger and Keith Richards and groups like *Freddie and the Dreamers,* and the *Hollies.* There was a potent mix of drink, drugs and sexual licence, aided by the increasing availability of the Pill, which formed a heady brew. One of my aunts asked me at the time if I practised free love, assuming that that was the done thing by all young people. She had read about it in the newspapers and, I thought, seemed rather envious of the greater freedoms that young people were supposed to have. Her question illustrated a widespread contemporary myth about the sixties which has persisted until the present. Traditional values were still held by the majority of young people but, as the years unfolded, the pressures to conform to a new set of behaviour patterns became increasingly difficult to resist. The seventies witnessed phenomena such as the anarchic Punk movement which openly mocked the old order.

It was still customary in the sixties for the man to ask the parents, especially the father, if it was agreeable to them that he married the daughter. There was little thought of going off to live together "in sin". A wind of change was beginning to blow, the effects of which were to have major repercussions in the following decades. I remember in 1962 asking my future father-in-law for his daughter's *hand.* Even when engaged there was a tight rein upon young couples. When Steff's parents had gone to bed and we sat in the sitting room for too long my future mother-in-law would bang her shoe on the floor as a signal that it was time for me to depart.

Getting married in 1964 had its particular traumas. A few weeks before the great day I telephoned Steff's minister who had agreed to marry us to check on details. He had completely forgotten and was otherwise engaged. Nevertheless, my minister (Rev Brian Barker) agreed to conduct the service. The invitations to the wedding had been duly sent out and we discovered that the printer had given me a totally false middle name. My mother had insisted that a nice piece of barathea cloth (she called it barracuda) which she had had for years would make me a perfect suit in which to be married. She duly commissioned one of her tailor friends to make the suit which looked fine until we discovered too late that one trouser leg was longer than the other by an inch or more. You can spot it on the black and white wedding photographs if you know what to look for! On the day prior to the wedding I went for a haircut; unfortunately, I chose a hairdresser who must have been in the army or who had been a sheep shearer for he left me looking like a convict.

Wedding Day , 4 April 1964, with my parents on the left and Steff's on the right.
Study my trouser bottoms carefully.

The day of the April wedding dawned rather cold and dull; in fact, it began to snow. Many couples married before the 4th April as it was the end of the income tax year so that a man could claim a full year's married allowance. The wedding itself proceeded without a hitch but at the reception the cork from a large magnum of champagne, which my father had saved for the occasion, erupted from the bottle with such force that it almost knocked a waiter unconscious. Whilst cutting the cake the whole edifice nearly collapsed. We got away on our honeymoon in a superb Riley sports car which my uncle had kindly loaned us as his wedding gift. Unknown to him and to us the tyres of the car had been stuffed by a previous owner with cardboard so that upon rounding a bend a front tyre burst and we skidded into a hedge. We were shaken and stirred, and it began to snow again. After getting the AA to help us the car limped to our hotel, the Bear Hotel in Chippenham, too late for a hot meal as the restaurant had closed. In the morning the car refused to start and in trying to push-start it the wretched thing ran away down a slope and ended up badly scratched. Married life had thus far been a disaster. We returned home, exchanged cars borrowing my father's (appropriately an Austin *Somerset*) and set off again for the West Country. At one small hotel the owner took one look at us, ascertained that we were really married by inspecting my wife's wedding ring, and proceeded to build us up with massive meat pies for the ordeals ahead. Things did improve from then on.

Those early years of marriage settled into a pleasant pattern and I was able to concentrate on my teaching. I did a certain amount of football refereeing on Saturday mornings. It has always amazed me how passionate people can get about sport. I remember one headmaster becoming apoplectic on the touchline when I gave, in his opinion, a wrong off-side decision. He ran on to the field waving his arms in a most peculiar fashion. One midweek afternoon I took the school football team to play at another Kettering school. The headmaster of this establishment was something of an eccentric who, in later years, became justly acknowledged as a novelist of genius. He brought his entire school out to watch the match. When we scored there was orchestrated silence; when they scored, there was joyous uproar. We lost by a considerable number of goals, and my boys were rather dejected by the unnecessary psychological pressure of the event. At the end of the game the headmaster swept his school back inside leaving us to find our way to the dressing rooms where he had thoughtfully written in beautiful calligraphy on a piece of card the Biblical quotation "Let not the Sun sink upon thy wrath". Byron Rogers, in his biography of the headmaster in question, J L Carr (known to us as Jim) makes reference to this incident. In *The Last Englishman* (2003*)* the author quotes me as being something of a critic of Carr; this is only half the story as Jim had an indirect positive influence on me, especially in writing and publishing. I could have added a postscript to the episode when Carr and I had warmly shaken hands soon after the event; he deliberately came to stand next to me at an open-air ecumenical service on a wet Good Friday in Dalkeith Place, Kettering and took my hand in a most disarming manner. It was his way of putting things right with me, and I appreciated the gesture.

Rogers writes at length about the battle that Carr had with the ecclesiastical authorities over the closure of the redundant

Church of St Faith at Newton in the Willows, near Geddington. It was during these middle years of the sixties into the seventies that the isolated church situated out in the fields was being vandalised. I knew much about and supported Carr's efforts to keep the church building intact and to find a use for it. He encouraged a poetry reading group and other literary activities to make use of the building. Part of Carr's outrage came over the maverick way in which a group of amateur archaeologists was allowed to dig up the nave. I was writing some articles at the time for The British Tourist Authority and together with the BTA chief photographer visited the church unannounced on several occasions. We discovered the nave ripped up, tombs opened and I identified the skeleton of an ancestor of Sir Thomas Tresham of Rushton (possibly Maurice Tresham who had owned the nearby manor) by the trefoil ring found on his finger. We made representations about our findings and were reassured that the remains were being re-interred at the church in Geddington. We termed the activities going on as "looting".

There was, however, another sinister aspect to the activities which went on at St Faith's; unknown to Carr and his supporters the building and the church yard had become a focus for the activities of a group of Satanists who were intent on using sacred ground for unholy rituals at night. This was one of the pressures behind the move to deconsecrate the decaying building and one of the concerns which the local vicar had to contend with. Out of his experiences at Newton Carr wrote and published a novel entitled *A Month in the Country* which was listed for the Booker Prize, won the *Guardian* Fiction Prize and was eventually made into a film starring Kenneth Branagh, Colin Firth and Natasha Richardson. I was delighted when the church was saved in order to become an educational field centre in 1975; I took several groups of children there over the following years to study the flora and fauna of the area greatly encouraged by the building's new role.

At the end of term just before Christmas 1964 I asked my headmaster if I might have the school Christmas tree which had graced the school hall for several weeks. He agreed, so at the end of term I carefully balanced it on my bicycle and took it home. It was rather too large for the house so I sawed off part of the trunk before bringing it through the front door. The tree had been subjected to central heating for a month and as it was pulled through the door the dried needles cascaded on the floor leaving a very bald tree. Having no Christmas tree decorations we set to and made some out of silver foil milk bottle tops in order to disguise the tree's nudity. We invited the two sets of parents round for Christmas Day. We ensconced ourselves under the gigantic skeleton of the tree on the only furniture we had available, namely some beach chairs. We were also so anxious to get everything right we forgot to take the bag of giblets out of the turkey; there was a flavour of plastic in the meal but, otherwise, it was a success.

1965. At home in Kettering.

Over the years I have noticed that people who are brought up in cities have a different attitude than a small town dweller as to how they treat other people. In a city it is not likely that you will meet up again with many a stranger so linguistic interchange could be bolder and more vigorous. In other words, you could be rude and get away with it. I had a small town outlook knowing that if one said or did anything untoward it could be revisited, sooner or later. The truth of this came home to me one Boxing Day when an elderly neighbour asked me to give her a lift in my newly acquired second-hand car to visit her daughter half a mile away. Two days earlier, on Christmas Eve, I had gone to the local shops to buy some vegetables. Whilst there, a rather arrogant woman had pushed in front of a child so she could be served first. It was one of the children from my class, so I intervened and piously pointed out that children should be respected. The woman sniffily took her place in the queue. Two days later, as my neighbour's daughter's front door opened, there stood the woman in question who icily thanked me for giving her mother a lift. Upon enquiries from her mother if we knew each other my neighbour's daughter affirmed that we were "acquainted".

The late fifties and early sixties witnessed the beginning of the consumerist society. Labour-saving appliances were more available and, as people's wages improved, living standards were heading upwards. When we married in 1964 we had one electric fan heater and no central heating or double glazing. Our only other source of heating came from coal which we kept in the outhouse. We did not own a refrigerator, a washing machine or a telephone. We bought a vacuum cleaner. I owned a bicycle and it took several years before we could afford to buy a second-hand car. It took a few more years before we bought a television. This was necessitated by me taking on a degree course through the Open University which to Harold Wilson's great credit commenced in 1969, the same year as the creation of Arpanet, the forerunner of the Internet. The purchase of a car led to the desire to build a garage. After studying the subject I purchased a *Banbury* pre-cast concrete structure which the manufacturers claimed would only take "two men with two spanners, two hours" to construct. In the event it took half a dozen of us several days. I built up a massive concrete base on which this proud edifice stood. In front I constructed a car port. Thinking that I would improve security arrangements I invented my own outside alarm which consisted of a number of tin cans on strings. Coming home late one night I forgot they were there and succeeded in waking half the street. That particular idea was rapidly abandoned. 1964 was the year that the Beatles recorded *A hard day's night.*

I vividly recall the death of Sir Winston Churchill and the state funeral accorded to him on 30 January 1965. Steff and I sat cosily by our new radiant electric fire in the dining room listening to the radio. It was a bitterly cold winter's day as the Royal Naval gun crew pulled the carriage flanked by the bearers, the Brigade of Guards, and the RAF escort. The solemn procession wound its slow progress through London to St Paul's Cathedral, symbol of the indefatigable courage and defiance which he and the nation had thrown at the might of Hitler. After the service the coffin was conveyed by barge and, as it disappeared from view in the mists hanging over the Thames on its way via train to Bladon, General Dwight D. Eisenhower bade farewell on behalf of us all to a great champion of freedom. It was the funeral of a hero, and a moment of history. That year another great conflict began with US troops being sent to Vietnam.

At Easter 1966 I left the Kettering school in order to take up my first promotion in a Northampton school. I was to be paid an extra £90 per annum, the cost I calculated being equal to the petrol I would need to use. Just before I left news broke that the Football World Cup (the gold Jules Rimet Trophy worth £30,000) had been stolen from an exhibition at Westminster Hall, London. Huge embarrassment followed until it was found on 27 March by a mongrel dog named Pickles out for a walk with its owner in south London. Later that summer the World Cup Final was played between Germany and England at a packed Wembley Stadium. Through the widening use of television some 400 million viewers watched as England won 4-2, the first time since 1930 when the tournament commenced. The country went wild. I was at home on holiday that 30 July and listened in on the radio. A plumber was doing some work for us on the bathroom. He would appear every day that week for an hour, then would quietly disappear to watch television elsewhere as the tournament unfolded. When I received his final bill he falsely claimed to have been at my house throughout the World Cup period and charged me accordingly. I refuted his claim and we came to an understanding; my bill was reduced by 75%

and I kept the old lead pipes which I promptly took to the scrap yard to cover some of the remaining bill.

Kettering, being the birthplace of the Baptist Missionary Society, hosted the Annual General Meeting of the Society not long after we were married. We volunteered to give hospitality to some visiting missionaries. They duly cane, a married quite elderly couple, and told us they had come from Africa. They were very tired as they had only arrived the previous day. They lived close to the Angola/Congo border which was heavily mined and barbed wired. The morning before they had set off for England the lady had had to enter the no-man's land to retrieve and bury the bodies of several people who had been blown-up trying to cross the border. She said that it was a regular occurrence. It was a stunning eye-opener on the real world and the cost of Christian commitment.

Over the years we were to meet many other intrepid people whose courage and strength of character were to deeply impress us. During the latter part of the 20th century it became fashionable to denigrate the work of missionaries as merely an aspect of nineteenth century imperialism. The true story is yet to be told, for the effect of Christian missionary commitment has been profound and positive for the world's good. It was at this time that Fr Trevor Huddleston was active in what is now Botswana; one day he stopped his horse beside some village women and raised his hat to them. It was this unusual gesture of respect from a white man that impressed one lady who became a Christian. I was privileged to work with her grandson more than three decades later. It was he who told me the story. He is now a minister himself and one of a new generation that gives hope to his country. During those years, the sixties, I became chairman of the local branch of Christian Aid, and with a group of other young people started an ecumenical organisation aimed at bringing churches together. We named it *Project One.* It was not without opposition from some denominational diehards.

I continued work in my spare time as a youth club leader at the church. There were many fine young people in the group, one of whom, a young soldier, instantly decided to go to help the people of Aberfan, near Merthyr Tydfil in Wales. On 21 October 1966 a huge slag heap shifted in heavy rain. Millions of tons of oozing black coal dust engulfed a farm, some terraced houses and a school. 144 people were killed, 116 of them children. It was a national disaster, the

Secretary of State for Wales declaring that a generation of Aberfan children had been wiped out. The young man from our fellowship tried to get to South Wales by hitch-hiking. I received a call the next day that on the way there he had been killed on the road in an accident. It was a devastating blow on top of the dreadful news from Wales. Going to his parents' house I did what I could to console them and still think of the effects such events have had on the Aberfan community and upon that young man's family; two separate tragedies yet linked by one terrible event.

Chapter Eight: Growing Responsibilities.

During the sixties and seventies it became increasingly necessary to have some means of transport in order to get to work. My father's generation walked or cycled to work as jobs were within a mile or so of their homes. Jobs became more geographically spread so that in order to obtain promotion I found myself buying my first car, a second-hand Ford *Prefect* which cost me £80. It was a temperamental vehicle and would often refuse to start in the mornings. Several times the windscreen wipers failed in the middle of rainstorms, and on one occasion Steff and I drove home whilst each alternately pulling a piece of string to keep the wipers going. We never travelled without a length of rope in the boot or a set of jump-leads in case of emergency. One neighbour had a technique of getting car engines started by hitting them with a spanner; miraculously the engines fired. Petrol cost about four shillings a gallon in the mid-sixties, yet the price inexorably rose during a time when the world's economies fluctuated due to the cost of crude oil from the Middle East.

Driving out of town to go to work was a new experience. I soon recognised many of my fellow commuters on the A43 which twisted and turned and caught out the unwary. One friend I knew always travelled at the same time in the morning and he would risk life and limb in order to overtake any car in front of him. He ended up in the ditch several times and wrote-off a number of cars. Coming home one evening in the fog I had to apply the brakes suddenly as a van had been abandoned without lights on the road. My wheels skidded and turned me one hundred and eighty degrees so that I was facing in the opposite direction. I had enough presence to drive onto the grass verge just before another car, a Triumph Herald, hurtled into the back of the van. Running across to the car I found that the driver was badly shaken and, as his engine began to catch fire, dragged him clear.

As the years passed, the A43, like many roads, was straightened and improved to keep pace with the growing volume of vehicles as well as the increased speeds at which they were driven. One snowy morning I set off at half past seven to do the usual half hour journey into Northampton. Reaching the steep Cransley Hill on the outskirts of Kettering I found traffic gridlocked. An enterprising farmer with his tractor was offering to tow each vehicle up the slope for £5 a time. But it was hopeless; snow always causes chaos in Britain. After four hours I reluctantly turned round and came home.

My first school in Northampton, Headlands Junior, was a large red-brick establishment built between the wars to house the child population of the eastern fringe of the town. It was surrounded by a mix of suburban houses, and classes numbered about 36 to 40 children each. The education of the town's children was the responsibility of the Borough Council, and the Director of Education knew his schools and the people who worked in them. The central organisation was housed in a large town house and there was an almost domestic atmosphere. Schools knew each other and there were many interconnections through sports and games and other activities. This was to change within the following six or seven years as the town began to expand rapidly and reorganisation changed the shape of local government across the nation.

Education itself was undergoing a transformation with an emphasis upon children learning through activity and experience. Yet at the same time the demands of the eleven-plus examination dictated a tight regime in the basic subjects. Good visual displays, particularly of children's work, were encouraged. The curriculum blossomed, especially in subjects like mathematics where rote learning of arithmetical calculations gave way to practical activities that covered topics such as geometry, weights and measures, number patterns and graphs. Children were encouraged to write creatively and to explore the locality. Keen on environmental studies I planned a nature trail around the school grounds, and bred some locusts and giant Indian Moon Moths in cages which I kept outside my classroom in the corridor. This latter project did not meet with everyone's approval and the thought of locusts hopping about, albeit in a cage, led some of my women colleagues to gather up speed when approaching my classroom door. Another of my colleagues built a bird table which he placed outside the classroom window; sadly, it collapsed on its first day, the headmaster reckoning that a sparrow had kicked it.

The headship of the school changed during my time there, and the new head was keen to be involved with some of the expeditions that we arranged. We used to take parties of the oldest children to South Wales, to Crickhowell in Breconshire, where we stayed in a youth hostel, walked on the hills, explored castles and generally had a wonderful time. The headmaster telephoned one Friday to say that he was leaving school in the afternoon and would be with us during the evening. He would stay for the weekend. He duly arrived and we found him a bed in the dormitory where the male staff and the boys slept. When we went to bed the headmaster dropped off to sleep instantly as he had had a long journey. The trouble was that he snored in a distinctive way. He would hold his breath then explode. After a few hours of this torture the boys began to complain, so it was decided to pick up the headmaster in his bed, luckily a single, and place him outside the door on the landing. This we accomplished, and the boys took it in turns to wake me up at 6am so that we could put him back again. We did this for three nights, and he never knew. Years later I met up with one of the boys, then a grown man with his own family, and we chortled at the comedy of the event and I confirmed to his disbelieving wife that it had actually happened. One of the girls from my class who is now a senior dental surgeon recently recalled the event; she described the condition as sleep apnoea, a serious disorder. At least the headmaster survived the youth hostel experience and lived until a ripe old age.

The late sixties witnessed huge expansion in Northampton. The whole of the eastern area was being developed with houses being built to accommodate the overspill from London and elsewhere. New schools were appearing and so there were opportunities for promotion. I was appointed to the deputy headship of Booth Junior School and worked alongside the head teacher, Jack Ward, who was one of my old teachers from my Junior School days. We opened a brand new school and part of my initial job was to order furniture and stock. Gone were the old desks; now children sat at tables in chairs that were designed for greater comfort and sized according to age. There was PE apparatus such as climbing ropes to put in the school hall. Instead of children having to perform somersaults on the hard floor there were thick rubber mats. Good quality papers, colourful paints, interesting books and carpeted areas for the children to sit on were all part of a new era in schooling. It was like paradise.

Teaching methods were able to change, and it was possible with the construction of the school to remove internal walls so that two classes were co-joined and teachers could work together.

108

Colleagues and I developed a Team Teaching approach which involved children being organised into ability groups whom we taught at their own levels of understanding. It took a great deal of motivation by the children as they were required to work on their own given tasks when not being actually taught. They were given certain free periods in which they could "choose" from a range of more relaxing activities once their set work was finished. The method produced a very satisfactory outcome for both children and staff. It is pleasing to see many of the children from those years in positions of responsibility and doing well in their chosen career paths; one is a broadcaster, another is a translator for the European Commission in Brussels.

On 15 February 1971 a new "D Day" arrived. For several years we had been preparing the children for this event, namely the official changeover of the country to the new decimal currency. Books that we had ordered as far back as 1968 had abandoned the old pounds, shillings and pence for the new pounds and pence system. Measurements were gradually changed to kilograms and grams, litres and millilitres yet the confusion that remained in the country at large was compounded when I went to a local timber merchant and had to buy ten metres of four inch by two inch wood. The children coped with the change better than the adults.

The official opening of the new school took place in the November of 1968. The Chief Education Officer and other dignitaries were present. He kindly noted my wife's advanced state of pregnancy and advised that we sat at the end of the row of chairs, just in case. Perhaps it was the bumpy journey home that did it because later that night Steff's labour pains began and I took her into hospital in Kettering. Things were happening quickly and as a mere husband the staff told me I was not required. Prospective fathers were then considered a nuisance and were not allowed to stay with their wives. So I departed feeling very concerned, leaving Steff to soldier on. After a glass of cider and a piece of pork pie I went to bed. The next morning the telephone rang to tell me I was the father of a baby boy whom we named Julian. It was a wonderful euphoric moment to think I had my very own son. Later that morning I went round to my parents to tell them the good news. I met my mother at the gate who told me that my grandmother had died during the night. It was a very strange experience with mixed emotions. Grandfather, who had never done any housework or cooking and was therefore incapable of caring for himself, moved into my parents' home where mother took on the burden of caring for him. His first attempt to boil a kettle led to an explosion as he forgot to fill it with water. Grandmother, who had carried the domestic routine of the home and, like so many of her generation, was at his beck and call died of a heart attack whilst kneeling down to unlace his shoes for him.

Steff with Julian.

It was good to get my wife and baby son home safely. I wanted everything to be right and made sure that the house was warm and all the things we had bought were available. We had redecorated a bedroom especially for him with Steff drawing and painting a delightful frieze of the alphabet with animal characters. We prepared for sleepless nights; Julian, however, was as good as gold and we soon got into the routine of the nightly feed and all the paraphernalia of sterilising bottles, and washing and drying nappies; this was the era before the disposable nappy.

Suddenly life had taken on an increased responsibility at a time when many things were happening in the world. Earlier in 1968

Martin Luther King had been shot dead and in the following year Enoch Powell had stirred up the issue of race in Britain. In the following year there were serious student riots in Prague which were brutally suppressed by the Russians. The image of a student, Jan Palach, burning himself to death in protest at the suppression of the Czechoslovak people captivated many minds. In Rhodesia in 1970 Ian Smith declared unilateral independence from Britain, and at home there was a state of emergency declared because of the dock strike. In the years 1968-72 there was an upsurge in industrial strike action reaching a peak of some 23.9 million working days lost. Disaffection was being felt within the teaching profession and amongst all sections of the community. In 1971 there was a major Post Office strike and in the following year the miners and dockers also walked out. Unemployment, which had been steadily rising for years, topped the one million mark for the first time. To add to the gloom the IRA bombed the Post Office Tower in London, the *Bloody Sunday* deaths occurred in January 1972 in Londonderry, and retaliation came by way of a bomb at the Aldershot Barracks in the following month.

Like many parents at the time we wondered at the wisdom of bringing another child into a world in turmoil. Many married couples seriously considered their responsibilities and decided to limit families or even forgo having any children at all. Concern at world population growth and the sustainability of the environment were becoming major issues for discussion. In 1975 Richard Briers and Felicity Kendall played the parts of Barbara and Tom Good who leave the "rat race" and turn their Surbiton home into a smallholding in order to become self-sufficient. *The Good Life* tapped into a gnawing anxiety with the usual brilliance of British comedy. One of my friends moved his family to Yorkshire where he endeavoured to find self-sufficiency by growing vegetables on a steep hillside. One day his greenhouse decided to slide down to the bottom of the slope where it disintegrated on a stone wall. Steff and I made a conscious decision to reproduce our own number. We were expecting our second child. This birth was going to be different! I was going to be involved!

During that time the health authorities actively followed a policy of encouraging confinements in hospital. Yet as Steff gave birth relatively easily it was agreed that her second confinement

111

should take place at home. We duly prepared and I read up on the duties of husbands and fathers. The midwife on her last visit expressed satisfaction that all was in order. Suddenly, in the middle of the night Steff's labour pains began and we used our neighbour's phone to call the midwife; she was not available. The doctor had told Steff that she was likely to give birth quickly "like shelling peas", so we began to get rather anxious. The doctor was not available either (it was rumoured that he and the midwife had gone off somewhere together for the weekend) so I prepared to do the job myself, scrubbing up, sterilising the equipment in the way I had been instructed and being the dutiful husband. Within half an hour of the birth a relief midwife arrived and took over rather officiously. I still feel miffed at her reaction to my efforts as she complained that I had sterilised the swabs in a bowl placed in a saucepan that had a tiny fleck of cabbage stuck to it. Yet, it was all worth it. We had a beautiful little girl whom we named Tessa. One of my happiest moments was to draw the curtains as the light faded on that October evening with my wife and baby girl tucked up safely in bed. The world outside could go hang.

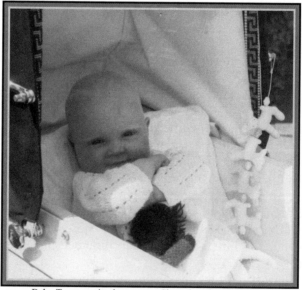

Baby Tessa awaits the unwary. She enjoyed twanging her
plastic lambs in the faces of admirers who came too close.

Yet the world outside was changing ever faster and could not be ignored. In the previous year, on 21 July 1969, the Americans Neil Armstrong and Edwin Aldrin were the first humans to land on the Moon. Armstrong had declared: "That's one small step for man but one giant leap for mankind". I brought my one year old Julian into the sitting room to watch the events on our first television set. I don't know what he thought as he watched the black and white pictures of the spacemen leaping about on the lunar surface. The moon landings received congratulations from across the world although the USSR reported the success with solemnity. The achievement marked the peak of the space exploration at the time with a further six missions landing ten astronauts on the Moon concluding with the Apollo 17 mission in 1972.

I reflected on how my early interest in astronomy had come of age with the actuality of space flights. Visionaries predicted vast developments with possible travel to the stars. Older children dreamt of becoming astronauts. My infant children would grow up in the Space Age and would become in 1977-8 enrapt by the sci-fi block buster *Star Wars* written by George Lucas. Set in "a galaxy far, far away" the fairy-tale story involved monsters, heroes and wizards in a good versus evil struggle. It was quickly followed up by *The Empire Strikes back* and *Return of the Jedi,* and in 1999 two further episodes of the saga. Back in the late seventies *Star Wars* riveted children's attention; the manufacture of children's toys linked to movies became commonplace, and parents thereon would be pestered continually for the latest must-have item. The all-pervasive television would see to that.

Life in the local school scene altered again. Decisions had been made to change the nature of the educational provision of the town. Nationally, a debate had been raging as to equality in education. It was an issue that had philosophical as well as political agendas. "Equality of opportunity" was the great slogan, and the growth of "Comprehensive education" had begun. Northampton had decided to change the two-tier to a three-tier pattern of schooling. Children would henceforth leave their Lower school at nine to proceed to a Middle school until they were thirteen then move on to an Upper school. The system would last for the rest of the century to be phased out in the early years of the 21st century. Back in the late sixties and early seventies all teachers were caught up in the changes, and I found myself on various working parties that designed the new middle and lower schools. It was an interesting time and great improvements were made.

On a personal level it became apparent that I had to choose whether to stay in the Lower Schools or to move into the nascent Middle School tier. A new ruling that dictated that male head teachers needed a female deputy, and vice versa, made it necessary for me to leave my current job. So I decided to apply for a different post, firstly in a Middle School which I didn't get, but then boldly I applied for the headship of Duston Church of England School and was offered the job. I remember driving there to get a sight of the school, situated in the old village, and feeling that life was about to change. Upon appointment I felt the time had come to stop commuting from Kettering. It was time to move house and take one's chances in a new situation.

Moving house in the summer of 1972 was easier said than done. Firstly, there was a huge demand for housing, especially in the Duston area which boasted that houses were a thousand pounds dearer than elsewhere in the town.. A house could be advertised early in the morning and a buyer might be forthcoming by the evening. I set out to find a suitable home and found that several houses I was interested in had been rapidly snapped up. Secondly, there was the price factor. Within eight years house prices had risen more than threefold and interest rates were rocketing upwards. The phenomenon known as gazumping had begun; this involved vendors breaking verbal agreements in order to accept higher offers. I found a three-bedroom semi-detached house for about £9750, offering a bit more than the market value simply in order to secure a home in which to live. That summer we left Kettering for Duston, a matter of some twenty miles as the crow flies; my mother thought we were moving to the other side of the world.

I began work as a young head teacher at the village school which had been founded in 1856 on land given by a former Prime Minister and his wife, Viscount and Viscountess Palmerston. It was a Church of England (Controlled) school which meant that the vicar and some of the foundation managers were appointed by the Church. In all other respects the LEA had responsibility. The buildings had been adapted and developed over the intervening years and I came at a time when the school had acquired new grounds and property ripe for imaginative development. Throwing myself into the job with great vigour I spent eight very happy years there. One of the happiest moments was when we had all trooped over to the church for an end of term Christmas carol service and came out to walk through a snow covered churchyard. There was a dedicated staff that did an exemplary job, the children were delightful and responsive and the school enjoyed the high esteem of the community. We developed the grounds into a wildlife area and an adventure playground; the children were encouraged to actively look after a number of pets. The range of ages of the children went from five to eleven, although as the three tier system arrived the oldest children left at the age of nine to go to a Middle School.

Life in schools involves dealing with a range of interesting characters whether they are teachers, ancillary staff, parents, children or visitors. A school is a microcosm of life and anything could happen anytime. At the end of the first week I was standing in my office looking out on the gardens thinking what a lucky man I was when the door burst open. A former psychiatric patient from the local St Crispin's Hospital came in and drew a bread knife from his coat and advanced upon me in a threatening manner. I was standing behind a lightweight table and had enough presence of mind to pick it up and run at the man, dropping it on his toes before escaping from the room. The man fled the building. Later a policeman, the vicar, a doctor and I cornered him in an old lady's greenhouse.

Folk in Duston were used to seeing patients from the St Crispin's hospital in and around the village. A former head master of the large local secondary school recalled that one day he received a surprise visit from one of Her Majesty's Inspectors. He apologised for the suddenness of his visit but indicated that he wanted to see the school in operation. The head master sent a warning message round the school and escorted the inspector around every department. Later that afternoon the inspector gave the head master his verbal report on the school commending it for its excellent work; a full written report would follow in due course. He then prepared to leave, his host escorting him to the door. On enquiring where was his mode of transport the inspector indicated that he lived opposite the school, namely in a section of St Crispin's Hospital. He had been an inspector but at the time was a patient. The head teacher saw the funny side of the incident but ruefully commented that his visitor had conned a free school dinner out of him.

There was one particular patient whom I got to know quite well. He had been a very senior officer in the Royal Navy and had had a distinguished service career. War had had its effect upon him and he spent his latter years often sitting in the church lych gate where he always had a large bottle of cider to hand. He was similar to many other older men who lived out their days suffering from the after-effects of shell shock. Other patients would arrive at the United Reformed Chapel in the village to attend the services where my family and I worshipped. I took my turn in lay preaching in those days and on one occasion had a patient standing and staring at me within a metre of my face throughout an entire sermon. He only disappeared when the collection was announced.

I found out that a cottage in the village, used in those years as a bank, had been once owned by my mother's Auntie Polly who had moved house to be near the hospital where her mentally ill husband had been incarcerated. The St Crispin Hospital, a Victorian edifice with a high brick clock tower, was situated on the Berrywood Road and an older generation had a dread of such institutions referring to the place in hushed tones as "Berrywood". I became very well acquainted with the hospital and visited many times. It was to be gradually phased out in the Conservative government's "Care in the Community" initiative and later closed. Housing developments have begun on the site, although the adjacent Princess Marina Hospital continues its valuable work intact.

There were many interesting child characters in the school, and one boy stands out in my memory. We'll call him Jack. Coming from a very deprived home which cut up the floorboards for fuel and threw rubbish out the window Jack's survival instincts were on full alert. One day he visited a local house where he managed to purloin a lady's collection of cacti. She was upset at her loss and went round to her neighbour's house for a cup of tea and commiseration. As she sipped the tea her eyes wandered to her friend's window sill upon which was a row of her cacti. Jack had sold them to the neighbour.

A worker at the local British Timken roller bearing factory called in to see me when his afternoon shift finished. He reported that a boy answering Jack's description had nicked his bicycle lamp. I called Jack into the office the next morning. Yes, he admitted the

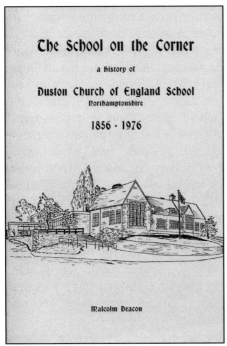

The School on the Corner

a history of

Duston Church of England School
Northamptonshire

1856 - 1976

Malcolm Deacon

theft and promised to have the lamp on my desk by the following day. Sure enough the lamp sat there on my desk; I phoned the man, but when he came to collect it he roundly declared that it was nothing like his. Jack was again sent for and he promised to return the lamp. Next day a lamp graced my desk and again the man returned. It was not his! After four different lamps I despairingly told him to choose the best one. Jack was a lovable rogue and I kept in touch with him until he grew up. Years later he came to visit me at my next school to thank me for the attention and the discipline I and his teachers had given him during his childhood. Local government reorganisation was proceeding apace in the early seventies. All the counties were reshuffled and local authorities amalgamated in a major shake-up. Bureaucracy was one of the results and paperwork began to increase. Every week head teachers would receive a brown envelope from the Education Department. In the early seventies it measured on average ten millimetres thick but by the end of the seventies was often four times that thickness. Circulars and instructions proliferated to such an extent that I kept all the papers sent during the year and took a photograph of them piled on my desk. The heap measured well over a metre and a half. The last straw came when we began receiving a weekly circular detailing the circulars we should have received. I sent the photograph to the Chief Education Officer protesting at the huge waste of paper. I was delighted to see the flood of paper diminish for a time, but as the years passed and Local Education Authorities and their schools became increasing targets for government attention the paper burdens became an avalanche.

The seventies were, however, a time of great enjoyment for me and the staff, and we were able to achieve good standards in all subjects. The school continued some highly individual activities such as Morris dancing, maypole dancing, handbell ringing and these were greatly sought after at local fetes and concerts. On the 120th anniversary of the school the children welcomed older generations who had been educated at the school. They came in large numbers and were entertained by the children on a sunny summer afternoon. The children danced around the maypole and played their instruments. The Morris Dancers performed and the whole event seemed as if nothing had really changed in essence. It was all about children growing up in an appreciative and caring community. In the light of the debate over obesity and children eating junk food some thirty years later it is interesting to note that all sweets were banned in our school; a very successful tuck shop was run by the children themselves selling carrots and apples. School meals were planned with healthy eating in mind, and I even inveigled one boy who would only eat chips to try cabbage as a "special green chip"; the ruse succeeded, to the delight of his mother!

An advisor came to the school one day and complained about the methods being used to teach reading. I pointed out the brilliant reading standards of all the children in the top year and suggested that such standards came from sound earlier teaching even though some might consider it old-fashioned. Educational theories abounded, one being the anathema to any form of competition. It was said that some schools during their sports' days instructed the children to aim to come last. This was a travesty, although it did point to a misdirected enthusiasm for certain visionary social theories about equality. Equality of opportunity in effect meant an equal chance of becoming unequal as no two people will behave exactly in the same way. We always kept a middle road approach, and as methodology has waxed and waned over the years it has proved its value. Children are by nature competitive little creatures that need to learn to lose as well as win in a gracious spirit.

Few people get the opportunity to educate their own children and I had hoped that our two children would have gone to a nearby school. Circumstances were such that Julian and Tessa were enrolled at my own school. We tacitly agreed to play the game of them seeing me in different roles, and they played it superbly. They received no favours from me at school and they fitted in with all the other children with no embarrassing problems. Thus I was able to see them at different times during the school day and listen to their views which, I am sure, benefited all the other children. It was a very happy school indeed, and I was well supported by my deputy, Matt Gordon, and a splendid staff.

One day many years after I had left that school I met up with one of the former pupils of those years. He told me that he had become an RAF pilot. While he was flying over Belgrade during the Kosovan War in 1998-9 his aircraft had come under attack by missiles. He told me movingly that at the height of the conflict he had reflected on happy moments of his life, one of the most meaningful being the time when at the age of five he and his classmates regularly persuaded me to go and sit with them on the library carpet to watch *Camberwick Green* on the school television.

The concept of schools as centres of communities was gaining ground. The local Upper School with its British Timken donated swimming pool, evening classes for adults and provision for pre-school children embodied this noble ideal. One of the great memories from those years was the establishment of a swimming

club which met over a two-hour period on Friday afternoons after school had finished for the week. Parents as well as children attended. It was very satisfying seeing, over the following years, parents training as life savers and children finding their way into swimming teams at their middle and upper schools. Our own children did extremely well with their swimming thanks to such an initiative. Over the ensuing years children we had taught to swim gaining honours for their later schools and themselves. I began a local history class in

1973 covering the history of Northamptonshire. The class met for formal lectures one week then on the following week would go out on an expedition to sites of interest. The illustration shows a group on location at Hunsbury Hill, an Iron Age camp close to Northampton. Full day expeditions on Saturdays took us across the county with lunch stops in local hostelries. The class became very successful with as many as forty adult students attending at its peak. Named *Off The Beaten Track* the course developed and continued for over nineteen years; I believe it made a distinct contribution to local history as many students went on to do their own researches.

Steff and I had come from a Baptist church background, but wanting to live and work in Duston decided to attend the United Reformed Church in the village. In that year (1972) the national Presbyterian and Congregational Churches had taken the historic step of uniting to form the URC. It was the right time for us to join and we began a period of our lives when we devoted ourselves to supporting not only the URC but helping to bring the Church of England and other denominations in the village closer together.

The URC ran a particularly successful youth programme through the Boys' and Girls' Brigades. There was a lively Sunday School which attracted many from both the old village and New Duston. Our own children took part in all the activities. I became an Elder and lay preacher, and Steff taught in the Sunday School. We supported the church by forming and editing the church magazine, and took part in the friendly social life of the church and village. Once I was invited to judge the apple pie competition at the Women's Institute, and having made my choice was nearly lynched; the pie made by the lady who had won the prize for the past decade or more was not placed. One year we invited folk to a Bonfire Party in our garden; forty came. The next year a hundred attended, so we switched venue to a field kindly lent us by Golby's Nurseries, a piece of land which now lies somewhere underneath Sainsbury's supermarket and its adjacent roads and car park. Within a few years the Bonfire Party attracted over a thousand people providing a good money raiser for the church.

For some years I was Chairman of *Christian Aid* in Northampton having held a similar position in Kettering during the mid-sixties up to 1972 when we moved to Duston. Created at the end of the Second World War in order to assist the millions of refugees on continental Europe, *Christian Aid* became a major charity with a global remit to bring relief to the poorest in the world by providing training in self-reliance as well as giving emergency relief. Some of the most heart-rending events over the years involved us in sending food relief to the starving of Ethiopia, lobbying the British government way back in the sixties over the suffering of the people in the former Portuguese colony of Angola (we even had a mention in *Hansard*) but generally organising an annual money raising Christian Aid Week in May.

Whilst doing my share of house-to-house collecting I found that the most generous people are usually the poorest in monetary terms. I have seen sacrificial giving by very ordinary humble people, and I have been treated with contemptuous disdain by folk from large houses with several expensive cars lining their driveways. On one occasion I called for the Christian Aid envelope at a well-to-do house. The male owner took great delight in putting five metal washers into the envelope before me; with great ceremony he popped them in one by one before licking it and handing it to me. It so happened that I was in need of some washers because I was repairing a fence that week, so I cheekily asked him if I could have them in exchange for a fifty pence piece. The following year I went to the same house and met the same man. "Wait there", he commanded and disappeared in the house. "That is for your cheek", he said, putting two ten pound notes into the envelope, and he added, "Please, come back next year". I returned to his house over the next ten years and we became good friends.

Over many years of involvement with Christian Aid two events stand out in my memory. The first was an extraordinary response to an appeal to assist the victims of floods in Bangladesh, a country frequently hit by cyclones and economically very poor. In Kettering we appealed for help in simply providing blankets for the hundreds of thousands of homeless who found themselves exposed to the elements. The people of the town responded by giving their spare blankets which were collected at Fuller Baptist Church. Children and young people of the church assisted in the loading of thousands of blankets into an articulated lorry kindly loaned free of charge by a local business man, the late John Billows. Within days the blankets had been flown out to the disaster area. It was an object lesson in human compassion.

A second vivid memory was the spectacular marathon run by young people starting from Westminster Abbey in London. The Archbishop of Canterbury commissioned teams of runners who carried lighted torches to many parts of the country. Relays of runners brought one torch to Northampton, the 11th (Duston) Company of the Boys Brigade taking over at Newport Pagnell. With police outriders in attendance the boys ran in formation to Abington Park in Northampton where civic and church leaders and the Christian Aid Committee awaited their arrival. A large crowd gathered for the ceremony of receiving the flame and the event concluded with a service, music and a carnival atmosphere. It was a brilliant start to Christian Aid Week 1977.

Before coming to Duston I had involved the school children in archaeological digs. With the local archaeological officer we were able to field walk sites before building developments took place; the town was expanding fast and this kind of work was called "rescue archaeology". Children with their sharp eyes are very useful. At Boothville the children had helped to sift the Roman temple discovered near the new roundabout on the A43. In Duston an entire Roman town had lain undisturbed beneath the allotments on the Weedon Road. Topsoil was taken off by digger and the children walked the site spotting pottery, a well, post holes where wood had rotted, a road, a draught piece, bones, coins, an earring and even fresh water oyster shells from the nearby River Nene eaten by the citizens so long ago. The site now lies underneath the developments at Sixfields. All was bustle as the town expanded.

In the wider world, too, much was changing with Britain joining the European Economic Union in 1973. In the same year Picasso died, and President Richard Nixon who had achieved an historic peace deal over the Vietnam War was seriously compromised by the Watergate Scandal. That year saw a personal triumph in that I was one of the first groups of Open University students to be awarded a degree. In 1976 there was a huge water crisis with reservoirs running dry and swingeing regulations brought out to curb the washing of cars and the watering of lawns with hoses. People were encouraged to use their washing up and bath water to water the gardens. One advertisement suggested that having a bath with a friend might be fun as well as a public duty.

In 1976 racial tensions erupted during the Notting Hill Carnival in London. Within a space of fifteen months in 1977-8 news came of the deaths of notable people: Mao Tse Tung, Benjamin Britten, Elvis Presley (at the premature age of 42) and Charlie Chaplin (aged 88). A bizarre follow-up to Chaplin's death was the theft of his coffin from the grave and its subsequent discovery. Celebrating the Silver Jubilee of her accession to the throne in 1977 was Queen Elizabeth II followed the next year by the accession of John Paul II to the Papacy. His visit to his native Poland in 1979 was to pave the way for the demise of communism. As the seventies unfolded the IRA stepped up its lethal bombing campaign on the British mainland. Places such as the Houses of Parliament, the Tower of London, the London Hilton as well as Edward Heath's home were bombed. I had been in London at the College of Preceptors and was making my way towards Euston when a small bomb exploded not far from me. I saw a puff of smoke and heard the shattering of glass, but was unhurt. Two of the most cowardly events of this period were firstly the shooting dead of the TV presenter Ross McWhirter who, with his twin brother Norris, edited the *Guinness Book of Records*. Secondly, Airey Neave MP was killed by a car bomb in 1979, the year that Margaret Thatcher was elected as the first woman Prime Minister. It was during the autumn of that year that I left Duston Church of England School to take up the challenge of the headship of a very different establishment.

Chapter Nine: Surviving the Eighties.

1980 began with a high degree of personal optimism: I had started a new job as the head teacher of Kingsthorpe Grove Lower School, we were moving to a more spacious detached house, and my first major book, a biography, was about to be published. Life seemed very rosy. Yet within the space of a few years we were to lose five family members by death. It was during the autumn of 1979 when I had just started my new headship that my parents-in-law, Phil and Phyll Loasby went to stay with relatives in Exeter. Whilst there my father-in-law had a massive stroke and ended up in the Exeter Royal Infirmary. Whilst I looked after our two children Steff travelled to Exeter to see her father who, sadly, did not recover. Her mother had been diagnosed with untreatable cancer. After treatment in a local hospice Phyll chose to die at home; Steff gave up her job to nurse her during the weekdays whilst her sister, Val, did the same on the weekends. If this were not enough Val's son Martin, our only nephew, was tragically drowned in a mysterious accident whilst swimming in Castle Ashby lakes. He left a wife with a baby daughter. Then my father, Bill, suddenly died, followed a year later by my mother, Betty.

A rare photograph of Gran and Grandpa Loasby with their grandchildren.
Front row: Tessa, Julian, Jenny and Alison; back row: Martin and Nicky.

So, over a few years the older generation of the family had gone. It was a coming-of-age, a sobering realisation that we were then the seniors of the family with no older and wiser heads to turn to for advice and support. The clearing of their homes of all the personal items, and the shock that a lifetime of work and effort could amount to so little in monetary terms, changed my outlook on life as I realised afresh that life is much more than a quest for status and possessions. This experience also had a profound effect upon my spiritual life. My mother-in-law had lain in a comatose state for some time but one day I timidly held her hand and prayed for her out loud. She suddenly opened her eyes, looked at me and whispered "Thank you". There was an immense peace in that bedroom. She died not long after this, released serenely into God's eternal care. I began to develop a strong sense of calling into this kind of ministry.

Meantime life had to still go on with our two children attending their schools and myself getting to grips with quite a tough educational undertaking. During this period when national affairs seemed to grow ever gloomier I drew much happiness from my family and friends. It was fun to watch our son and daughter growing up. We taught them to swim, and as a family swam at least three times a week. We built a canoe, walked the dog (and got him lost), visited many places, tried to help the children with their studies and shared their joys and sorrows; in fact, we did all those things which a normal family does.

We were very much involved with the United Reformed Church in Duston and took a full part in its varied activities. One lively side of the church's life was its annual pantomime in which we were all involved over the years. Having a reasonable ability with the piano I became the pantomime's orchestra, sometimes supplemented by a drummer. One year the Mayor of Northampton, John Gardner, attended and was persuaded into playing the drums as part of the slapstick, complete with mayoral chain of office. So much did he enjoy it he came back the next night and played for the whole show. The pantomime played for three nights, Thursday to Saturday with an afternoon matinee on the last day. Rather than go home between the two Saturday performances the cast would stay on, and a volunteer would go to the local chip shop to purchase forty or so portions. I used to wear a tailed dress suit with black bow tie. One year it was my turn to get the chips and I duly rolled up to the local "chippy" complete with evening dress. The proprietor was something of a wag and enquired what I was doing so dressed up. "My dear chap", I said with a straight face," I always dress for dinner on Saturdays". The entire shop full of customers rocked with laughter. They were good times, and it is pleasing to see the continuation of the pantomime (The Duston Youth Theatre) led by some very able and talented young people.

It was a culture shock going from a relatively placid church school environment in Duston, where I had everything at my fingertips, to a much larger and more urban school serving a wide cross-section of society in Kingsthorpe. The social milieu was changing and over the next decade it became increasingly apparent that the disciplining of children by some parents was deteriorating. Although this was always a minority, and as a school we exacted good discipline, the task of the reception teachers over the period became increasingly more difficult. Vandalism from older children from outside the school was a problem so I set about establishing myself; whenever windows were broken they were immediately mended and when trees and shrubs were damaged they were replaced. Individual culprits were tracked down and spoken to. Gradually we won through and established the security of the school. One night when fetched out at midnight by the police to attend a suspected break-in I met a police constable who was plastered with non-drying paint which we had placed on the tops of gates to deter intruders. "My sergeant will moan at me when I get back to the Nick", he complained. I helped him clean up.

One of the tricks of the trade I developed was to ask staff not to send any child out to the toilets at a certain time. This was usually within the first few weeks of a new school year. So with no-one about I would then stand in the corridor and with upraised voice bellow at some imaginary evil-doer. Then I would visit each classroom in turn asking the staff if everyone was being well behaved and working hard. It was all very much tongue-in-cheek. Yes, they were doing well, I was assured, and I ended up encouraging anyone doing good work to be sent to me at any time to get "a good try sticker". So by throwing an imaginary "wobbler" everyone knew where they stood. It supported the staff, kept down the bullies, set a framework that school was there to enjoy and to help everyone learn, and it worked! Children like praise, and I

126

enjoyed them coming to me to show good work. Some of the happiest times were when I had the whole school to myself for "a Deacon spectacular". The staff liked it as they had a rare hour to themselves. The children and I shared stories and news; on their birthdays they would bring one of their special presents to show and we would sing Happy Birthday to them and they would get a clap. It was simple recognition of human worth and individuality.

One of the first major tasks we had was to finish a project started by my predecessor, namely, the building of a swimming pool. An indoor location in the shape of an old wartime building was available, but it needed total renovation. The pool was to be a free-standing one measuring some fifteen by five metres. It consisted of metal panels, pipes, filters and other equipment and a pile of sand. We completed the necessary money raising and with staff and parental help had the pool operating within four months. It was pleasing to timetable in every class for a weekly swimming lesson. Over the next decade more than a thousand children learned to swim in that little pool. When the thousandth child received her ten metres certificate I thought it appropriate to ask the local press to cover the event. What better encouragement to the school and the children, I thought. One local newspaper chose, however, to headline me as some ogre for disciplining some children who had turned all the taps on in the cloakrooms, flooding a large area, and had sworn at and kicked a dinner lady. I had banned them from attending school dinners for a week; a fairly mild punishment, but one of the mothers had complained to the newspaper. There was no mention of the success of the swimming pool. Such treatment outraged the majority of the others parents who wrote numerous letters of protest to the newspaper concerned supporting me for upholding discipline. Some sort of grudging apology came in the following week when the newspaper printed a piece on the swimming pool.

Some years earlier I had had a skirmish with the national press over reporters barging into my previous school attempting to take photographs and interview a child who had been the subject of a matrimonial dispute. Declared a Ward of Court by a London magistrate the child had been rapidly tracked down by the media who descended on the school like a pack of wolves. I ordered them off the premises and they waited menacingly at the gates until school closed for the day. Unknown to them I had phoned the child's guardians and they had spirited her away by a back exit. One national newspaper called me "unhelpful".

Such experiences of the media were becoming commonplace. There was a growing and voracious thirst for reporting on anything that was seemingly scandalous at the expense of the positive good work that so many in society did day by day. One head teacher colleague had been headlined, accused of some dreadful sexual impropriety. The subsequent court case completely exonerated him yet the press hardly reported on his acquittal. In fact, I was one of a delegation to a newspaper editor to protest that a five-line mention of our colleague's exoneration on an inside page was out of all proportion to the front page coverage of his accusation. Over the following two decades media intrusion and unfair coverage were to become a major feature in all our lives influencing the rise and fall of celebrities, politicians and even the course of wars.

The Thatcher government which dominated the eighties developed a hard-nosed attitude to society in general. It was partly a reaction to changing values and events but mostly an outcome of the personality of the Prime Minister and her cabinet. "Our Margaret is an astute politician and a strong personality; we are proud that she is our country's first woman PM", said one of her relatives to a friend of mine, "but she has a tendency to go too b***** far". There was no doubt that we had a strong leader at the helm. 1980 saw the infamous Iranian embassy siege in London. The government acted decisively by sending in the SAS. Two years later war fever gripped the nation as the Task Force set off to fight the Argentineans who had invaded the Falkland Islands. As the fleet sailed into the icy waters of the South Atlantic many hearts quickened as the bloody conflict unfolded. As part of the task force there were former pupils of mine; one serving in submarines, another in the Fleet Air Arm on board HMS Hermes which, when it returned to Portsmouth from the war, was greeted with rapturous emotion.

During these years schools became increasingly exposed to the public gaze, their work and curricula more than ever a political football. No longer were schools left to proceed quietly with their work. The education of the nation's children was considered in deadly earnest. As in the nineteenth century when Britain realised it had to keep up with the rest of the world so the education of the nation's children was deemed vital to survival in the new technological age.

I met most of the Secretaries of State for Education in an official capacity. In fact, I entertained one such personage for several hours prior to her addressing a head teachers' meeting in Northampton. Whilst head teachers, in the main, were supportive of the government's drive to increase standards in education my suggestion to the Secretary of State that the government should be careful not to weaken the morale of the teaching profession by pressing changes too rapidly, was met with a withering dismissal. Over the following years the number of teachers who retired early upon health grounds or who simply quit the profession became an alarming issue. The increasing pressure on the schools was a major factor then, and has continued with a changed government into the 21st century.

Although the nation had been successful in defending the Falklands Islands serious domestic troubles were brewing. Margaret Thatcher successfully took on "the enemy within" in the person of Arthur Scargill, the General Secretary of The National Union of Minerworkers. The situation led to violent confrontations at pit gates. Many police forces sent officers to help control the dispute which lasted for a year starting in March 1984. It was during these years that I served as a head teacher representative on one of the Police Liaison Committees that covered the Borough of Northampton. The general public was not aware at how flimsy the thin blue line had become with upwards of a hundred police officers (out of a total force of a thousand) absent from the county at any one time. The strike was one of the longest and most damaging disputes in British industrial history. It marked a great watershed as the decline of heavy industries was moving apace. From 170 major coal pits operating at the time of the strike by 2002 only 13 survived, and the once mighty National Union of Mineworkers numbering 187,000 fell to 5,000.

Behind this confrontation lay a deep worry which affected everyone in the nation. Unemployment had inexorably risen from 1972 when it reached one million. In spite of a brief improvement in 1975 mass unemployment became a feature of British life during the late seventies and early eighties. At the end of January 1982 more than three million people were out of work, a situation which had not prevailed since the 1930's. I recall attending a lecture at the University Centre in Northampton during which the speaker predicted that mass unemployment would be a permanent feature of life thereafter. It was unnerving having children growing up and having to face a bleak and uncertain future. Like many parents at the time Steff and I were very anxious to encourage and motivate our own children who were into their teenage years. Some predicted that the rise in computerisation would reduce the need for many workers, but I am glad to say that subsequent experience proves that computers create the need for more rather than less work.

It was a breath of fresh air to get away from time to time with the family. We used to rent a cottage in the delightful North Norfolk village of Aylmerton close to the sea near Sheringham. We spent many a happy time there away from the demands of daily life. We lived in an old cottage next door to the owners, an elderly couple. The husband, well in his eighties, was still active and would "look after my old gals" in the village by doing their gardening for them; "the old gals" were probably twenty years younger than him!

How lovely to walk along a beach with the waves rolling in. One needed a tough spirit very often on the North Norfolk coast as the wind off the sea could cut like a knife. Blue with cold our children would doggedly face the cold North Sea. Sand castle building is a noble art distinctive of the British seaside experience. So I would often have a garden spade in the car boot ready to assist in doing full justice to the enterprise; many children from all around the beach would eventually join us in our magnificent creations. We walked the footpaths along the cliffs and trudged through the deep banks of leaves from ancient beech trees in the nearby countryside.

The woods, fields, the sea and the sky did much to restore the human spirit.

From school some of the staff and I took parties of children to enjoy the same experiences in that area, going pony trekking, walking the seashore, travelling on the coastal railway, living and learning together, meeting the local fishermen and seeing the sights. These times are so important for children, and I was determined to keep such experiences as part of the school's commitment to them. Many school expeditions had their comical experiences, and I well recall the trip we made during the Duston school days one Easter on the Oxford Canal when we woke to find two inches of snow covering the canvas of the longboat and the "butty". One boy in particular, noted as "a human dustbin" delighted in finishing off every scrap of food leftover; for his breakfast one morning he finished off half a dozen boiled eggs and the remains of the previous night's supper, the entire contents of a large saucepan of cold macaroni.

Dog dirt has long been a big issue with me, ever since I fell in some as a child in the local park. As dog owners ourselves during the seventies and eighties we did our best to clean up as we went along. I was involved in a County Council initiative in Health Education. It was a time when research pointed to the roundworm *toxacara canis* being responsible for serious illnesses in children, and I pressed the matter on the local authorities. It was while the family and I were on the beach at Sheringham that I became enraged by irresponsible dog owners. We had built a great sand castle which was fouled by every dog in sight. That was the last straw. So I wrote a letter to *The North Norfolk News* just signing it "M. Deacon" and saying that as a holiday maker I was disgusted with the state of things. The letter provoked a furious row which lasted more than two years with letters flying back and forth supporting or raging against "Mrs Deacon". Our Norfolk friends sent us numerous press cuttings of the issue which eventually reached the Sheringham District Council chamber. The final cutting reported that a new regulation had been passed banning dogs from fouling the beaches and the promenades. The report stated that the council were in agreement and that "the motion had been carried".

When *The Race Relations Act* was added to the statute book in 1976 I was heartily glad as I had encountered a number of incidents in which members of ethnic minorities had been grossly abused. My Christian background taught me that all are God's children. One Saturday morning I was at a house which the family owned and rented out in the town centre. As I was painting the front door two builders verbally attacked an Indian lady and her children in the street. She was visibly shaken. I intervened on her behalf and was lucky not to have been beaten. It showed me painfully what racial abuse is like.

Ironically, a week later I was phoned by a race relations officer who had had a complaint about myself for alleged racist language. What on earth had I said, I wondered. The dreadful words were: "Even Jim couldn't fix it". The reference was to Jimmy Saville who had a popular programme called *Jim'll Fix It* on television which granted people's dearest wishes. A lady from an ethnic minority had asked me to severely beat a child for allegedly spitting in her son's school lunch. I had reminded her that corporal punishment in schools was being abolished at that time (1986) and that I needed to investigate the matter for her. She then changed the subject and told me that she had written to Jimmy Saville for him to speak to her son in order for him to keep his bowels open. Hence my quip. My strategy of defusing the situation with humour had backfired, and I was glad that when I met the race relations officer he had enough common sense to see the funny side of the situation and the whole thing was dropped.

Yet it was a reminder of a new age in which we were living where we had to be careful of how we spoke and acted, however innocently. Words were changing their meaning so that new associations were added to them. No longer would "gay" mean happy or "black" simply refer to a colour. A new age of political correctness was dawning and there were traps for the unwary. The following years were to see a flowering of the compensation culture in which alleged or actual wrongs were pursued in order to exact monetary gain or to gratify simple spite. I am reminded of the man who deliberately walked into a tradesman's ladder in order to claim financial compensation for injury.

There were, however, real tragedies which occurred without warning. The family of a girl in the school told me they were going to spend a short holiday break in Belgium. It was early March 1987. As the ferry *The Herald of Free Enterprise* left Zeebrugge harbour on the return journey it capsized. The ferry loading doors had been left partly open and the ship rapidly sank as the cargo holds filled with water. The little girl and her family were fortunately saved, but the memory of that event will stay with them. In school, her teacher did her best to let such experiences come out in her writing, talking and illustrations. We tried to help. I remember her coming into my office to cuddle Oscar the Owl, the school's mascot. I used to tell the children to tell Oscar all their troubles. It was amazing how effective such a strategy was.

Other events crowded the eighties, one such being the 900th anniversary of the writing of the Domesday Book. The school took part in a national effort to record the country as it was in 1986 with information that could be put on computer disc. The school was asked to survey the Althorp Estate. I was pleased with this assignment as I knew the Earl Spencer personally and had visited Althorp on a number of occasions. Telephoning the estate office I arranged to take a party of children to Althorp to meet the estate manager. The Earl himself turned up and was his usual gracious self with the children who asked a battery of questions as to the acreage, the crops, the livestock and so forth.

Althorp in 1986 had begun to change from a decade earlier. Living close by in Duston during the seventies many of us locals occasionally saw the Lady Diana Spencer driving around the area. She might sit beside you at the uni-sex hairdressers, or you might meet her in a local shop. She had passed her driving test and like any other young person was enjoying her life to the full. My local history course led me to explore the site of a Roman villa close by the hamlet of Nobottle, on the Althorp Estate. I had sought and was granted permission to lead a party of adult students to the site. It had been originally excavated early in the twentieth century. A hoard of late Roman coins in a leather bag had been discovered. Going one sunny evening when the wheat was well advanced it was easy to pick out the course of the old Roman track that crossed the field. This led to the villa site and we discovered a number of masonry pieces in nearby hedgerows. The Earl had asked me to visit him to report on our expedition. I duly went to the house one evening and was ushered into the house by Diana herself telling me her father was waiting for me in the library.

It would have been in 1980 when Steff and I attended a soirée organised by Diana's stepmother Raine Spencer. Whilst we were there a helicopter landed on the lawn and out stepped the Prince of Wales with Diana. We were all agog as they had not long announced their engagement. They married in July of the following year. Reflecting on all that has happened since those innocent days I am saddened that her girlhood freedom was all too brief. Soon she would be the mother of the heir to the throne and one of the most tragic and iconic figures of the twentieth century, known and respected throughout the world. Only four years before the school children and I were conducting the Domesday census of Althorp in 1986 the term Acquired Immune Deficiency Syndrome (AIDS) was used for the first time. In 1988 Diana stunned everyone by meeting and shaking hands with AIDS sufferers. It was a great act of courage and humanity.

Our own family life proceeded with Steff working for a friend, Brian Malkin, who started a chemical company in his garage and within a few years had established a firm employing over a hundred people. The children proceeded through the education system, surviving the years of the Punk fashion of spiked hair and black clothes and make-up. Popular culture in 1980 included the beginnings of breakfast television and we moved house to the sounds of Sheena Easton singing *Modern Girl*. Teenagers require their own sacrosanct spaces, namely bedrooms. As our children grew up they wanted to try their hand at decorating their own rooms so we agreed and gave them their head; Julian painted his room all black and Tessa managed to cover her walls in red gloss paint! We had a distinctive house. When Julian was about fifteen we bought him a two-man tent for his birthday in November which he insisted on pitching on the back lawn that night; he and a friend tried to sleep through a howling winter's gale. By three o'clock in the morning they were frozen so gave up the attempt until the Spring.

All parents worry about their children as they move out into the adult world. Tessa would be out until quite late with her friends; I kept awake until her footsteps were heard crossing the tiled floor of the kitchen to have a late-night snack. She was home safe and sound. One night Julian returned home minus a tooth. It had been knocked out by some lout. Barclay the dog found it on the floor of the car, and after some coaxing was persuaded to give it up. Early the next morning I rang the dentist who agreed to see him straight away. I proceeded to the cloakroom sink in order to wash the tooth but it pinged out of my fingers and fell down the plughole. So I took off the U-bend and flushed it out. Taking the tooth triumphantly to the dentist I was amazed when he threw it away saying it could not be re-fixed and proceeded to fit a new tooth. Upon returning home we found I had left the tap running with the U-bend unscrewed. It took a few hours to clean up the resultant flood.

DUSTON

NORTHAMPTONSHIRE

A PHOTOGRAPHIC RECORD
c1880 TO c1920

In the mid sixties I wrote occasional articles for publications and was pleased to have written several pieces for the Northampton *Chronicle & Echo* on the growth of popularity of folk music during that period. The local folk music scene was extremely exciting with folk and Morris dancing making a comeback. Local bands enlivened the scene, and venues such at the Artichoke Inn at Moulton became popular meeting places. Interest, too, in local history was growing. Apart from a few writers like Arthur Mee, and Tony Ireson of Kettering, Northamptonshire's rich history had not been given its due attention. I pressed the British Tourist Authority to include material on Northamptonshire in its prestigious magazine *Coming Events in Britain* and, for my cheek, was invited to contribute some articles which were accepted for publication. One of the articles, on Rockingham Forest, prompted me to revisit the Eleanor Cross at Geddington one afternoon where I met a man, complete with expensive Hasselblad cameras. He turned out to be Brian Boyd, the chief photographer for BTA, who had been sent to photograph the

135

monument and the village for my article. We became good friends going out on several other assignments in the county. Such beginnings led to a number of other small historical publications, but more than that I developed a keen eye for items of historic value which were being thrown away. One day, passing a builder's skip in Duston village, I espied some wooden boxes containing old photographic glass plates. The builder was just about to drive off to the tip but allowed me to retrieve the boxes. They turned out to be unique photographs taken by a noted local photographer, H. H. Garrett. Together with David Foster and Stephen Garrett I set up DFG Publishing and the resultant publication *Duston, Northamptonshire: a photographic record c1880-c1920* sold out its entire print-run within a short while in 1990.

It was during 1978 that I was asked to join a small committee at Doddridge & Commercial Street United Reformed Church situated on Castle Hill in the historic core of Northampton. They were planning a celebratory event to commemorate the 250th anniversary of the ordination of Philip Doddridge. I knew of Doddridge as an important hymn writer but of his life story precious little.   Inspired by a booklet on the 350th anniversary of the birth of John Bunyan I was asked if I would produce a similar item on Doddridge.   The originally planned slim volume turned out to be a substantial biography. It took nine months to research and write, and a further nine months to check the manuscript.   John Munro, deputy chief librarian at Northamptonshire Libraries who had agreed to publish the work, gave me a meticulous training in how to put a book together and how to ensure it was fit for publication.   Like Doddridge I tried to rise at five in the morning to do several hours before going to work, but the effort nearly killed me!   I recall having private access to the Local Studies Room at the Central Library when everyone had gone home.   In the stillness of the library I worked on often late into the night.   Eventually *Philip Doddridge of Northampton* was published in March 1980 and launched at an official event at County Hall.   The family accompanied me to a dinner hosted by the Chairman of the County Council.   It was gratifying to see favourable reviews in the religious and literary press and to receive appreciative letters from many people.   The National Free Church Women's Council presented a copy of it to HM the Queen Mother when she attended their annual conference that year, and the evangelist Dr Billy Graham made favourable comment on it. Such an experience had an eventual life-changing effect.

I continued my commitment of helping where I could within the local church.   The Free Church tradition emphasised very much the responsibility of individuals to make a contribution to the life of church and community.   It was part of the belief in the "priesthood of all believers" in which every faithful person, whether lay or ordained, is called upon to exercise a ministry, using the circumstances, talents and opportunities of life to encourage and care for others.   So there was a deepening sense of calling into the ministry of the church which became more and more insistent as the decade unfolded. Some words of Charles Simeon, the Cambridge theologian, were a great encouragement; he said: "God does not choose the fittest for his tasks, but makes fit those whom he has chosen".   I duly started a training course on a part-time basis through the United Reformed Church; it took over three years to complete using techniques such as annual summer schools and local tutors who worked me hard.   Fine ministers such as Rev Conrad Husk, Rev Derek Fitch and Rev Stephen Harris and others energetically put me through my paces. My ordination as a Non-Stipendiary Minister, originally termed Auxiliary Minister, took place at Duston in May 1988, the presiding minister being the Rev John Slow.

Ordination at Duston United Reformed Church
4 May 1988. Presiding Minister was the Rev John Slow,
Moderator of the East Midlands Province of the URC.

Such posts mirrored changes within other churches; the Church of England was ordaining Non Stipendiary Ministers and the Roman Catholic Church had long used worker priests. The idea was simple; suitable people were ordained to the ministry of Word and Sacrament in order to serve the needs of the Church whilst continuing to earn their livings in the community. St Paul could do it whilst earning his daily crust as a tentmaker; so could we. Amongst my fellow students was a farmer and a sewage works manager, and I was to meet others such as a former racing car driver, a coal miner and a stock broker. Becoming an NSM was a step along a winding road which had taken me from my early days in Kettering, giving talks to groups, and moving on to preach in the village and town chapels of the county. There was a great fellowship of common purpose amongst the Free Church communities that comprised, in the main, Baptist, Methodist and United Reformed churches. There was a constant interchange of preachers so it was easy to be invited to take services in their representative places of worship.

Harvest Festival service at Byfield Chapel c1992

Over the years I visited numerous chapels and had some comical experiences from time to time. One such Baptist chapel, way out in the country, asked me to go at short notice because the preacher was ill. I travelled many miles to get there only to find no-one there. The doors stood open so I went in, found my way to the vestry and waited. No-one came until one minute before the service was due to start when the organ started playing; the church secretary popped her head round the door to tell me we should start. Entering the sanctuary I found a congregation eyeing me quizzically. Panic overtook me; where was I to lead the service from, the lectern or the pulpit? Choosing the pulpit I stumbled my way up the steps. As I began to speak a voice reached me from below; it was the secretary giving the weekly notices. I got through the service well enough, I suppose, and was about to depart when the secretary came to thank me for coming. She solemnly handed me a pound note which I had put in the Gifts box in the church porch when I had entered saying that the preacher always received the contents of the box as his or her fee.

Once I went to preach at a town church and was welcomed by an elderly lady church secretary. We prepared ourselves for the morning service whilst the church filled with people. Spot on the minute she went to open the closed vestry door when the door knob and its spindle fell off on the outside. Speechless she simply held the remaining door knob in her hand. No way would the door open. The organist kept playing and no amount of thumping on the door or shouting could alert the congregation to our plight. Neither of us was fit to climb out of the window, she because of her age and I thought it a bit undignified for the preacher to clamber out of a window. After the best part of ten minutes a rather bewildered church Elder turned up to rescue us. On another occasion in a very old chapel I announced the first hymn and then promptly disappeared through the wood-wormed floor boards; I was more shocked than hurt.

I found in the churches and chapels of the county many dear souls who were the salt of the earth. Their fellowships held fast to deep-rooted human values which had been nourished in the soil of Christian England. The spirit of the New Testament was hot in their veins, and they had a commitment to the communities in which they lived. Many were to be found in the caring professions, in supporting charities and being involved with all kinds of community activities especially with the young. Some of these fellowships struggled on with a faithful few; others were packed to the doors with activities going on every day of the week. One church on the point of closure, namely Creaton chapel, burst forth into new life thanks mainly to a few families joining and the regular support of ministers and lay preachers. As with many churches the foundation of a Sunday School or Junior Church for the children inspired remarkable growth and a new lease of life. Many a time have I been welcomed into people's homes after a service in a village chapel and regaled with refreshments and tales of all that was taking place in the locality. Fortunate to have a car I recalled the preachers of earlier times who would walk many miles to lead worship.

As I became more ecumenically minded I discovered that the same spirit suffused other denominations and I developed a wider sympathy and understanding of the Universal Church in which all who have a faith in Jesus Christ have more that binds them together than anything that divides them. In reality, all Christians work for the same firm although in different departments. It is the vagaries of upbringing and limited opportunity for meeting others from different traditions, together with fringe fundamentalists, that have been the major factors in retaining divisions. Over my lifetime there has developed a stronger togetherness within the mainline churches; this is one of the most significant and positive changes that took place in the latter half of the 20th century. Back in the eighties significant changes were being made in the position of women. Although the Free Churches had had women ministers for decades it was a controversial vote in the General Synod of the Church of England in 1987 that cleared the way for the ordination of women to the Anglican priesthood.

As the eighties came to an end the pace of change seemed to quicken even more. The vulnerability of the individual to deliberate malicious activity or accident was brought home in a series of disasters. In 1984 the Conservative Conference was targeted when it met at the Grand Hotel in Brighton. Twenty pounds of gelignite, planted by the IRA, exploded killing five and injuring thirty-four. It was a grim reminder of a seemingly endless problem. Two years later the Kings Cross underground station fire erupted under the escalators killing thirty-one firemen and passengers. It was the same year that saw a severe set-back to the US Space Shuttle programme when on 28 January the Challenger rocket exploded seventy-three seconds after launch. I recall the event because a young teacher, Christa McAuliffe was on board; she was scheduled as the first teacher in space; many of our pupils were following her progress and were stunned by the disastrous outcome.

One of my teacher colleagues, the late Ron Wilson, was a charismatic figure who was not only the warden of the Everdon Field Centre and a great authority and prolific writer on wildlife but also a broadcaster of note. He and I prepared a fifty minute programme for the BBC marking the 400th anniversary of the execution of Mary Queen of Scots (8 February 1587). So on the very day in 1987 we stood together on the grassy mound, the remains of the castle at Fotheringhay, where Mary met her death. A chill wind whipped across the nearby River Nene and whistled into the microphone. The programme was duly broadcast. Ron was delighted with the response receiving accolades from the BBC management and the Advisory Council one member of whom "had tears streaming down my face by the end of the programme". There was one tongue-in-cheek complaint from a lady who phoned in to say that my vivid description of the actual beheading of Mary had coincided with her Sunday lunch. As I described the necessity of the executioner in using the axe to saw through the partially severed neck she was at that moment trying to slice her joint of beef. It quite put her off her meal.

Significant events were to crowd the closing years of the eighties. There was the Great Storm of 16 October 1987. Michael Fish, the former weather forecaster, will be forever tarred with the brush of getting his predictions so wrong. Although we did not suffer quite as badly as the south east of England I remember having to replace tiles blown from the roof, repair fencing and collect up branches ripped off our trees, resulting from the centre of the intense depression tracking eastwards across Buckinghamshire. We had a sleepless night listening to the howling wind. Fifteen millions trees were uprooted and whole forests destroyed. It was fortunate that the storm occurred during the night otherwise the death toll of sixteen would have been higher.

As if this was not sufficient to rattle people's sense of well-being anyone with money in stocks and shares was in for a severe shock a few days later. What has been termed Black Monday saw the crash of world stock markets on 19 October 1987. With some money left me in my parents' estate I had invested in unit trusts which had performed very well. All seemed rosy, but for some reason I sold most of them a week before the crash, and thus saved ourselves from greater loss. It was a salutary reminder of the volatility of money markets, and how all of us are bound up in events often beyond our control.

Although the Clapham rail disaster of 1988 seemed to happen to other people far away several folk known to me had been involved. The terrible events of 21 December 1988 will ever stick in my mind. Friends of ours were travelling home to the USA and when PanAm flight 103 exploded in mid-air, the result of a terrorist bomb, we feared the worst. Debris had showered the Scottish town of Lockerbie, directly under its flight-path. We spent an anxious time and were somewhat relieved to hear that our friends had taken an earlier flight. The same sense of relief was felt when another friend escaped death whilst driving to Nottingham on the M1 motorway. If he had been driving slightly slower he would have been caught by the crashing British Midland jet which ploughed across the motorway just seconds after he had passed.

Earlier that year, on 15 April a gate was opened at the Hillsborough football ground in Sheffield in order to allow crowds of tight-pressed fans to watch the FA semi-final. What followed was the worst disaster in English sporting history with ninety-four people killed and 170 injured. All were crushed by the huge crowd that pressed forward trapping them against the metal barriers erected to prevent hooligans invading the pitch. On that very day we sold a house that we owned in Hillsborough, close to the football stadium, and coincidentally to one of the policemen who had been on duty at the football match. He subsequently suffered from severe depression, as did many others, following his experiences that day.

Steff and I had been planning to travel to China on an extended visit. We had hoped to take a trip along the Yangtze River and were hoping to be in Beijing in the summer of 1989. The mighty Tiananmen Square is the largest in the world, capable of holding a million people. We wanted to experience that vista from the famous Gate of Heavenly Peace. Our trip would have taken us to Beijing but news of unrest in China and other factors made us abandon the trip. It was just as well, for on the 3-4 June the student protest for democratic reform was brutally repressed by the Chinese government. Tanks sent into Tiananmen Square were temporarily held up by the courage of a lone student who stood in their path. Yet bloodshed ensued with thousands being killed. We watched the events unfold by television news and counted ourselves lucky not to have been there. The nearest we got that year to China was the local Chinese takeaway shop.

The fact that we should seriously contemplate a trip to the Far East was in itself a major shift in our thinking. Long-haul travel was getting easier and affordable. Folk who had gone out to find the sun on Mediterranean coasts in the sixties and seventies were often now looking towards other more exotic and adventurous places. It was possible to holiday in the Maldives or Sri Lanka, visit the Himalayas or trek the Sahara Desert, snorkel off the Great Barrier

Reef or ride the Trans Siberian Railway. The world was opening up and many young people took a year out to widen their experience by back-packing. Our daughter Tessa had visited the United States; our son Julian had travelled as far as Australia. If the younger generation could do it, so could we!

So, in 1989, Steff and I went on a new venture, going to Israel, a trip which was a turning point of experience. Landing at the Ben Gurion airport in Tel Aviv having endured the intense security checks of El Al we were hit by the heat and noises of the Middle East. It was late at night and our coach deposited us at our Palestinian-run hotel just outside Jerusalem on the Mount of Olives. We fell into bed and were awoken by a braying donkey and the sound of the muezzin calling the faithful to prayer. It was six o'clock and the city was astir before the heat of the day became too intense. The sunlight was blinding and as we looked out of our window the extraordinary sight of Jerusalem awakening to the morning sun was breathtaking. From our vantage point on the Mount of Olives we could see the city, ringed by its ancient walls. Rising above them was the Temple Mount, with the Dome of the Rock mosque and the Al Aqsa mosque dominating the space where once stood the Temple of Solomon.

It is hard to describe the intensity of emotion that the experience of first going to Israel evoked in me. The Christian culture of Britain as mediated in my youth through school, home and church, had given me a sound grounding in the events and people depicted in Old and New Testaments. Now I was treading the dusty soil of the Holy Land itself, walking where the feet of great leaders like Elijah had trodden and where Abraham had been the father of what were to become the three great monotheistic world faiths, Judaism, Christianity and Islam. Above all, it was the place where Jesus of Nazareth had walked and talked, lived and died, and had been resurrected. Would I be disappointed, nay disillusioned, I wondered by finding that my Western perceptions of the lands of the Bible were based on myth and misunderstanding?

It was staggering to find so much of the biblical record literally lying at our feet. In AD 70 Jerusalem was destroyed by the Romans under Titus. Over the centuries synagogues, churches and mosques have been built across the city reflecting the chequered history of this amazing place. Like so many other cities it has grown to accommodate a burgeoning population. So to find the city that Jesus knew one has to go underground. Many feet below the present surface there are numerous archaeological discoveries which vividly bring out the narratives of the Gospels. One such is a pavement of red stones situated below the present-day Ecce Homo Convent of the Sisters of Sion on the Via Dolorosa. This is the site of the Antonia fortress which Herod the Great dedicated to Mark Antony. The fortress was the residence of the Roman Governor and the pavement, or *lithostrotos,* is most likely the very place on which Jesus and Pontius Pilate confronted each other at the former's trial. Scratched into the stones by the guards is a game called *King* which it was customary for soldiers to play when they had prisoners awaiting execution. The game involved the mockery of the winning soldier's prisoner, his dressing up and wearing of a crown of thorns. To stand in such a place is to draw upon the deepest emotions. The authenticity of the Biblical narratives shouts aloud.

In the crowded and narrow streets of Jerusalem there was a ferment of life, diverse, argumentative and passionate. One day in Old Jerusalem we met a beautifully dressed young couple; they had just been married and were leading their wedding party into the city from the Damascus Gate. An international and multi-faith crowd gathered around us and congratulated the couple; there was clapping and handshakes, a water seller came to ply his wares and one nearby market stall holder offered them a gift of fruit. It was a magic moment of racial harmony, a paused movie image which sadly soon moved on. Such was the experience of the Holy Land, not only in Jerusalem but right across the country with so many places evoking the memories of the past. There were numerous surprises, such as seeing the Arabic graffiti which plastered every wall in Bethlehem, and the realisation that the Shepherds' Fields are situated not on the hills but in the valley where the grass is most likely to be. Walking the shore of the Sea of Galilee I was surprised that there is no sand but only pebbles. Being a lake the water is not tidal. Yet crossing the water on a little boat the biblical story of the Calming of the Storm came home with dramatic suddenness. Within a matter of ten minutes the wind, funnelled from the Mediterranean through the Valley of Jezreel, whipped up large waves which put the boat in some danger. Just as quickly the storm subsided. Along the shoreline of black pebbles there are occasional large black stones. I was reminded of the words of Jesus when he declared that Peter should be his rock, strong, solid and immoveable rather than a pebble which could be easily thrown around. The whole experience of the Holy Land at that time worked its own fascination upon us. Within two years we would be back, but in that time much was to change.

Chapter Ten: A New Calling.

As a social phenomenon the disco has dominated partying since the mid seventies when *Saturday Night Fever* set a new trend in music. Whatever the event, whether it is a wedding reception or coming-of-age party, the ubiquitous disco may be found. Many discos are nothing more than a din of noise that makes it impossible to hold any conversation whatsoever. Steff and I have always considered that parties need to be more mentally challenging and require a mixture of relaxed bonhomie, music, and even a few games and puzzles. Over the years we have had some splendid parties such as our Silver Wedding when we hired a Country & Western dance band, and my fiftieth birthday when we had a French evening with appropriate food and drink; everyone dressed up, remarkably most men as Napoleon and most women as tarts! There must be some deep reason for this!

I'm celebrating half a century.

We're celebrating quarter of a century.

A party is a time to enjoy some good food and drink in a convivial atmosphere, not to get "bladdered" with alcohol or sit numbed by the endless, mind-blowing throb of loud music emanating from the home music centre. Indeed, I reflect that the phonograph of my parents' day gave way to the gramophone of my youth, the record player of my young married life and to the music centre of my children's era. This has moved on to the karaoke, the personal walkman and the downloading of music from the internet via an iPod of our grandchildren's generation.

Thus the New Year's Eve party that we organised at the end of 1989 had its usual lively ambience. The house was full of friends who were set on having a good time. Every room heaved with people and many were intent on finding the clues to the quiz that we pinned up around the house. As the night wore on there was a lot of singing especially as the midnight hour struck. The old tradition of someone dark bringing in a piece of coal to herald the new year had long gone within our particular circle of friends. We sang *Auld Lang Syne* and everyone kissed and hugged everyone else. Going out into the garden in the early hours when everyone had gone home I felt strangely apprehensive of the new decade we were entering. What would the nineties have in store for us all? The children were both young adults now and beginning to make their own way in the world finding new friends, working and studying.

The New Year was only a month old when the dramatic news came on 2 February that President de Klerk of South Africa had announced the end of Apartheid. Within another week or so, on 11 February, Nelson Mandela was released from his long imprisonment. The struggle for racial equality in South Africa had finally achieved a favourable outcome. It was stunning news, and reminded me of my student involvement back in the late fifties when mass demonstrations filled Trafalgar Square in London. South Africa was to bravely embark upon a self examination of its failures led by the indomitable Archbishop Desmond Tutu. The Truth and Reconciliation Commission throughout the following years was able to exorcise much of the hatred that had fuelled Apartheid. It remains an all-time model for the reconciliation of the apparently irreconcilable, relevant to so many issues throughout the world.

An even more exciting change came later in the year, on the 9 November, when the Berlin Wall was knocked down. Thousands clambered over the wall with hammers, pick-axes and bare hands to destroy this symbol of the division between East and West which had been one of the terrible legacies of the Second World War.

Relations between the Soviet Union and the West had thawed considerably. It was the age of what the Russian President Gorbachev called "glasnost" and "perestroika". Margaret Thatcher had declared that she could do business with him, and the extremely personable approach of the US President Ronald Reagan had convinced the Soviets that America was sincere in wanting to disarm the huge stockpiles of nuclear weapons which only promised mutual destruction. Thus, in the opening year of the nineties, two great divisions, Apartheid and the Berlin Wall had fallen. By the end of 1990 even the seemingly unassailable Margaret Thatcher was ousted by members of her own party in favour of John Major.

For me it was a year of transition. I had returned to my head teacher duties after the Christmas break. All was seemingly well; the school had a good name in the community. The new nursery that we had opened two years previously was proving to be successful. It was a joint venture with Nene College (later the University College of Northampton) and provided a training opportunity for the college as well as affording local children a nursery place, albeit half time. My plan was to develop the nursery as a full-time institution, but that would cost a lot more money.

So, why was I feeling unsettled? I asked. Undoubtedly, the pressures on schools were worsening. I had always managed to teach every class in the school for one period a week. It gave the staff at least one free period and I practised what I preached in being a head teacher. In that way I knew every child and kept my finger on the pulse of the school. But the pressure of paperwork increased to such an extent that I had to give up my teaching commitment, consequently gradually becoming more remote from the children and sometimes not knowing many of their names. Even my deputy, Audrey Foulger, had to relinquish her teaching commitment to keep up with the ever-increasing flow of administrative tasks. There was a general unease within the teaching profession especially regarding the attitude of authority towards employing expensive teachers. Young teachers did not cost as much to employ as more senior staff. It was the age of getting "value for money" and "accountability". Head teachers and senior staff were encouraged to retire early to make way for younger and less costly staff. One was considered as getting old at fifty. It was the age that courted the young. The frightening statistics of life insurance actuaries stated that the

149

average male teacher retiring at age sixty-five had sixteen months to live. A former deputy head of the school, struggling on to sixty-five in order to get his full pension, lived exactly that amount of time after his retirement. All who attended his funeral returned with sober thoughts.

The issue for me came to a head one morning when an official called to see me to tell me that ever more changes were on the way. He noted that head teachers might well be called "line managers" in the future for our role was changing to that of a bureaucrat in chief. We had to learn office skills and management techniques. We would have to set the budget for the school and be accountable for it. It was to be a different task, although the standards of education not only had to remain good but had to improve. The pint pot would have to hold the quart. I recalled the words of our former family doctor in Kettering who had brought both me and my wife into the world. He was a kindly soul, a committed Christian who had told me that he believed his calling from God was to be a good doctor. He had seriously considered going into the ministry in the Church but felt he could do more good in the world of medicine. His words rekindled in me the sense of Christian calling that I had long felt in the cause of education. The conviction grew that my life had to change. There was much to be done outside the narrow world of school. One morning I picked up the telephone and spoke to the Education

Department, known to staff as "the office", and announced that I wanted to take advantage of the early retirement scheme. Within the hour a very senior official was sipping coffee in my office and sharing my feelings with which he fully agreed. It was within only a matter of months that I had announced my intention to retire from the profession. Fond farewells were said and I left teaching after thirty years without a backward look. One of the wonderful presents I received was a trip in a hot-air balloon. Quite a number came to bid me farewell as I ascended skyward.

It has been often said that when one door closes another opens. The truth of that statement came home to me within a matter of weeks for I was invited by the United Reformed Church to apply for full-time stipendiary ministry. My original idea had been to take life a bit easier, do some more publishing and writing, spend some time in the garden and with my wife, and continue as a non-stipendiary minister serving the church as best I could. I went for several interviews and was offered various college options for a one year full-time course. Never in my working life have I had to prove my qualifications by showing certificates, but the church wanted to see everything, including GCE O levels certificates. I joked that perhaps I could show my first swimming award. The church, rightly, wanted to be sure. So did I, and I went through a whole period of thought and prayer as to what was the best for me. I was accepted at Westminster College, Cambridge and was told that I was welcome for an academic year beginning in the September of 1990.

Meantime, the summer was with us, and apart from taking a holiday I worked with Julian doing contract decorating and landscape gardening. We did the same the following summer. It was a refreshing return to the bustling everyday world of physical work where the completion of a task can be seen. Unlike the teaching of a child, the success of which is a long-term commitment, the results of painting a ceiling, the building of a garden wall or the laying of a patio can be seen in relatively quick time. It made me reflect that so many in the caring professions such as social work, psychotherapy, teaching or the Church, never really see the final outcome of what they are trying to do.

September 1990 saw me start my Cambridge course. The plan was to spend the weekends at home with Steff, before driving into Cambridge via the developing new A14 late on Sunday evenings and coming home on Friday evenings. It was a marvellous year that gave us both a refreshing boost to our married life, giving both space to develop our interests yet (using the current in-phrase) sharing some "quality time" together. Kalil Gibran, in his brilliant book *The Prophet,* likens married life to the two pillars that supported the roof of the Temple in Jerusalem. Each stood apart yet both were united in supporting the structure above them. The Cambridge interlude was a time to reassess the whole direction of our lives and we were prepared to move home and serve the Church wherever we felt God wanted us to be. All options were open.

Westminster College is an impressive building situated at the intersection of Queen's Road, Northampton Street and Madingley Road. The college originated in 1844 in London as a college of the Presbyterian Church of England and came to Cambridge in 1899. It owes its establishment in 1897 (the year that the Cambridge Senate had voted against conferring degrees on women) to two remarkable sisters, Mrs Lewis and Mrs Gibson, who gifted the land on which the college was built. They were noted linguists and biblical scholars who were awarded honorary doctorates by several universities for their work which included the discovery of valuable manuscripts in the St Catharine's monastery in the Sinai, and in Cairo. The manuscripts are now housed in the college library together with numerous other ancient artefacts. When the Presbyterians came to Cambridge they did so in style, and it is said that the college tower was then the highest in the city. Since 1972 the college has been one of the training colleges of the United Reformed Church dedicated to initial and continuing ministerial and lay training. The college is home to the Cheshunt Institute for Reformed Studies which holds the most comprehensive collection of material relating to the Presbyterian and Congregational traditions within the Christian Church. Amongst the manuscripts is the original *Westminster Confession.*

On my first day I drove through the stone gateways, past the wrought iron gates and round the obelisk that dominates the forecourt. Ahead lay the brick built college with it stone mullioned and transomed bay windows, and the arched doorway over which are the quaint windows of the library. It was like entering another world with the vaulted corridor, the great dining hall with its timbered ceiling with plaster motifs and walls lined with oil portraits of its founders and great theologians. In the heart of the college is the chapel with its curious stained glass windows by Strachan and brass memorials of ministers who went out across the world as missionaries. The study bedrooms had little changed from the times when coal fires were lit in the grates. The women "bedders" came daily to keep the place tidy.

I soon got used to the new life. First thing was the morning service in the chapel; we were all expected to take our turn in leading the worship. Then there was breakfast in the great hall served by a cheery staff and taken at long wooden tables and benches. A whole timetable of lectures and discussion groups had been mapped out for me and the first thing for all students was a crash course in Hebrew. It was expected of me to take on a number of courses some of which were taught in other colleges of the University, so I found myself sitting in lectures and seminars not only at Westminster but at St John's and Trinity, and the colleges of the Theological Federation such as the Methodist Wesley House and the Anglican Wescott House. Students from all the colleges of the Federation came to Westminster for specialist lectures so that the common room and dining hall were often packed with new faces. It was good to be training alongside students of the Methodist and Anglican churches, and since my day the Federation has grown to include Orthodox and Roman Catholic students.

The college had a reputation of having the best meals in Cambridge and attracted many students from the Federation. I put on a considerable amount of weight due to the fine suet puddings available. One evening at supper an unfamiliar face was noticed, mainly because he helped himself liberally to many second helpings. After a few weeks the bursar asked him who he was and he turned out to be a student from Magdalen College who happened to think he could eat his way through our menu. The bursar presented him with a hefty bill and we didn't see him again.

Life in Cambridge seemed idyllic, and I recall walking in the early morning through the snow covered grounds of St John's College and across The Bridge of Sighs. I took the opportunity of attending evensong in Kings College Chapel with the choir singing the office amidst the twinkling lights. One could be forgiven for thinking that little had changed over a century or more. A sudden fall of snow in late January had brought the usual chaos to the country and one particular weekend we found ourselves snowed into college. No-one could get home. I had to see the college Principal over some matter or other and found him in his study, sitting in front of a roaring fire, reading a book on Saint Paul. Outside snow hung thickly on the trees and looked picturesque through the leaded light windows.

Yet the world outside was in deep trouble. It was my turn to lead the morning worship in chapel on 18 January. I heard the news on my radio the previous night, some half hour before midnight, that Allied aircraft had begun bombing Baghdad; the Gulf War had begun. That morning the college common room was agog with anxiety over the war, and as several PhD students from Kuwait and Iraq were lodging in the college there was a natural concern for them. The newspapers had printed lurid details of the capability of Saddam Hussain to wreak terrible injury on the Allied forces. According to them there would be mass carnage and huge numbers of casualties. Preparations were being advanced to prepare hospitals for the expected influx of severely injured service personnel. Chemical and nerve gas warfare was greatly feared. In Addenbrooke's Hospital some wards were cleared ready for casualties, and I was one of several students trained and put on standby as emergency chaplains. The war did not last long and thankfully the worst scenario did not occur, but it was an indication of a new direction in international relations. The war left many unfinished problems and fears which a decade or so later would return with traumatic results.

One of the unfortunate effects of the building of the M11 motorway linking London and Cambridge was that it led to an influx of homeless beggars into the city. To them Cambridge represented rich pickings from its tourists. The city appeared to them as the crock of gold at the end of the rainbow. During the eighties and nineties begging on the streets became a major problem for most town and

154

city centres. Sleeping rough in doorways, huddled in sleeping bags many young people took to a life of homelessness. One young man asked me for any spare change. "No", I said, "but I will buy you some lunch". He accepted, and we went to the *Town and Gown,* a local pub at the back of the college where I bought him fish and chips. I met him several more times and became quite friendly, so much so that he told me that he made over one hundred and fifty pounds every day by his begging. He had a much bigger income than me. The sad part was that he squandered it all on drink and drugs. Some five years later when taking a group to visit Cambridge I saw him again, looking twenty years older and very ill. He is probably dead by now, a casualty of a modern phenomenon of self destruction. More like him crossed my path when I began my ministry later that year in Northampton.

All too soon the Cambridge experience was over. The round of lectures; seminars and retreats; late night study in the hushed atmosphere of the great library amidst its massed tomes; the writing of essays; leisure activities that included a rowing trip or two on the

Cam; visits to colleges and churches; a bike ride to Grantchester to see if we could spot the controversial author Jeffery Archer at the Old Vicarage; a dinner at Kings College as guest of their rowing club; a memorable Ascension Day Eucharist when the service started with the launching of giant sky rockets; the traditional end of year Summer Ball; the camaraderie of fellow students from many backgrounds, countries and different denominations that gave a rich seam of experience to fuel a new phase of one's life.

I passed all the courses to which I had committed myself and was "commended to the United Reformed Church for stipendiary ministry". During the spring of 1991 I had discussed the possibilities of where I would serve. In the URC the system is to look at one church at a time, to be invited to preach and to accept the Call of a congregation. In spite of initial doubts as to the wisdom of going back to Northampton a clear call from the congregation of Doddridge & Commercial Street URC (Castle Hill) in Northampton came in the form of a document signed by all the members. It was the corollary of the time spent working on the Philip Doddridge biography. If he had laboured there until he was in his fiftieth year then, I thought, I could serve (however humbly) from that age for as long as I was able or needed. I accepted, and was inducted to the church on 31 August. Many of the Cambridge students and friends from far afield turned up to wish me God speed.

My new ministerial role included spending seventy-five percent of my time with the Doddridge, Castle Hill congregation and twenty-five percent with the joint URC/ Methodist Church at Wootton. For this purpose I was "recognised and regarded" by the Methodist Church as one of their ministers. In addition I was to be a chaplain at the former Nene College and also Parkside Independent School in Northampton; the latter was founded by my friend Lynn Madden and known for its high standards in music, dance and drama. So I had plenty to do.

Before getting stuck into my new tasks Steff and I returned to the Holy Land for another visit in the autumn of 1991. I was one of the pilgrimage leaders so had to do quite a lot of preparation. We planned a similar itinerary to our first trip staying in Jerusalem and then moving into Galilee centring our visit upon Tiberias and making expeditions into the Golan before moving westward through

Nazareth to Caesarea and southward hugging the Mediterranean coast back to Tel Aviv. It was an ambitious programme.

In the two years since we had visited the Holy Land the political temperature had changed. Jerusalem, the epicentre of Judaism and Christianity and one of the major centres of Islam has long been a place of passionate interchange. When we visited the Dome of the Rock and later the Al Aqsa Mosque the atmosphere was terrifying. Hundreds of young Palestinians had come for the Friday prayers. We gladly passed through the armed Israeli guards at the gate from the Temple Mount to enter a totally different world of Jewish devotion at the Western Wall. Things were getting ugly when we were there as stones had been hurled down on the Jews from the walls of the mount.

Palestinians had begun to protest against the Israelis by starting a strike, the Intifada, which took place every Wednesday from midday. All Arab shops and businesses were closed, although we were welcomed by Arab friends into their shops surreptitiously through rear doors. Hearing that an Arab/Israeli dance troupe was giving a show in Jerusalem that night we arranged for six Mercedes taxis to pick up our group at the hotel to take us there. Sure enough, six white limousines arrived and took us to the show which was absolutely captivating. We had agreed to meet our taxis at 2330hours at a certain spot. Five were there; the sixth had not arrived. As leader I stayed behind with several others to await the arrival of our taxi. Sometime after midnight one of the other taxis arrived. The driver told us to put our heads down and draw the curtains over the windows. He drove us through red traffic lights at breakneck speed around the city's outer road, past the Damascus Gate and up to the Mount of Olives. Only when we were safely back at the hotel did he tell us that our first taxi had been stoned and burnt out as he had broken the Intifada.

Next morning at six o'clock I led our intrepid group down into the Kidron Valley to find the entrance to Hezekiah's tunnel. It was a pre-breakfast jaunt. We duly found the tunnel, went into its depths until we came upon the water course that leads to the Pool of Siloam. Mission accomplished we returned to the daylight. As we emerged shots rang out over our heads. High above us on the upper road Israeli soldiers were firing rifles and waving to us to go. We quickly went back to the hotel. Later that day when we were installed in our Tiberias hotel we saw an Israeli television news bulletin which described in graphic detail the riot that had taken place that morning half a mile from where we had been. Two members of the Israeli parliament, the Knesset, had staged a sit-in protest in the village of Silwan (Siloam) and had caused mayhem.

At the Dome of the Rock, Jerusalem.

Examining Roman remains with Pat Barber at Caesarea.

We had seen the tension between Jew and Arab on our previous trip, but the atmosphere was getting much more serious. The Israeli army raided the Jerusalem hotel in order to roust out any Palestinians breaking their curfew by working. One was discovered and had to spend the night in the lounge under the watchful eye of a soldier and his Alsatian dog. One waiter hid in a large wardrobe as the army searched the hotel and made good his escape. Out in the street a young Palestinian boy had been forced to stand under a lamppost with a fierce dog held on a leash guarding him. His home was but a few hundred metres away, and his anxious family waited until he was allowed to proceed after more than an hour.

It was not hard to see the injustice of a system which gave instant citizenship to Diaspora Jews immigrating to Israel whereas Palestinian families who had been there some hundreds of years were denied the same rights. Yet our visit to Yad Vashem, the Jewish holocaust memorial, with its stone bunker in which a permanent flame is reflected in a mass of mirrors tells the harrowing story of the Nazi persecution of the Jews. A recorded voice intones the names of the million children out of the six million killed in Hitler's *final solution.* Such memory lies deep in the Israeli mind and is reflected in the hawkish stance they play in the politics of the region. Sitting in a boat on the Sea of Galilee I asked an elderly Israeli couple why it was that Jew and Arab could not co-exist in such a beautiful land. Their chilling reply that the land was too small for both epitomised the nature of the conflict which has caused so much bloodshed and anguish. Since then the phenomenon of suicide bombing against the Israelis has lost the Palestinian cause much support from the West.

Those who seek to involve themselves in the politics of the Middle East do so at their own peril. It was in January 1987 that the Archbishop of Canterbury's special envoy, Terry Waite, was kidnapped in Beirut. A man of immense courage and a great humanitarian he had been involved in negotiating the release of captives in Tehran and Libya. In his own captivity he spent 1,763 days of which the best part of four years were in solitary confinement. We were conscious that Terry was not that far from us as we drove northwards through the West Bank and up into the Golan Heights. This area had been captured by Israel in the 1967 war. There were empty buildings and burnt out tanks still evident. We travelled through Druze villages high up in the mountains that bordered Lebanon and paused awhile on the Syrian frontier where we prayed for Terry's release. We were physically as close to him as we could get. It was a very moving visit as we renewed baptismal vows in the waters at Banyas, the Biblical *Caesarea Philippi* where the apostle Peter had declared Jesus to be the Christ. The melting snows from the slopes of Mt Hermon form the pools which are the source of the River Jordan. It was from this spot that Jesus set his face to go to Jerusalem, and all that that meant in terms of suffering and sacrifice. Three weeks after our arrival home in the UK Terry Waite was released from his ordeal; he arrived at RAF Lyneham on 19 November to a rapturous welcome.

Chapter Eleven: A Town Centre Ministry.

When I left teaching, the usual jibe was that we had short working days and long holidays; when I entered the ministry the general view was that we only worked one day a week. So whatever I did I had a "cushy number", according to contemporary folklore. With the children grown up and independent we should have fewer commitments, I thought. In theory, life would be a lot easier! I felt that I could comfortably make several visits every day and soon work my way through the congregation with plenty of time to study, write sermons and visit the sick. It was not like that in reality, as numerous calls upon one's time came, not just from within the church but also from outside. I seriously underestimated the pressures that ministers were under. Dietrich Bonhoeffer once said that the church should exist to serve those who are outside it, and it was clear that there were issues in society that needed the Christian voice and helping hand.

Castle Hill United Reformed Church where I had the privilege of being Minister 1991 – 2002

Any church fellowship needs to be spiritually and numerically strong in order to serve the world, so I set about trying to build up the work of my predecessor in enlarging the congregation, welcomed all kinds of people and tried to provide interesting and lively services. It was good having the support of a dedicated group of people who had been the strength of the church over many years. One of the changes in society is the diminution of the pool of dedicated people willing to give themselves in the service of others, particularly the young. I was fortunate to have in the church folk who would week by week lead in the Boys and Girls Brigades, the Youth Group and the Junior Church. There was the music group *Discovery,* which month by month led services for the young and the young at heart providing lively exhilarating music. There was *The Bright Hour,* a group of retired ladies who met on Monday afternoons; the origins of the meeting went back more than a century. Church members sang in the choir and took part in leading worship. Others dedicated themselves to all the myriad jobs that are needed in keeping a church building intact and a fellowship of people together.

It was a privileged position to be able to meet people in their own homes and share their sorrows as well as joys. One of the hardest tasks is to sit throughout the night at the hospital bedside of a dying friend and to minister to the family as well as the patient. I did this at various times and have been aware that such shared experiences have formed strong bonds of friendship between the family and me. This is the heart of ministry for one tries, in spite of one's own inadequacies, to be the Christ-like presence in the midst of the world's woes.

Yet there are many happy occasions which also weld together minister and people: anniversaries of all kinds, and the round of social events which are part of the life of any healthy church. There were the traditional Harvest Suppers and other similar occasions. During my time at Castle Hill two General Elections were held. We took the opportunity of inviting to the church all the candidates for the Northampton South Constituency for public hustings' meetings. Both events turned out to be lively affairs with a variety of opinions being given. The church was very much in the thick of social life, concerned with contemporary issues and problems.

Young people's work has always concerned me, and I went on several Boys'/Girls' Brigade camps at various locations in England and Wales. I persuaded Steff to come to her first camp. We ended up in a Welsh field under canvas. The first night was spent pinning the tent sides down with stones from a nearby dry-stone wall; the wind was so strong that as I lay on my camp bed our dog Barclay steadily moved past us in his basket blown by the wind; he had a most quizzical expression on his whiskered face. On another camp occasion Steff helped as one of the cooks. The mess tent was situated on a hill with a distinct gradient. When the Sunday Yorkshire puddings were cooked the variable thickness of one end of each tin to the other reflected the steep slope. They were great times of high adventure: pony trekking, building rafts to cross rivers, abseiling down a slate quarry, playing the famous Lobby Ludd game when the officers went off into the town in disguise with the youngsters in pursuit, and the inevitable camp concerts on the last night.

The shortest and most memorable sermon that I have ever heard was preached by a Baptist lay preacher, George Green of Rushden, who once announced his sermon text as "Horsemuck". Yes, the congregation had heard it correctly, he was going to preach on manure, and as our gardens thrived when we put a good helping into the soil so did our lives when we bothered to pray. "Prayer", said the preacher, "is the fertiliser of the soul". Having spoken for less than two minutes George finished his sermon. Members of my family who were present and who were farmers still remembered that sermon forty years later. So did I, and believed the simple truth of what had been said. Trying to follow George's advice, and also to emulate Philip Doddridge who spent a regular time in his vestry praying for his people and the wider world, I invited anyone at Castle Hill who would like to join me first thing on a Wednesday morning to do so. From the start, the Morning Prayers attracted a regular group numbering between a dozen and twenty who shared in that vital ministry

The growth of better understanding between Christians of different traditions has gradually brought about an interchange of ideas. The strong Puritan tradition which regarded imagery in church as being idolatrous has mellowed; it is recognised that worship and the expression of faith often need colour, sound and movement as well as simplicity. Worship has thus become more lively and expressive, and joint services with other churches have brought about some fusion of liturgical practices. At least with new hymn books such as *Mission Praise,* Christians from many traditions have widened their common musical ground.

Steff and I travelled to Poitiers in France with a large group of Christians from Northampton; we were guests of the Roman Catholic, Reformed and Baptist Churches, and were welcomed in their churches and at the city hall. They came on a return visit to Northampton bringing with them a choir of over seventy men and boys who sang at Castle Hill. I tried to preach a sermon in French and by the wry smiles on their faces I reckon I made a few gaffes. It was delightful sharing the hospitality of our homes with French Christians.

The church welcomed many other groups such as Amnesty International and the Scouts, and a particular series of services had a list of guest preachers that included the chief officers of the Police and Education. One mid-week morning I walked into the chapel and was surprised to find it filled by hundreds of Barclaycard personnel. They had been evacuated from their nearby headquarters due to a bomb scare and had used the facility we offered them to provide an emergency meeting place. I quipped that it was an unexpected pleasure seeing them in church and announced that the sermon would only last an hour. At this, they all roared with laughter. A second bomb scare within a matter of weeks led to the wry joke that perhaps it was the minister putting in the hoax calls as the church received a fee every time it was used as an evacuation centre.

One of the great Sacraments of the Church is that of Baptism. Through baptism one is initiated into the church fellowship, the Body of Christ, and receiving the gift of the Holy Spirit. The United Reformed Church very wisely kept a balance between the dividing issue on whether it is applicable for infants or is for those who are older "believers". The simple rule was to use one's common sense; the families who attended church had no problem as they could honour the promises they made. Moreover the congregation, who also made promises to God and to the parents in helping to nurture their children, would be able to carry out their commitments.

I presided over many lovely services of baptism of both adults and infants. With the latter I would take the child from the mother, administer the sacrament and then carry the child through the congregation who stood as I moved amongst them which signified their acceptance of the child into "the household of faith". Steff usually assisted me by presenting the parents with a lighted candle as a symbol that the "light of Christ" had entered that little soul's life. These were great moments and ones which drew families into the Christian fellowship.

However, general cultural sentiment in wider society viewed Christening as simply a social occasion. A lady telephoned me on one occasion to state that I was to Christen her baby at a specific time on a certain Sunday afternoon. When I asked her why, the answer was that the child needed to be "done" and, anyway, the party was set for that day at the local community centre and the invitations had already gone out. I pointed out that Baptism should be carried out in a public service of worship and that it involved others in making promises. She didn't want that, or to come to any interviews over the meaning of the Sacrament; she did not have any intention of ever coming to church apart from this occasion. Instead, I offered her a service of Dedication in which we gave a blessing to the child during which she and her husband made promises regarding its upbringing. That was not good enough. She was abusive when I refused to budge.

Such an incident points to a social phenomenon which still clings to the trappings of a past Christian culture when the birth of children and their upbringing as well as the state of their immortal souls were considered of vital importance. Perhaps my greatest disappointments as a minister centre on the baptism of children when parents start attending church, express keenness in matters of faith and then the week after the baptism they never darken the church's doors again. I have failed to find an answer as to why they take the trouble and how they can make promises which they do not intend keeping. It is their own children that they are letting down in not letting them develop a faith life; it is almost an abuse of the nature of the Sacrament which they claim they want.

During the eighties and nineties many churches began to cease meeting on Sunday evenings. This was simply due to dwindling numbers in an age when so many other attractions abounded. Lack of public transport on Sundays also had an effect upon some who did not have a car of their own. We managed throughout the nineties and into the new century to keep a successful evening service going. Like evensong in the Church of England the evening service was a conclusion to the Sabbath day and also a beginning of the new week. There is nothing lovelier than seeing the lights of the church blazing forth in the dimming twilight. There are many happy memories of the chapel with its polished box pews suffused by candlelight and resounding with the sound of the reading of the great scripture lessons and carols of Christmas.

Keen to ensure the rhythm of the Christian Year we began the annual cycle of worship every Advent, singing Doddridge's great hymn *Hark the glad sound the Saviour comes* and other seasonal carols. Throughout Lent into Easter and then on to Pentecost the weekly services drew the faithful from many parts of the town. One particularly poignant service was Remembrance Sunday when the congregation gathered at the war memorial in the church vestibule to lay a wreath in memory of those from the church who had perished in the world wars. A bugler stood on the stairs and played *The Last Post*. The church was a gathered community and we tried hard to draw in folk who lived in the vicinity, especially the children and young people.

It was tough work in the town centre with the increasing problems of the urban jungle. Policies of local authorities often do not help matters, and I witnessed at first hand the changing demographics of the immediate church area. Older folk, once content to live in the high rise flats, gradually left because of the disruptive behaviour of their younger and less sociably responsible neighbours. Over the years I helped a number of elderly friends transfer to Bethany Homestead, a unique residence for the elderly founded by local Baptist and Congregational churches and opened in 1926.

Drug taking and prostitution in the area around the church worsened in spite of valiant efforts by the authorities to stop kerb crawling by motorists. I got to know a number of the street girls who usually kept their distance from the church premises. Many were only teenagers yet they were hooked on drugs and controlled by evil pimps. However, I managed to get one or two out of "the game" but only with great daring and the co-operation of local authorities. One woman in her forties who had several beautiful children came to see me one day. She told me that she had been abused by her own father as a teenager and had been a prostitute since then. She wanted to escape, but was in the clutches of an unscrupulous pimp. She had no employment record, no savings and no confidence in living a normal life. She said, amusingly, that all she did was to dress up in her leathers and get paid for beating middle aged men with a whip. "They stagger away from me black and blue", she said with ironic amusement," and they pay me for it". Yet there was disgust as well as desperation in her voice. With the pimp due to appear in court on serious criminal charges the opportunity presented itself to do something. When the court verdict of several years in prison was announced a taxi from social services arrived to meet the children and their mother. They were whisked away to start a new life with new identities in a new place. Within a matter of hours a different pimp had moved into her flat. She had escaped by a whisker. Months later I received a postcard thanking me for my support. She had found a job, had somewhere to live and the children were doing well in their new schools.

On 28 August 1994 thousands of shops opened legally for the first time on Sundays following a change in the Sunday trading laws. Even major stores such as Marks & Spencer and Waitrose who had opposed the new law bowed to the inevitable and opened their doors. For decades shops had opened contrary to the law on Sundays, and there were glaring anomalies that demanded redress; it was perfectly legal to buy, for example, a pornographic magazine from a newsagent yet it was illegal to purchase a Bible. Many saw the change as another step in the secularisation of society, a further break with the traditional past when the Sabbath had been the time for worship and a day of rest and family get-togethers. On 21 August, as I had done for some years, I drove into the town centre to lead church worship. There were few cars on the roads at mid-morning, and by lunchtime traffic had increased to a reasonable amount. The effect of the Sunday Trading Act was instant as the roads the following Sunday were busy from an early hour and by lunchtime there were queues of cars waiting to get into the car parks of B & Q and other stores.

From that date Sunday became as busy a day as the rest of the week. One effect was that regular worshippers at the town's central churches had to vie with an increased demand for car parking spaces, and even face the inevitable charges which the Borough Council began to levy on Sunday parking, hitherto freely available. It was all part of a changing culture in which shopping had become an aspect of leisure and the new cathedrals of modernity were the opulent shopping malls that had begun to spring up across the land. I had mixed feelings about such a change and certainly supported many of the views of the Keep Sunday Special campaign that fought a losing battle against the matter. There was a real sense that another aspect of our national life had gone for good and serious concerns that employees would be forced to work on Sundays. There was disquiet that the frenetic pace of daily life would have no times of quietness and placidity. In fact, church life carried on much as it did before and I took the view that it was much better getting up and about on a Sunday morning rather than laying in bed; ever being the pragmatist I argued that coming to church to thank God for all the benefits of a consumer society should be the priority before one went off to spend one's money.

One of the great joys of my life was to conduct the wedding of our daughter Tessa to Richard at Castle Hill Church in 1993. Her brother Julian was away in China but managed to telegram his good wishes from Beijing. So our great friend Roger Tame deputised in order to give the bride away. The photograph shows us at the church door with bridesmaids Sarah and Laura. Later Julian himself was married to Giuliana in Melbourne and we did not get to meet our new daughter-in-law until they came to England for a holiday in 1998.

Our grand daughter Hannah was born to Richard and Tessa in 1994 and grand daughter Natasha to Julian and Giuliana in 1998. So a new generation had begun opening up a fresh and hopeful dimension in our experience.

Over the past twenty years or so weddings have become big business with numerous interested parties determined to make money out of a lucrative market. Dress makers, costume hirers, chauffeur services, caterers and the like bewitch the unmarried into thinking that the wedding day itself is all there is to getting married. Wedding exhibitions are held at local hotels and other venues. I have seen fathers take out huge loans against their mortgages to pay for the expensive finery and reception deemed necessary for their children's Big Day. As a minister my task has been to counsel the couple to look to the marriage itself as a life-long commitment, a long-term investment in each other. The wedding service with its vows and promises is the vital part, but the culture in which we live dictates that the trappings are the things that matter.

The most annoying personages who turn up at weddings are often the amateur video camera operators. At one wedding I conducted in Duston an over zealous guest with a camcorder stood on a chair to get a better view, over-balanced and crashed to the floor just as the couple were about to take their vows. I resolved to be strict on such matters, so at Castle Hill welcomed the sensible cameraman and told him where he could be inconspicuous. Most professional photographers were discreet although some had the habit of dominating proceedings if allowed. One day I found a maverick character armed with a video camera ensconced just behind the lectern from where I would be conducting the wedding. Aggressively he refused my request that he move himself out the way. The groom, best man and guests were all seated, and the bride was on the point of arrival. Being equally stubborn I told the camera man the service would only start when he removed himself. There was an uneasy stalemate for five minutes until the best man whispered something in his ear (I shudder to think what it was) that made him shift. The wedding then proceeded very happily.

Brides have long had the privilege of being late for their weddings. For one wedding I asked a new organist to play. It was her first experience of a wedding so I advised her that she only needed some introductory music to cover the ten minutes or so as the congregation gathered, plus the usual hymns and wedding music. The bride did not appear for well over forty minutes. The organist was getting desperate playing the set piece in different keys and octaves and with several variations. In an age of mobile phones it was easy to track what had happened to the bride. She had had a beautiful hair-do and all her make-up done to perfection. Ready in all her finery for the wedding her father had thoughtfully tried to spray her bouquet to keep it fresh. Unfortunately, the spray had hit his daughter full in the face. Hair-do and makeup were ruined. The air was blue. The bridal party finally reached the church breathless and disconcerted as the organist, much relieved from playing her prepared pieces over and over again, launched with verve into *The Bridal March*. I knew how the organist felt; years before I rashly promised to play the organ for a wedding in another church. The bride was very late and I had played Elgar's *Chanson de Matin* so many times that I still shudder when I hear it now.

It is in the area of marriage and relationships that social change can be seen most clearly. Few marriages that I conducted were for young first time couples; most were for couples, one or both of whom had had a previous marriage. I realised that many came to my church as the regulation then in the Church of England was not to marry divorcees. My remit was to judge the merit of each application, and there were times when I had to refuse. If the relationship seeking marriage had been the cause of divorce, in other words adultery, then I could not in all conscience undertake the wedding. On the other hand, innocent parties who had been divorced through no fault of their own had a right to happiness. It was much better for their relationship to be blessed and honoured in God's sight than to live "in sin".

Since the sixties a greater awareness has developed that some marriages do fail for a variety of reasons. The greater freedom that women have gained has meant that they feel no longer tied to loveless and unhappy marriages, as in the past. The same can be true for men. Some critics have argued that divorce has become too easy and that perseverance is a lost art, but few couples really want the anguish of breaking-up. Most couples live together before they seek to marry, and those who have been through the mill of a separation and divorce are careful not to repeat past mistakes. Wedding services have changed to include the recognition of the children of one or both partners so that they are united in their new family. I have conducted many weddings that have resulted in happy fulfilled marriages with couples determined to honour their vows. It is surprising how many weddings conducted at Registry Offices, or in other secular places now licensed for weddings, still want a religious blessing for their civil contract.

One of the great dividing issues within society in general and the Church in particular is the issue of same-sex relationships. Throughout the nineties and into the present the issue of accepting gay people into the ministry or priesthood has caused great controversy. The word "gay", I think, is unfortunate and misleading in that it has more than a hint of irresponsibility about it. The majority of gay people of both sexes whom I have met are not promiscuous; they are loyal and faithful to their partners and very caring, responsible people. In my experience most of my fellow Christians are broadminded accepting people on their character and personality rather than on sexual orientation. The sexuality issue is part of a wider social obsession which has grown since the sixties.

One of the first funerals I conducted, I remember with great clarity. It was for a young man, one of my former pupils, who had been killed in a scooter crash. Hundreds of young people gathered at the crematorium in great dignity to lay him to rest and to say farewell. It was obvious that out in the busy world many had little connection with church but had a spiritual need. Their usual comment was that they were "not religious", but what they meant was "we are un-churched". The depth of spirituality in many people is amazing. One married couple who had been brought up in Northern Ireland, one a Roman Catholic, the other a Presbyterian, had been virtually excommunicated by their respective churches. Theirs was a "mixed marriage" not tolerated in the fifties. In spite of staying away from the church for the best part of forty years they still said their prayers, taught their children and grandchildren to do the same and regularly read their Bibles. When one partner died the family asked me to conduct the funeral service at Castle Hill. Hundreds turned up as the family was large, and I remarked at my respect for their spiritual life adding that the church was the poorer for not having them inside it. It was a provocative comment which resulted in a number starting to attend church, several of them remaining members to this day.

Funerals, of course, have their amusing sides and I recall the funeral director whose top hat was cremated as a joke, or the time when both the handles on one side of a coffin fell off so that the quick thinking funeral director had to whip it round so that the congregation, who all sat together on one side of the chapel, did not see. On another occasion a hearse left whilst the funeral director was inside a house rolled silently along the street and came to rest in my friend's front garden. The unexpected may happen at any time. One funeral director friend was carrying a coffin up to a church door when he tripped and turned several somersaults down a slope to disappear completely into the long grass. The entire procession of vicar, bearers and family froze in horror only to hoot with laughter when the unfortunate man reappeared with his hat and dignity much battered by the incident. The son of the deceased declared it the best funeral he had ever been to and wondered if the director did it regularly.

A most memorable funeral I conducted was that of a former drag artist. Hundreds turned up, many of them dressed as Teddy Boys. It was requested that Bill Haley's *Rock Around the Clock* should be played during the service, and when the music started they all got to their feet and began to jive. Bewildered, I wondered how the service would end, but I did not need to worry for they all sat down when the music finished and listened as good as gold. It was a burial and, as the service at the graveside concluded, a large middle-aged Teddy Boy with velvet collared draped jacket, bootlace tie, crepe soled shoes and drainpipe trousers placed his hand on my shoulder and said: "Padre, I never believed in God until today". He almost had me in tears. I learned a valuable lesson that day, not to "judge a book by its cover".

Such occasions bring out great dignity in most people. Over the nineties and into the new century I realised that many funerals were for a generation who had experienced hardship and war. They had survived into old age keeping intact their own integrity. Many women had had a rough time, often bringing up their families in wartime and the post war world, being widowed at a relatively young age and keeping a stiff-upper lip attitude to life. Like my mother they threw nothing away and kept store cupboards full of tinned food and bags of sugar in case of emergency. There were men who were the silent heroes who had returned from war to carry on their lives, their jobs and their family life. One elderly man I knew modestly kept his Military Medal and his Distinguished Conduct Medal tucked away in a drawer. He was a Dunkirk and D Day veteran. At such funerals a dwindling number of comrades from the British Legion and service organisations dutifully came to honour their comrades. In 2004, on the 60th anniversary of the D Day Landings the last great commemoration took place in Normandy. It made me realise that I have been privileged to be involved in the honouring of a generation whose faithfulness and loyalty remain as an example of service and sacrifice, and a reproach to a later age grown soft in its own self interest.

John Warwick of Collingtree, who served in the 2nd Battalion Support Company, Northamptonshire Regiment during World War Two gave me the following extract from an Irish Women's Land Army Christmas card for 1943. The card reached one of John's comrades on the banks of the Garigliano River, south of Rome in January 1944. John remembers the exact words which poignantly put life into perspective:

"Be gentle when you touch Bread.
Let it not lie uncared for, unwanted;
Too often Bread is taken for granted.
Beauty of sun and soil;
Beauty of patient toil;
Wind and rain have caressed it;
Christ has blessed it.
Be gentle when you touch Bread".

Funerals also bring out the little idiosyncrasies of people. One coffin builder I knew would make a pipe rack for any deceased smoker and fix it inside the coffin; a little personal touch. Funeral directors' attempts to let family and friends carry coffins sometimes come to near disaster. One early morning I was asked to conduct the interment of a habitual drunkard. Four of his friends from the town centre hostel where they lived were asked to do the honours of carrying the coffin. They were still inebriated from the previous night so swayed and lurched with their burden, finally succeeding in giving their friend a fitting if bumpy burial. One elderly friend had the last laugh on me when I conducted her service. In her will she had instructed that the hearse taking her from the church to the

173

crematorium should go at full speed. Zooming along the bypass to make a detour through a housing estate in order to get in front of the hearse I arrived at the crematorium in a somewhat breathless and dishevelled condition.

Sadly, funerals are also occasions when the simple greed of people manifests itself. One elderly lady who had no relatives whatever told me years before her demise that she wanted me to conduct her funeral and that she was leaving her considerable estate to certain friends and charitable causes. On the very day of her funeral I was standing at the crematorium door when a taxi pulled up at the end of the drive. Out stepped a man with a suitcase who proceeded to hurry along the drive to the chapel. He told me that he was the deceased's long lost great nephew who had travelled all the way from Canada to pay his respects to his darling auntie. He enquired as to the identity of the solicitor handling her affairs! In another instance one family had virtually cleared the house of furniture and effects within hours of their relative's demise even before I could get there to organise the funeral. I have known others who have had locks changed in order to keep other family members out so that they could pick over the goods and chattels left. Human greed is amazing. Where there's a will there's relatives!

Over recent years funeral services have changed. The addition of music on CDs or tapes has personalised them but not without some amusing overtones. The curtains at the crematorium closed one day as the tune *Blaze Away* was being played. Another coffin made its exit to Gracie Fields singing *Wish me luck as you wave me goodbye*. I have lost track of the number of times that Frank Sinatra's *I did it my way* has been requested. At a traditional West Indian burial the family sing many hymns as they fill in the grave themselves, before covering the mound with flowers. One such service took four hours to complete, but once finished they had worked out their grief and went home much cheered by their community spirit and family solidarity.

Other quirks can be seen in the way cremated remains (ashes) are treated. One lady kept her husband's ashes in an urn on the mantelpiece. For some unknown reason they ended up in a Boys Brigade jumble sale and were only retrieved after much desperate searching. Another friend who was a hot-air balloonist had his cremated remains scattered from the air over Northampton. But the most comical scattering of ashes was done by a Church of Scotland colleague who had the task of blessing one man's ashes at his request. They were loaded into 275 Caledonian Classic 12 bore shotgun cartridges with No. 6 shot with plastic degradable wadding. They were fired by all his friends and family at the beginning of the 2004 shooting season. The deceased had been a sporting and vintage gun expert working for Sotherby's and had died of severe food poisoning. The minister commented that "It was a normal scattering of ashes, a few words and prayers. After all, he had a lifelong interest in ballistics". The cartridges accounted for seventy partridges, twenty three pheasants, seven ducks and a fox.

The widow of one of our friends who was blessed with a great sense of humour asked me to conduct his funeral service. His ashes were to be buried at a later date. The day before the interment the funeral director delivered the urn to my house ready for the service. On arriving home after an evening meeting I found Steff, the urn placed on the coffee table before her, watching an old episode of *Steptoe & Son*. "I thought we would share one last laugh together", she explained.

There are, of course, tragic events resulting in the call upon a minister. There are the stillbirths and cot deaths, the suicides and the accidents. On one occasion the brother of the deceased arrived handcuffed to two security officers; he had a tattooed line across his throat with the instruction "cut here". He had been allowed out of prison for the occasion. On another day I conducted the funeral for a young man in his thirties whose common-law wife had registered him as a "drug dealer". The service was packed with a particular segment of society; many were addicts of drugs and alcohol and not a few were prostitutes. Yet the intense way in which they listened and took part in the service brought out in me an overwhelming compassion for a lost generation whose lives have been ruined by the pressures of society.

One amazing fact is that many people have no-one close to them to mourn their passing. Apart from the carers in residential homes, the Social Services, funeral directors and the ministers there are often no friends or family present. I led the service for a lady aged 104 who had outlived all her family including children, grandchildren, brothers and sisters, nephews and nieces. To add to the situation staff from her residential home were stuck in heavy

175

traffic and arrived at the end of the service. Only the funeral director, organist and I were present.

The supernatural is a basic interest of many, and as a minister I was expected to have a view on the subject. I went with a colleague to a house where a woman claimed she was being haunted by a poltergeist in the shape of a man who entered her bedroom. We came home rather amused as the woman didn't object to the man's presence but complained that he wouldn't get into bed with her. There were other times when I did have a tingle run up my spine as I sensed an uneasy atmosphere. One Saturday afternoon I was called out rather urgently to investigate a disturbing presence in a child's bedroom. It was much more than the imaginings of the child so I prayed aloud and demanded it should remove itself, and it did. It was good to do house blessings, especially for folk who were moving into a new home; these usually finished with a cup of tea and much laughter.

Whilst doing some photocopying in the church office someone walked past the door and into the church sanctuary. It took me a few moments to realise that I was alone in the building and the doors were all locked. Following the dim figure into the church I saw it was a man who disappeared into the Old Vestry. I made enquiries and was amazed by several elderly ladies who told me who the man was and that they regularly saw him. He had been associated with the church within living memory and had died about twenty years previously. It became commonplace knowledge and no-one was bothered by his occasional appearances. One morning I called into the church to meet up with some builders who had been doing extensive renovations for us. Like all builders they started work early and then had a breakfast break mid morning. They sat in the church kitchen and were all as white as sheets when I entered. Our ghostly friend had walked down the stairs and along the corridor into the church; they said they had heard his footsteps which had echoed on the hard floor. I explained that we knew who he was and he was friendly, but I don't think I convinced them.

In 1991 at the beginning of my ministry at Castle Hill I was invited by the Bishop of Brixworth, Rt Rev Paul Barber, to represent the Christian Churches on the Major Incident Team within the Northamptonshire County Council. It was becoming clear that local authorities had a responsibility to make sensible preparations in case of a major incident. Such events included motorway pile-ups, chemical spillages, air and train crashes or natural disasters that severely stretched the resources of the County. Northamptonshire itself was straddled by a major motorway, railways, and overhead the endless northward flight of aircraft taking off from London's Heathrow Airport. Events such as the Grand Prix at Silverstone had enormous potential for disaster so had to be taken into consideration. The thinking then was based on the possibility of major emergencies such as had happened in the spate of the disasters that had occurred during the late eighties.

The task involved organising volunteer clergy across the religious denominations into a system able to respond in case they were needed. I was supported by Canon Bill Kentigern-Fox, and we attempted to involve leaders from other faith communities holding training days every year. As clergy posts changed with great speed, the task of updating the list was on-going. Sometime during the mid nineties the emphasis changed from "if" to "when" an incident would occur. Local authorities had begun to step up their arrangements following a number of natural disasters. Live exercises were arranged which tested the resources we had at our disposal. We were pleased that in an emergency we could place chaplains in several temporary mortuaries or rest centres in different locations over a 48 hour period with shift changes in order to support victims, their families and the emergency services themselves.

In 1993 the folk at Castle Hill began to think of what the church might do to mark its Tercentenary. Built in 1695 the chapel had served the town ever since and had a startling history. With many connections within the local schools I wondered whether it might be possible to get together hundreds of children's voices in a choral festival. I recalled my earlier teaching days when the place had been filled for local music festivals and eisteddfods. Coach loads of children from virtually every school in the town would arrive at the chapel to be crammed into the wooden box pews and in the gallery. Their young voices filled the spacious interior. So if we were to repeat such an event we needed someone well-known to be the guest of honour.

Through a contact I had good reason to hope that there might just be a chance that the Princess of Wales might grace our presence if she came to visit Althorp sometime during 1995. Such a

177

visit would be a major coup. However, I received a letter from her secretary in early December 1993 telling me that the Princess had made a major decision to stop her patronage of many charities and good causes. She sent her best wishes to the good folk at Castle Hill and apologised that she was unable to attend. Within a few weeks the reason for this became public knowledge as press intrusion into her life had become intolerable. The Princess had been secretly photographed whilst working out in a gymnasium. She intended suing the perpetrator and her withdrawal from some of her public life was a reaction to all the other pressures, notably her separation from her husband, which she was facing. In her letter the Princess sent the church her "warmest greetings and very best wishes for your tercentenary year". She had been interested in the connections the church had with the Royal Family. Philip Doddridge and his wife Mercy were welcome guests of Augusta, Princess of Wales, in the 1730s and 40s. In fact the royal children were educated partly on Doddridge's hymns and the future George III knew his verses by heart. The then Prince and Princess of Wales gave Mercy a ball gown in exquisite silk, portions of which are still preserved at Castle Hill. Diana, Princess of Wales, expressed her interest in all this and was appreciative of the admiration expressed to her for all her charitable work, especially amongst children.

Malcolm Deacon

The Church on Castle Hill
the history of Castle Hill United Reformed Church
Northampton

We duly celebrated the church's 300th birthday and inaugurated proceedings with children releasing three hundred coloured balloons. 1995 was filled with special services, events and publications that moved the church on into another period of its history. I was pleased to be able to research, write and publish a history entitled *The Church on Castle Hill* which told the story of the fellowship which emerged in the dark days of 17th century persecution and has kept its faithfulness to the present. As minister I can proudly say that I attended and took part in the vast majority of church events, ably and enthusiastically supported by Steff who constantly encouraged me at all times. She has tirelessly given me every support and has contributed her own inimitable ministry wherever we have been, particularly in hospitality at our home, in brilliant illustrations for publications, in superb floral decorations and many other things both social and spiritual.

Events during 1995 were organised by the *1995 Committee* which sponsored a play especially written by Rev Keith Spence on the life of Philip Doddridge. *Entitled All for God* the play was performed in the church to enthusiastic audiences. Steff was involved with other ladies in making a commemorative patchwork, and she produced specially illustrated booklets for the children. All the church members gathered for a special photograph, and guest preachers came from far and near. One of the many services that year was a reaffirmation of wedding vows; all couples married in the church, and still alive or together, were invited to attend the service and a special supper. The menu was based on 18th century dishes. We mounted a display of differing styles of wedding dresses worn by brides married in the church throughout the 20th century. 1995 was packed with enthusiastic effort and concluded with a service attended by civic and other dignitaries and the county's Boys Brigade Battalion.

Not to forget the outside world, that year the church supported two of our young people, Wendy Robinson and Chris Hewitt, on their trip with the East Northants Land Rover Club on an act of mercy to help the desperate plight of the people of Belorussia; many children had been born with terrible deformities following the catastrophic destruction of the Chernobyl nuclear power station. We later began giving regular support to the Ukraine particularly in the supply of clothes and household goods and the sponsorship of children. 1995 also marked the fiftieth anniversary of VE day which concluded World War Two and we held special services.

Concluding that eventful year and referring to T. S. Eliot's poem *The Journey of the Magi* I wrote in Castle Hill News: "Some people feel that it is easier being a Christian in other better and easier times. The modern secular world with all its facile commercialism, its criminal activity and the general disinterest in matters of religion seems to be a difficult time in which to follow Christ. But it is now

179

that the star shines for us; now, and no other time. Like the Magi we do not choose the time; we simply must take our courage in both hands and follow the light wherever it leads".

On the front of Castle Hill Church is a sundial dated 1695, the year of its foundation, with the motto "Post est occasio calva" derived from the Roman poet Cato. It has been translated: "opportunity has locks (i.e. hair) in front, but is bald behind", or alternatively: "Take time by the forelock". In other words, if we don't grasp opportunities when they present themselves we shall have left it too late and our fingers will slip off a retreating bald head. This summed up so much of the church's history and my ministry there.

As a minister during these years I frequently met characters who would exert enormous energy and time trying to wheedle money from me. My experiences in Cambridge had led me to treat this urban phenomenon with some caution. In my student years I once visited the British Museum in London and gave half-a-crown to an old beggar lady at the gates. Coming out of the museum later that day I observed the same person transform herself into a much younger woman who jumped nimbly into a taxi.

The Christian understanding that one treats one's neighbour with dignity, respect and kindness brings a daily moral problem when one encounters street beggars. One day outside the church as I was getting into my well-worn car a new Transit van drew alongside. Inside was a man with a woman and children, all well dressed and stuffing themselves with fish and chips. He wound down his window and told me he was on his way to see his dying mother in Nottingham. Coming past Northampton on his way north on the M1 motorway he noticed that he was getting short of petrol; to his consternation he had left his credit card at home. He knew that people in the town were generous and considerate. Would I be so kind as to let him fill up his tank using my credit card? He would, of course, pay me back with interest when he got back home. The grin on my face and my sceptical response elicited a diatribe of unprintable expletives.

One man came into the church at the end of a communion service and using foul language deliberately caused a commotion. A church Elder gave him some money to get rid of him, which was just what he wanted. A taxi driver friend told me that this individual hailed his taxi minutes after the incident and had produced a wad of bank notes asking his way to the nearest vicarage. One particular character did manage to get our sympathy but was caught out when the ministers of the town centre had a meeting and it was discovered that he was cadging money from eight different churches. All of it was spent in the local pub! Even he tried the old chestnut that his mother was dying of some unspeakable illness and he just wanted his bus fare to Norwich. When I offered to take him to the bus station and buy him his ticket he soon disappeared. It was then that I decided to never give money but offer practical help in giving a meal voucher which could be used at a local café, and advice as to accommodation and free food at excellent church-run centres in the town.

The phenomenon of begging on the streets of so many British towns and cities during this period had many causes, but mostly came from a cynical exploitation of basic values of good neighbourliness upon which our society is built. As unemployment began to decline in the late nineties and continued into the new century, begging on the streets and the sight of people sleeping rough in shop doorways began to lessen. Yet there were those who were genuinely homeless and really in need, and their cause was damaged by the confidence tricksters. The real needy were often not the ones going begging. Trickery, however, was not confined to the streets. There were more externally respectable folk who saw the clergy and the church as a means to an end. There were those who put my name down as a reference for jobs or for getting their children admission into popular schools without asking my permission; I only knew about the matter when reference letters came through the post. One couple had their marriage at the church with all the usual trimmings only to default on paying the very modest fees which the church required. They spent a small fortune getting drunk in a local pub after the wedding yet thought it acceptable to cheat on the church.

Yet in spite of all this I met many folk who were the salt of the earth; people who were caring, considerate and loving. They were the givers and not the takers. There were many who gave their time and efforts in leading young people and tirelessly working to support all that churches, charities and community groups strived for. Living in relative poverty there were elderly folk who had seen hard times in the past who were the most generous folk I have ever met. When visiting them there would always be a cup of tea or coffee on

181

offer. If all occupations have their hazards such as farmers getting "farmer's lung" the clergy must get "ministers' bladder". I politely declined too many cuppas when on my rounds.

Grand-daughters Hannah and Natasha. 1998

Grandpa and Barclay.

Chapter Twelve: Crossing the Millennium

Why is it that we do the things we do? Take, for instance, moving house. We had moved from our house in Kettering to Duston, then once again within Duston in order to obtain a bigger property and garden. Every house we have had has needed some major repairs and renovations. In Kettering I became familiar with the replacement of gutters, the erecting of fences and the building of a garage. In Duston our first house had problems with the central heating; the builders had mixed copper with galvanised piping and the consequent chemical reaction had furred up the pipes so that the gap left could hardly fit a needle. Our second Duston house in Park Lane necessitated us doing a major refit of windows, kitchen, redecoration and the building of another garage and study. At every house we have owned we have redesigned the garden adding in shrubs and plants, constructing ponds and other features. We have enjoyed the work immensely and have left each property much improved.

So why move again when we were well settled? One day in the early months of 1995 Tessa called on us with an estate agent's leaflet; the property advertised might be of interest to us! An old farmhouse dating from the early 18th century had the charm of metre thick stone walls and oak beams, an old pump and a deep well and lots of what estate agents call "potential". Behind the charm, however, lay decades of neglected maintenance, so that it was necessary to gut the house and restore it from top to bottom. Treatment for woodworm, new wiring and plumbing systems and the demolition and rebuilding of one section of the house were essential. It was a challenging prospect. We bought it, leaving Park Lane upon which we had just spent a fortune putting in a new bathroom. We must have been mad!

I moved in first, setting up my office in one of the bedrooms and sleeping on a mattress in a sleeping bag on the landing. There followed two years of steady work put in by all the family in which we restored and developed the Grade II listed building, Diary entries record work starting early in the day and timed to balance out with other duties and pressures. It was salutary pondering the problems of putting in new radon sump and sewer pipes, plastering walls, fixing joists and clearing upper ceilings of old thatch that had fallen in. I remember driving into Northampton to have a word with a demolition gang who were taking out old stables at the back of a public house making way for the building of a multi-storey car park. I did a deal and later that week a lorry backed up the drive and deposited over ten thousand reclaimed bricks in a massive heap. These were sufficient to rebuild sections of the house and all the garden walls, the broken "bats" forming hardcore. All this work had to be balanced with ministerial duties of visitation, preparing and leading church services, going to meetings and coping with the on-going tasks of one's job. My son-in-law Richard did sterling work and we shall be always grateful to him for all his help. We finished the main task in two years, yet have spent the years since making improvements as time and money allow.

The house was a building site for two years.

It is significant how much time and money people are now willing to spend on Do It Yourself. DIY represents huge business, and the ready availability of power tools has transformed the interests and capabilities of many householders. I still have many of the old tools that my father used like a brace and bit, a set square and a wooden plane. They seem quaint when set next to the electric planes, saws and drills which I have in my workshop. Dad's old hammer still resides in my toolbox. He always reckoned it was the same one he had had as a boy; over the years, however, it had had several replacement heads and half a dozen new handles!

Winter scene in the garden. C 1998.

I found some spare time to collaborate during this period with Charles Ward in producing an aerial map of the centre of Northampton showing its historical features in cartoon form. We called ourselves *Highsight Maps*. The task required high-level aerial photography from a helicopter by Charles and some brilliant graphics by Tim Parker to achieve a startling image. The result was a map of Northampton the like of which had never been seen before! In the decade or so since, Northampton altered considerably so that the map remains a fixed image of how things were in 1994.

On Sunday 31 August 1997 I woke up early. It was a fine sunny morning and I was due to go into the studio of Radio Northampton to make a short broadcast item. I switched on the radio to hear the stunning 6 o'clock news that the Princess of Wales had been killed in a car crash in Paris. My planned broadcast turned out to be an impromptu tribute to the Princess. As the days unfolded there was an extraordinary outpouring of national grief. I led a special service at Castle Hill for those who wanted to express their sorrow. Countless flowers were left outside St James Palace and the funeral service at Westminster Abbey on 6 September was watched by millions across the world. The reaction of the general public was quite alarming and the local authorities decided to activate the Major Incident Plan. I was involved, and arranged to have chaplains on duty with the Red Cross and the WRVS at two reception centres. There was genuine concern over the possibility of public hysteria as the cortege passed through the western edge of the town.

We all watched the televised events from London, admiring the forthright way in which Charles Spencer gave the tribute to his sister. His sentiments were echoed far and wide, with applause within the Abbey itself that resonated across the nation. As the hearse left north London to move towards Northamptonshire along the M1, I took up position on the Collingtree bridge that spanned the motorway. It was eerily empty of moving traffic apart from the occasional police Range Rover that patrolled up and down. Cars were parked on the hard shoulders and people had climbed the grassy banks to get a better view. Then the hearse appeared, a black Daimler, registration number B626 MRK. Behind, holding back three lanes of close packed traffic which stretched southwards into the distance, were three police Range Rovers blue lights flashing.

People ran forward onto the motorway throwing flowers at the slow moving hearse. Too slow, I pondered, and my thoughts were confirmed by my police colleague on the bridge. The Daimler, weighted down by a lead-lined coffin and travelling in low gear, was finding the journey very heavy going. Evidently, another hearse had been ordered to shadow the first one in case of breakdown. At Junction 15A the cortege left the motorway to move uphill towards Duston. The crowds behaved themselves impeccably; there was no panic. Along the A428, through Harlestone and through the entrance of Althorp went the hearse. Millions worldwide saw two British police officers firmly closing the wrought iron gates. Round the corner and out of sight continued the Daimler only to break down within sight of the house. Her brother Charles, who had arrived by train ready to welcome his sister's body, exclaimed that Diana would have loved such a farcical situation. It was as if she had had the last laugh and her irrepressible spirit had freed itself from all that had weighed her down.

Within a week of the death of the Princess of Wales came news on 5 September of the demise of Mother Teresa of Calcutta. The two women, from starkly contrasting backgrounds, were both powerful icons of a Christ like approach to caring for the poor and underprivileged. Mother Teresa had declared that by blood she had been born an Albanian, by citizenship an Indian, by faith a Catholic nun but as to her calling she belonged to the world. "As to my heart, I belong entirely to the heart of Jesus", she roundly declared. Her death was greatly overshadowed by the media's concentration on the Princess of Wales, especially speculation as to the cause of the tragic car crash in the Paris underpass.

The deaths of these two women, so different in age, life-style and culture yet united by a common humanity, had a profound effect globally. With instant and world-wide coverage of news events billions of people felt they knew them personally. Many, fed by the growing influence of the internet, speculated in the growing trend of conspiracy theory. A new era of suspicion of authority was dawning. The extraordinary outpouring of public grief over the death of the Princess of Wales eventually subsided. Local people living around Althorp, where the Princess was buried, were relieved when the crowds began to lessen and life returned to normality. The causes for which the Princess had laboured continued to be supported, and Mother Teresa left her own legacy with numerous organisations and thousands of co-workers dedicated to the heroic task of caring for the poor. Her place of burial at the Mother House of the Missionaries of Charity became a place of pilgrimage. In December 2002 Pope John Paul II permitted the cause of her canonisation.

With Julian living at that time in Australia the opportunity presented itself to travel long-haul to the other side of the world. In 1998 the family set off to fly to Australia via Bangkok. All our senses were on full alert as the aircraft flew a great circle south of Moscow, above the Caspian Sea, across Afghanistan, India and southward over the Bay of Bengal. Our grand daughter Hannah was with us and with her striking thick curly auburn hair she resembled the eponymous *Anni*e. We were all shocked by the attention she received in Bangkok; several offered to buy her which made us very wary, and we were glad to leave.

Moving over the Indian Ocean I will always remember the thrill of sighting the Australian coast thinking we had arrived; it took several more hours to cross the continent, its orange brown landscape whitened by parched saltpans far below, until we arrived in the relatively green ocean side of Sydney. There below we spotted the distinctive outline of the Danish architect Joern Utzon's Opera House, its design based upon the segments of a peeled orange and resembling the white sails of the many yachts that ply the harbour. We went on to stay with Julian and Giuliana in Melbourne. Giuliana was expecting a baby at any moment and we had come for that reason. But babies take their own time and, as we had planned a visit to the Red Centre of Australia, we eventually set off by rail from Spencer Street Station in Melbourne. Natasha was born that night as we travelled by *The Overland* train into Adelaide.

Leaving Spencer Street Station, Melbourne on the night train for Adelaide. March 1998.

It was an exciting trip thrusting northwards on the "legendary Ghan" railway, a single track that then led from Adelaide to Alice Springs. It is one of the world's great railway journeys. In 2004 the railway was opened as far as Darwin thus linking the south and north. The Ghan had been named after the Afghan camel drivers who, in the nineteenth century, transported travellers through the outback and helped to build the railway. Millions of wooden sleepers were laid, transported by specially imported camels that each carried several sleepers; these were secured crisscrossed on each animal's back so that it could rest at night without having the burden removed each time. Numerous descendants of these camels inhabit the Outback to this day. We travelled through the night only stopping once to deliver the milk, newspapers and other supplies to an isolated farm. In vain did we look for any kangaroos amidst the endless scrub; only the occasional cow wandering in search of vegetation caught our eye. We were to encounter kangaroos elsewhere.

Alice Springs is a modern town and far from the image we entertained from Neville Shute's *A Town Like Alice.* Time had moved the settlement on, and we were made painfully aware of the adverse impact of western values upon the Aborigines whose way of life has been turned upside down. In the town we discovered a Uniting Church dedicated to the memory of one of Australia's great pioneers. The Rev. John Flynn, known as "Flynn of the Inland", was a Presbyterian minister who in the 1920s built a hospital in Alice; he sent nurses out on camels to minister to the settlers scattered across hundreds of thousands of square kilometres of bush. Flynn's pioneering work, together with a colleague's invention of radios with electricity powered by means of bicycle pedals, eventually developed into the Royal Flying Doctor Service. As we looked around the church and the hospital (now a museum to Flynn's achievements) we marvelled at the courage and faith of so many Christians who took the Gospel across this enormous continent in conditions of incredible hardship.

Alice Springs can reach uncomfortable temperatures. When we were there the hairs on my bare legs seemed to singe in the searing 40 degrees centigrade as the roads and pavements sweltered like oven plates. An annual boat race, the Henley-on-Todd Regatta, is run in Alice along the dry bed of the River Todd; bottomless boats are used so that the participants can run. Once, in its history, the race was abandoned due to rain flooding the river bed. From Alice we journeyed for some four hours across the parched reddened landscape, stopping once at a remote camel farm, before reaching one of the most evocative sights on the planet, the giant smooth rock known as *Uluru* by the Aborigines, or Ayers Rock to westerners. Unusually, rain was falling high above the rock yet did not reach the ground as it was evaporated by the intense heat. As evening approached this gigantic outcrop gradually changed colour from a dusky orange to a deep red, and a profound mystical hush fell across the landscape. Some twenty-five kilometres west of Uluru lay a dozen massive rocks, known to the Aborigine as *Katajuta* (many heads) or The Olgas. Such massive features as Uluru and Katajuta are impressive symbols of Aboriginal ritual and myth and exude the same mystical feeling that one is part of something that stretches back to the dawn of time. Lizards scuttled at our feet in the spiky grass as night turned from purple to black and the stars of the southern hemisphere blazed in all their glory.

Uluru (Ayers Rock) March 1998

Into the vast emptiness of inland Australia came the intrepid explorers of the nineteenth century. Men like Charles Sturt were perplexed by the strange directions taken by the Murray and Murrumbidgee rivers believing they drained into an inland sea. John McDouall Stuart (whose memorial can be seen on the Stuart Highway leading northward to Darwin) crossed the continent from south to north at great physical cost. He travelled twenty thousand kilometres through some of the harshest terrain on the planet, much of it on his grey mare Polly. At least Stuart survived; others were not so lucky. Steff and I became imbued with the bizarre story of Robert O'Hara Burke and William John Wills who led an expedition from Melbourne in 1860, the aim being to forge a route across the continent to the Gulf of Carpentaria. The cavalcade of camels that set off from Royal Park, Melbourne, serenaded by a band and the cheers of a huge crowd, soon found itself beset by harsh terrain, bad weather and the results of incompetent planning. Burke eventually left the party at Cooper's Creek to complete the journey with three companions. They succeeded in reaching their goal but upon the return journey perished at Cooper's Creek having missed their back-up party by a matter of hours due to a misunderstanding of messages cut into the trunk of a coolibah tree, the famous *Dig Tree.*

Such are the stories of the early pioneers and their echoes are to found out in the bush and in state archives. Now bustling cities such as Sydney, where Captain Cook first landed on the Australian east coast, belie the epic struggles and hardship that went into their foundation. One only has to visit the Immigrants Museum in Melbourne to obtain a vivid glimpse of how hard it was to leave all behind to go out to such an unknown land. As in North America the rush to find gold and the scramble to acquire land led to outlawry; in Melbourne's old jail we paused at the hanging beam where Ned Kelly was executed and viewed his suit of iron armour in which he defied the Victorian state constabulary.

Artists have depicted the Australian story in telling detail; it is greatly moving to see work like the triptych by Frederick McCubbin entitled *The Pioneer* which shows in the first picture a young man and his wife with their cart making a home for themselves in the forest. The second picture shows them with their primitive home, garden plot and with a child. The last picture shows the man looking sadly at a grave; perhaps his wife and child have died worn down by hard work or disease. The man is alone. Many artists entitle their work simply "Lost", showing a solitary individual in a relentless landscape. Russell Drysdale's pictures are classics of social history showing the occupations of the generation that settled the land through the forties and fifties; young country folk dress up to drive into the distant local town for a Saturday night out. One stunning picture shows two children looking forlornly over a gate towards a landscape that contains a single tree and nothing but endless barrenness. Such were the deep impressions made upon us on this first visit to Australia, as much as the vivid colours and wildlife of the Great Barrier Reef and the pulsating cosmopolitan life of its cities. We were to return to Australia several times.

As the nineties began to pass preparations were being made for the celebration of the Millennium. In Britain much was focussed on the Millennium Dome being constructed at Greenwich on the Meridian Line. Its subsequent chequered history involved political intrigue, controversy and gross over-spending and left it in the public mind as a huge white elephant. In 1997 the Prime Minister, Tony Blair, declared that the Dome would be "The most exciting thing to happen anywhere in the world in the year 2000". Events left this dictum sounding very hollow. Like many others I went with the family to see the Dome and found it a bag of mixed delights. Even more disappointing was the River of Fire which was to take place on the Thames; this happened so quickly that almost everyone missed it.

To some, catastrophe loomed. The history of millenarian speculation is a long one. William Miller had predicted 22 October 1844 as the day the world would end, but Charles Taze Russell, the founder of the Jehovah's Witnesses, tried his hand at predicting 1914. His successor predicted 1926. This pessimistic view continued with Hal Lindsey declaring 1981 as the year of Armageddon, and Lee Jang Rim stuck his neck out for 28 October 1992. As the year 2000 loomed the end of the world was seen as imminent by many millenarian sects and some took up residence in Jerusalem and other holy places waiting the world's final hours.

At a different level dire predictions that a "bug" would wreak havoc on a world grown dependent upon computers caused near panic in some circles. It was conceivable that entire governmental technological systems running key defence, industrial, commercial, health and social services would all collapse. One family in Montana, USA, began preparing for what became known as "Y2K" as early as 1997, storing vast stockpiles of dehydrated food and tinned chicken chow mein. They even bought water beds to store extra water and shotguns in case civil order broke down. They learned self survival skills and had weekly family emergency drills. Comical as these notions appear there was a common global concern that all computers would stall and chaos would ensue. In the event, the world went on much as it did before. Wisely, preparations were made well in advance so that satellite tracking systems affecting aircraft and shipping movements passed the awaited hour without a "glitch".

With all this as background in the local scene we were concerned to ensure that the Millennium was marked as the two thousandth birthday of Jesus of Nazareth. Knowing all the arguments that the calendar might be wrong by several years what really mattered was to celebrate the real thing. So if the national events lacked any spiritual or ideological focus then at the grassroots level ordinary people ought to have a chance to give thanks for someone whose life and teaching was worth celebrating. Many churches, including our own, gave out Millennium candles with a prayer card, and we held memorable special services as the new era dawned. It was also a time at Castle Hill to make a start on planned developments to buildings and facilities to bring us up to date to face a new era. New legislation meant that all areas of public buildings, including churches, such as upstairs rooms and toilets would have to be accessible to the disabled. Major work beckoned.

During 2000 we also went to the Millennium presentation of the Passion Play in Oberammergau with a group of friends. Every ten years all the men, women and children of Oberammergau in Germany perform a drama of a very special kind; the passion of Jesus. They are fulfilling a vow made by their ancestors in 1633 when their lives were spared from the ravages of the Plague. The drama was a very moving experience in itself, but also because of the sense of contrition which most modern Germans feel over the horrors which spread beyond their own borders during the past century. It was an act of atonement, and it was appreciated by the thousands who travelled to see the play's 105 performances spread over five months. It was fascinating seeing the lead characters during the breaks between performances going about their daily business in the town; Jesus might cycle past, or St John be seen cutting up meat in his butcher's shop.

June 2000 brought together two major events, one local to Northamptonshire and the other national. At Pentecost that year (11 June) well over ten thousand Christians from across Northamptonshire gathered in Abington Park as an act of solidarity and witness. I had been part of the organising group and was delighted that all our planning had come to fruition. Coach and car loads from far and near descended on the park. At that event which had an almost carnival atmosphere on a bright, sunny Sunday all the leaders of the main Christian churches were present to pledge their mutual support of one another. History was in the making as the county's Churches Together (itself part of a wider national movement) signed a covenant pledging that from that moment they would work and plan together for the future. It was deliberate policy to not bring any banners that would proclaim differences. Sadly the appearance of one fringe group who were asked to remove an

193

inappropriate sign was seized upon by the local press who, in seeking to sensationalise, missed the point of the whole event. I wrote to the editor lamenting the trivialisation of newsworthy events and missing defining moments. Future local historians will look back at the files of local newspapers and will be totally misled by such inadequate reporting. Nevertheless the event was an outstanding success and one which brought together the greatest gathering of Christians ever held in Northamptonshire.

Of much greater moment nationally were the events which took place two days later (13 June) in London. A movement had gathered momentum aimed at alleviating the crippling debts burdening much of the Third World. The Jubilee 2000 campaign brought Christians and others to large gatherings in Trafalgar Square, at Lambeth Palace and formed a human chain across Lambeth and Waterloo Bridges. A boatload of petitions was presented to the G8 summit meeting in Cologne on the following weekend. Many supported these events by wearing badges in the form of a broken chain. With the Biblical concept of Jubilee, a wiping out of the burden of debt and the chance to start again, the campaign made inroads into political thinking and some practical action ensued with significant debts being cancelled on a global scale.

The first day of the new millennium I felt much as I had the day before. It was interesting to reflect that we were entering the third Christian millennium, and when the second was imminent in 1000 AD Christendom viewed the event as a major shift in ridding the world of evil and a stepping forward into a new age of peaceful civilisation. With another thousand years on the clock the idea of using the event as a universal party or money-making enterprise had won little popular support. Most people I knew had decided to stay at home with family and friends. In spite of the firework displays and other public events there was a quiet disappointment that there were no great expressions of hope for the future of civilisation and little confidence that humankind was progressing. The wars that had disfigured the 20th century, especially recent wars in Kosovo, Rwanda and Chechnya, left a sense that the new century would have troubles enough as injustice, organised crime, global warming, mass malnutrition and disease were issues that needed to be tackled.

This sober mood was reflected in a radio interview I had with Paul Needle on BBC Radio Northampton back in May 1999.

We had reflected on the pernicious war raging in Kosovo and spoke of how Jesus had taken upon himself the violence and discrimination that the world inflicts, yet had triumphed. I wrote later in *Castle Hill News*: "It is right that the civilised world stands up for humane values and unites against oppression and discrimination. None of us wants to see war but unless people like Milosevic [president] are stopped by united action by the nations the 21st century will open with even more horrors than the present".

On the 11th September 2001 I was visiting a church member during the early afternoon. His mobile telephone rang; it was his wife telling him to switch on the television. As the picture appeared we saw what seemed to be a screening of the film *Inferno* where a huge American skyscraper catches fire. It took a minute or so to realise that the images we were viewing were live. Aircraft had been hijacked and deliberately flown into the twin towers of the World Trade Centre in New York and the Pentagon in Washington. It was a savage act of terrorism that was to define the course of the new century. From it war in Afghanistan and then Iraq would swiftly follow and everyone would be made aware that no-one and no place were safe from the fanatic.

In a piece that I wrote for the BBC at that time I said: "A strange thing happened to my computer on Tuesday; its clock stopped working at a few minutes before the terrorist strike on the World Trade Centre in New York. I only realised this later in the week, a week which everyone will remember as one of the most infamous in all human history, and one that will be seen as a huge paradigm shift in our view of the world. I heartily wished that time itself had stopped those few minutes before those fatal plane crashes. Welcome to the Twenty-first Century everybody when the advances of technology and ease of global movement make it possible for fanatics to unleash indescribable evil upon innocent people. The shock is felt across the world; the reality that we live in a global village and are all interconnected. It is not only America that has lost its citizens but people of some thirty nationalities died or are missing presumed dead in this appalling act of barbarism. One thing that few have mentioned is that this week has been One World Week. How bitterly ironic, yet so prophetic; the world has no place anymore for fundamentalism in any form".

195

In the immediate aftermath of such events a great fear gripped many people. My own son and his family were about to return to Australia. We drove them up to friends in London from whence they would leave for Heathrow International Airport. The tension was palpable, the threat looming in a city that was unable to be protected. I recall feeling sick at the thought of them travelling on the underground to Heathrow, or of the stopover they had booked in Penang. They were glad to get back to Melbourne having stayed in a hotel devoid of any westerners all of whom had evacuated. The only other occupant of the hotel was President Mugabe of Zimbabwe who had taken over the top floor with his entourage. (The regime in Zimbabwe had only recently seized a cousin's farm under the so called "land reforms" with tragic consequences).

It was amazing how the 9/11 outrage brought people together. Within three days all the town centre church leaders in Northampton, myself included, led a vigil for peace on the steps of All Saints Church in Northampton. At least a thousand people stood in silence for three minutes. Specific prayers were offered for people who were known to us and who had died in the catastrophe. The smallness of the world community was underlined by a deep sense of shared tragedy. We felt one with the chaplain to the New York Fire Brigade who had perished alongside his men, and with the Archbishop of Canterbury preaching at an impressive service at St Paul's Cathedral, and for the powerful words of the Pope on a visit to Kazakhstan urging people of all faiths to practise tolerance and understanding.

The following Sunday I said in my sermon: "Whatever its origins fundamentalism in any guise turns its back on even discussing how to live in a modern plural world. It turns to intolerance and embraces violence as a means of change thereby edifying the terrorist as some kind of hero. Committing suicide must be the ultimate act of desperation, and committing suicide taking thousands of others with you thinking it is God's will must be the ultimate blasphemy. Christianity, Judaism and Islam must recognise their common origins, beliefs and aspirations and, together with other faiths, take a lead in the vital task of reflecting on our common humanity and condemning violence. We need a global day of atonement and repentance in order to start again".

196

I like to think that in the various activities of my life one golden thread has been a commitment to my Christian faith. So there has been no contradiction in pursuing different occupations and activities. They all point in the same direction. This underlines a distinct concept of ministry being the effort put in by all "the people of God", whether lay or ordained, for the betterment of the world. Such an understanding always informed my teaching and was made manifest in my ministry within the church. I have always felt that versatility in life saves boredom and staleness.

Sometime in 2001 I felt that I needed to move on from Castle Hill; ten years is a good stint in ministerial terms. I felt I had supported the church members as well as serving the URC District Council as member and President, its Executive and Pastoral Committee and other duties of visitation to local churches. I had preached in most of the county's URC churches and knew many people. It would be a wrench to leave. Should we move to another church elsewhere? The United Reformed Church had decreed that stipendiary ministry should conclude at one's 65th birthday so it was not practicable to look elsewhere as time was fairly short. In the meantime there was much to occupy myself with the major refurbishment of the church buildings, so I resolved to make that a priority for my final year. An ambitious scheme to modernise the buildings had been gradually worked out by the church members and the time was ripe for its accomplishment. One of my last acts was to help in a modernisation fitting for the new century.

In 2002 the three hundredth anniversary of the birth of Philip Doddridge was marked at Castle Hill in the newly refurbished buildings. I hosted a seminar on Doddridge's life which brought eminent speakers to Northampton; one was a friend, Professor Françoise Deconinck Brossard from the University of Paris-X who simply travelled to Northampton by the Eurostar train via the Channel Tunnel to be with us. Another was Dr David Wykes, the director of the Dr Williams's Library in London. During that period I attended the University of Leicester to deliver a lecture myself on Doddridge to *The Hymn Society of Great Britain & Ireland.* At the end of September 2002 I retired from my ministry at Castle Hill after eleven years of service. Steff and I were deeply touched by the good wishes of so many friends. We had done our best.

Church Treasurer Fred Bird and Church Secretary Ian Stewart
Present me with some power tools for a busy retirement.

Retirement is a dangerous thing; one either does nothing or takes on too much. Keeping out of things for a while my interests centred on my own family, house, garden and village.   Steff and I were welcomed by the folk at our local Anglican church and the change was very refreshing. I resolved to support the church there as well as doing all I could to help the local Baptist chapel and to do some preaching from time to time for the URC and anyone else, so I became a kind of freelance. It was also good picking up local historical interests, writing, doing some broadcasting, supporting local activities and helping to establish the Milton Malsor Historical Society. Becoming involved with the local primary school and helping them with specific projects was a refreshing return to the school situation. One day I taught a science lesson on air pressure and we made a rocket out of a plastic lemonade bottle and a foot pump. The children were amazed when it took off and flew more than fifty metres across the playing field.

One of the most memorable events I initiated with Milton Malsor Parochial School was a *Living Nativity* which involved many people in the village. Katherine Patterson the head teacher and her staff prepared the children and Kathy Kempley and I did the rest. Just before Christmas 2003 during a brilliantly sunny afternoon I dressed up as a Roman centurion and with Kathy and several sixth formers costumed as Roman soldiers, marched to the sound of a drum to the Little Green in Milton Malsor, to be known for the occasion as Bethlehem. There a large crowd was waiting. We stopped and I read out the proclamation that all should return to their home towns for the census ordered by the emperor. At that moment a mule borrowed from a local circus, together with Mary on its back and Joseph by its side, appeared from behind the cottages. Two children from the school were ably taking these parts.

December 2002. The Living Nativity. Milton Malsor.

Led by the soldiers the crowd followed the mule along the street to be met by the entire primary school who sang carols before leading everyone through the village, knocking on the doors of "innkeepers" until we arrived at the field near the church. There shepherds danced on the grass which I had cleaned of cow dung that morning with a shovel. As the church clock struck three and the sun shone, angels in white and gold appeared on the church wall. They pointed the shepherds to an old barn which had been set out with straw bales where everyone gathered for a stunning finale. To add to the realism of the stable church farming friends provided goats and a new born lamb. Everyone ended up at the church for refreshments. Local radio covered the occasion and ran a programme of the whole event on the following afternoon. It was a lovely way to mark the Incarnation and to bring many in the village together. It was also a good start to an exciting Christmas as Julian, Giuliana and Natasha flew in from Australia via Vietnam on Christmas Eve for a family celebration.

Family get-together. Christmas 2002/New Year 2003.

No-one yet knows whether the bombing of the Tora Bora caves by the Americans in the Afghan War succeeded in killing

Osama bin Laden. It is suspected that he escaped. From time to time he, or someone purporting to be him, has issued bellicose declarations. One such came out on Boxing Day 2004 urging terrorists to do their utmost to destroy the impending democratic elections in Iraq. But this was rightly relegated to short comments on inside pages in most newspapers as more important and pressing news began to emerge. The world had suffered a major catastrophe. On a personal level as we took down the Christmas decorations and packed our suitcases for a family get-together in New Zealand news began to come in that a Force 9 earthquake centred in the Indian Ocean and west of Sumatra had occurred. We realised that we were heading in that direction!

Unknown to us in Phao Lak, north of Phuket, along Thailand's western coast elephants giving tourist rides became agitated, began trumpeting and broke free. Flamingoes on the Indian coast suddenly left for safer forests, and in Sri Lanka hundreds of species ranging from water buffalo to lizards reacted to instinct as they sensed the imminence of some major global catastrophe. Within hours a huge tidal wave (tsunami) engulfed the shores of eleven countries. Hundreds of thousands of lives were lost in one of the greatest tragedies of human history.

By this time we were already on our way, and as we crossed the Indian Ocean, above the Andaman and Nicobar Islands and the northern tip of Sumatra, we could only guess at what had happened below. Reaching Singapore we found great relief that the huge bulk of Sumatra had shielded the city from the tsunami, although locals told us they had felt the shock of the earthquake. Soon survivors had begun to arrive at Changi airport and a massive airlift of aid was clearly beginning to build up across the region. In the busy Orchard Road, preparing itself for the usual New Year's Eve festivities, we met young people from the Salvation Army collecting funds for the disaster victims. As the days passed the terrible scale of the tragedy shocked the world.

On our outward flight from Singapore to Christchurch via Melbourne a number of tsunami survivors were allowed priority in clearing customs and immigration control as they had escaped with only the clothes they were wearing. Whilst in New Zealand a minute's silence was held on 16 January at 1.59pm local time, the time the earthquake struck. Similar events, we gathered, were held in London and many parts of the world. Such multi-faith and multi-national events expressed a commonality of approach to global tragedy. It was salutary as we sat on the beach at Russell in the beautiful Bay of Islands to reflect that if the epicentre of the quake had shifted further along the Pacific tectonic line the beach we were on could well have been devastated as had the coasts around the Bay of Bengal. One person chillingly commented: "It could have been us".

The belief that the world's weather is changing is widespread, the cause being seen as global warming. A giant iceberg which had drifted northwards from the Antarctic was causing considerable concern to New Zealanders at this time (January 2005). We found other locals in New Zealand bemoaning the worst and wettest summer in decades, although farmers were pleased that on average they had saved ten thousand dollars by not having to irrigate their fields. Following our family holiday in New Zealand we split up, Tessa and Hannah coming back to the UK and Steff and myself following Julian, Giuliana and Natasha to Melbourne where we stayed with them for a time. Melbourne has become familiar territory to us and we occupied ourselves with a variety of visits and social functions. One evening we decided to go to the beach at Brighton, overlooking Port Phillip Bay. The waves that evening had an unusual force behind them; an ominous array of clouds was massing all around. The wind had begun to rise and the temperature had dropped over the past day from the mid thirties to eleven degrees centigrade. The news media warned of a massive cyclone. That night we were awoken by the sound of torrential rain and violent winds. The palm and gum trees outside Julian's apartment swayed and bent under the terrifying force of the wind.

As morning dawned Melbourne's city centre was flooded and brought to a standstill, the River Yarra was overflowing its banks and hundreds of trees had been torn up by their roots. Steff and I had been contemplating taking the overnight ferry to Tasmania for a few days but had decided not to. Good thing we did, as the *Spirit of Tasmania* ferry putting out for its evening run, dressed overall with twinkling lights, soon encountered in the Bass Strait twenty metre high waves which dashed in portholes and left terrified travellers soaked and stranded in their cabins. The ship had to turn back into Port St Phillip. As far away as Adelaide hailstones rattled down, and to the north in high country snow fell. This was during Australia's high summer season. Although Melbourne is noted for experiencing four seasons in one day the talk on the streets and in the media during the following days centred on the unusual climatic changes which were being experienced.

Upon arriving back in the UK in February 2005 we heard of a major demonstration being held pressurising the United States administration to agree to the Kyoto protocols, planned to come into force within weeks. As most other nations had agreed to some limitation on the emission of greenhouse gases into the environment the Americans, seen as the world's largest polluters and reluctant to agree to the protocols, were essential to make them have any effect. The issue of global warming has become one of great urgency.

Milford Sound, South Island, New Zealand. January 2005. Unspoiled environment.

Mt Cook, South Island, New Zealand. 2003.

Chapter Thirteen: How have we changed?

"Did you have toilets when you were young"? enquired a little girl when I was talking to her class in a local primary school. "Oh yes", I replied, "but they were not as nice as the ones we have today". I had been talking to the children about life "in the old days". It was a useful reminder that in order to grasp the effects of change one has to set reference points in order to make comparisons. It is a matter of "then" and "now", because somewhere between those two points change has occurred, often cumulative and imperceptible.

The child told me that her house had a bathroom, a shower room and a separate toilet; in all there were three toilets in her house, and they were all carpeted. Then I told the children about the great joy my family had in the fifties when we had a bathroom for the first time with a linoleum floor. My father had broken through a wall and by sheer hard work had transformed the coal shed into a toilet. He later converted a spare room into our first bathroom, although it took years to get any heat put in it. The school children agreed with me that it would not have been pleasant having to rise in the middle of the night to go outside in rain or snow to get to the outside lavatory which boasted no heating nor light. I told them about chamber pots, known by various names such as "guzzunders" or "jerries" which graced most homes. "Urggh", the children reacted. They were also interested that the bedrooms at my grandparents' house boasted a matching set of a Victorian wash basin, jug and "po" each decorated with lurid floral patterns.

Warming to their theme the children asked other questions such as to whether we had mobile phones, computers and televisions in those far off days. They were amazed that we had none of these things; neither did we have central heating and double glazing. I told them about my grandmother whose hands were red raw with the Monday washing in her dolly tub, adding that many women developed rheumatics and arthritis of the hands because of wringing out the heavy wet washing and having to squeeze out the water using a mangle. The advent of the washing machine and the tumble drier were great steps forward for them. Now, the proliferation of labour saving gadgets ranging from food blenders to microwave ovens makes the kitchen of my mother and grandmothers' generations seem positively primitive.

Undoubtedly, material improvements in better housing and work conditions, public health and domestic appliances have made life a lot easier for everyone. Women have greatly improved their lives over the past half century. The advent of the Pill and other contraceptive methods has reduced the one-time endless pregnancies which were the lot of earlier generations. I have an old photograph (see p 30) of my great grandparents on my father's side of the family showing them sitting in their backyard surrounded by their ten children. Grandmother was worn-out by continuous pregnancies and confined to her role at home. World War Two changed women's opportunities and roles. Many went out into the "munition" factories and served in the armed services.

Since then they have fared better in the work environment. No longer do women who marry have to give up their professional teaching jobs, for instance, and there has been a steady improvement in the equalisation of pay for the same work, although there is still a long way to travel before full equality is reached. Once married my mother's generation left work and concentrated on their home and family. The husband was the bread-winner. Now women often have to work because it takes two incomes to pay off the mortgage on the house, or to buy all the gadgets that we want. Yesterday's luxuries have become today's necessities. Whilst women rightly have their own careers there is a different pressure on them to work, often full-time, and bring up their families as well. Many men have had to change their attitude to home life and do their part in domestic chores, fetching and carrying the children from school or other activities. Yet there is a real sense in which men have lost their confidence in their one-time roles as bread winners and the head of the family. The ability of women to conceive babies through IVF procedures is alleged to have brought upon many men a sense of male redundancy. As if to underline the issue male sperm counts have been steadily falling for years. Huge moral dilemmas have arisen over the possibility of cloning human beings; the arguments range from the chance of eradicating major inherited diseases to the frivolous designing of babies for cosmetic purposes. Pressure groups on this and other issues such as abortion, euthanasia and animal rights have become increasingly more intractable and militant.

Some commentators have argued that the sixties began a process of social fragmentation which threw off personal restraint. It is a much more complex issue because pressures on individuals, families and indeed communities and nations have changed and multiplied over the past half century. The modern era witnesses a significant   rise in the number of single people; it has become acceptable to belong to agencies and use the internet to find a date. Housing demands for single accommodation reflect the trend and even restaurants have begun to recognise that many customers need to sit alone so adjust their seating arrangements accordingly.

In the area of marriage and family life there has been profound change. It has become socially acceptable to live together without being married and to openly maintain same-sex relationships. Many marriages founder and lead to divorce and new family bonds are created by subsequent remarriage. Many children live with a single parent or learn to accept as siblings children who are the offspring of the new partner of either mother or father. Even grandparents have taken on a new role often being second parents to children whose own parents are out at work.

In a review of wedding gift lists from 1954 to 2004 the John Lewis store chain noted that the newly-weds of the post war era wanted practical items such as white cotton sheets and pillow cases, plain white tablecloths, toasting forks, saucepans and alloy cutlery. Twenty years on in the fifties the choice was upon coloured towelling to match coloured bathrooms, floral country style patterns, ovenproof Pyrex dishes, Tupperware and duvets as an alternative to sheets and blankets. The early 21st century now demands white dinner services, top of the range cutlery and stainless steel kitchenware. Guests are invited to chip in by buying items of an expensive dinner set or even in contributing to a state of the art plasma television. Fewer cooking utensils feature in the lists either because couples already have them, or because they intend buying ready-made meals or eating out. As so many couples have lived together before marrying they require an upgrade rather than the basic models. Now that places other than churches and register offices are available for weddings exotic locations such as a beach in the Seychelles or a Scottish castle may be places where the misty eyed might tie the knot.

A generation or so ago divorce was considered anathema and most couples stuck together through thick and thin, yet many unhappy marriages struggled on unable to break the misery, trapped by the social milieu of the times. The liberation of women, particularly by having their own employment and incomes, brought about a major change. My parents had a very happy marriage, but when my father died my mother had not been out to work for decades, could not write a bank cheque and, in spite of bravely learning to drive in middle age, had lost the confidence to do so simply because father always did everything.

Life expectancy has changed with most of us hoping to survive to an older age than previous generations. There is concern that the number of people over retirement age will outbalance those of working age, with consequent economic problems in affording care facilities for the elderly. My generation are relatively well-off compared to our parents and grandparents; we have our own homes, pensions and some savings built up over lifetimes of fairly stable employment. The inexorable rise in the value of houses makes us rich on paper, although property has to be sold or downsized in order to realise any capital. The developing trend in the early 21st century is to encourage longer working lives in order to build up any shortfall in pensions. The pension age for women as well as men will soon rise to sixty-five, a consequence more due to economics than equality. It is government policy to encourage at least part-time work after that age. Older folk now enjoy their retirements doing things other generations only dreamed about. Many now take up new hobbies and studies and have an enormous potential and opportunity to rebuild community activities. The sky is the limit!

Food is another subject of huge change. I recall during the forties and fifties the small slice of cold meat, the mashed potato, the Brussels sprouts and the HP sauce which we regularly had for lunch on Mondays, or the stew and dumplings, or meat pie on Thursdays; frugal fare yet sufficient. How I lusted for the tins of pork and baked beans that we saw advertised in the American comics we acquired as children. Fifty years later the fast-food culture which has been the outcome of the Americanisation of western life is under attack for its effect on public health. The rise and fall of the burger culture is a social phenomenon reflecting the need for fast food in a lifestyle revolution where many people have little time to cook at home. At one time the woman of the family geared her life to the meals the family needed and the husband's cycle of work. Now increasing concern with the effects of fast foods is leading to the greater use of salads and less fatty fare like the growth of Japanese-style sushi bars. Statistics released in the *Freedom of Information Act* stating that more than a quarter of the British population in 2005 is obese sound a warning note that the trend of longer living may well reverse itself in the years ahead. A TV series by celebrity chef Jamie Oliver shocked the government into reversing the nutritional decline of school meals by providing more cash for better ingredients.

The proliferation of food has had a curious effect upon the traditional Harvest Festival. No longer is the notion of "all being safely gathered in" at the close of the summer and the beginning of the autumn season relevant; as food comes from all round the world there are multiple harvests. The growth of frozen food and its preservation means an all the year round provision. Sadly, such bounty in the western world hides the fact that the Third World still relies on the natural cycle of seasons and blunts our sensitivity to our real dependence upon the bounty of the good earth. The same can be said of flowers as they can be flown in from many an exotic location. The prediction that half the world's population will be living in urban surroundings by 2050 is another startling change that distances us even more from the natural sources and production of food.

In my childhood we were glad to eat what we could and a slice of bread and pork dripping with a pinch of salt on it was deemed sufficient to keep out the cold and give nourishment to a growing boy. In those days families ate tripe, fried giblets and rabbit. Now I can visit my local supermarket to wander down the well-stocked chasms of goods, or even order online a vast array of foods gleaned from every part of the world and have it delivered by van. When I was a grocer's delivery boy pedalling away on my bike my customers considered themselves a cut above the rest as they could afford such a service. Now, a huge industry exists to deliver to a consumer society where instant service and instant credit is offered, expected and demanded.

Most children are now taken to school by car or travel on public transport. In my childhood I had to walk or go by cycle. Although my parents had a car from before the war it was only used for holidays and visits to relatives. Gradually, owning a vehicle became an imperative for employment and keeping in touch with relatives who had moved away, so that everywhere now is busy with traffic. The opportunity to travel widely across the world is another huge development. Men of my father's generation went abroad because they were drafted into the armed services. Their experiences in the jungles of Burma, the deserts of North Africa or in the battles across Europe for ever changed their lives.

I recall sitting in school as a child with world maps on the wall showing the countries of the British Empire marked in red. Many children enjoyed collecting postage stamps and were conscious of the diverse world that owed allegiance to the British Crown. Stamps from exotic places such as Tanganyika and Ceylon, the Seychelles and Mauritius worked their own particular magic. The world was changing then as the Empire was disintegrating but the Commonwealth was emerging. There was also the United Nations and many young people, including myself, joined the United Nations Association which encouraged an international outlook. Having had the privilege of travelling to other countries I am amazed at how our forebears colonised many parts of the world taking with them a distinct culture and outlook on life. In Canada, Australia, New Zealand, India, Hong Kong, Singapore and many other places the British made their indelible mark. It is a remarkable achievement reflected in the universal use of English as the world's prime language.

It is clear that people are speaking in a different way. Language itself is constantly changing with new words added to our vocabulary much of it coming from the world of computers. We can now "log on" or change "default mechanisms", "browse the net" or "download". Certainly, I tell myself in the wake of some research by Leeds University in 2005, my concerns when young over my regional accent were wasted energy. Ease of travel, entertainment and communication has changed the ways in which we speak. We are used to the accents of *East Enders* as much as *Coronation Street*. Since the sixties accents have merged, the Yuppie phenomenon of the eighties spawning the hard talking, money making, wheeler dealing language of Estuary. Extreme accents, including the one-time plum in-the-mouth RP (Received Pronunciation), or "posh", are now decried. I'm glad my elocution teacher failed to make me speak in this way. Now regional dialects are fashionable! Even the Queen has toned down her accent; a study of her Christmas Day speeches over the past half century will attest the fact!

Emile Durkheim the sociologist once said that the process of education was the mechanism whereby one generation passed on its values and knowledge to the next. He was speaking in the late fifties well before the communication revolution got into its stride and the education system became a political football. A whole range of influences from government, the media, the internet and their peers diminishes the control that home and school have upon the young. Parents and teachers, youth leaders, religious leaders and social workers are only a part of the input into the lives of developing children and young people. As they grow older the less likely they are of being influenced by an older generation and more by those who have something to sell them. Fashion and pop culture see children in terms of potential adults who have money to spend, if not their own then their parents'. Even very young children want designer labelled clothes and the latest in electronic gadgets or toys. One of the greatest dangers is the all-too prevalent drug culture which is one of the most vicious evils of the age.

In reflecting on that recent lesson I had with those primary school children I was struck by the fact that they are better fed, better dressed, have many more opportunities to indulge in sports and other activities, travel more and live in materially better homes than my generation could ever have dreamt about. Yet parental work patterns, home situations, the pressures of an increasingly urban society and the perceived threat from social deviants have led to a cotton wool culture; most children are not let out on the streets and not allowed to find their own way around their neighbourhoods.

The concept of authority has diminished. As a child I had a range of figures to look up to: there was my father, my teachers, the local policeman, the church minister and a range of others who kept my exuberant naughtiness in trim. There was a moral and spiritual ethos which worked in the same way meted out through Sunday School, youth club or uniformed organisations like the Scouts, Guides, Boys' and Girls' Brigades. This framework has largely gone and is due in part to a lack of commitment by a generation of adults who have lost a sense of service to the community; this is in itself an aspect of the diminution of the influence of religious faith which has traditionally taught that life has a vocational aspect.

Throughout my lifetime organised religion has been losing ground; I sensed it in my youthful years and I am well aware of it now that I am of retirement age. Yet in spite of rumours that the Christian Church is on the brink of collapse religious faith still continues and always will do so.

What has changed is that a broad range of faiths other than Christianity have been introduced into British society. The enthusiasm of their adherents often shames the lack-lustre commitment of some who call themselves "Christian" but never go anywhere near a church. Yet within Christianity itself there has been a huge surge in independent congregations, often meeting in school and community halls and homes, advocating a Pentecostal or charismatic style of worship. The last quarter of the 20th century saw many new hymns being written and the introduction of all kinds of musical instruments into worship. Whilst congregations in the "mainline churches" in Britain have generally declined new shoots of growth constantly emerge, and the Alpha course, originating at Holy Trinity Church in Brompton, has become a worldwide phenomenon. If mainline Christianity in Europe is in some decline the Church in Africa and Latin America is advancing at a rapid rate.

In spite of the apparent domination of secularism the latter part of the 20th century and the beginning of the 21st is an age of spirituality even though much is "unorthodox". *New Age* type ideas have developed over recent decades and are inherent in much modern film making; Superman's power is generated from crystals and many of the themes contained in Steven Spielberg's blockbusters are said to be *New Age* in origin. Astrology has become popular and it is commonplace for folk to identify themselves in terms of their star signs; they clearly half believe the generalisations by tongue-in-cheek articles contained in the mass circulation newspapers and magazines.

Many people from numerous walks of life are thinking in the same way, that somehow society as we have it in Britain lacks focus and direction. There is a feeling of disappointment that in spite of so much more affluence we are no happier than fifty years ago. The desire to acquire the latest designer possessions, especially clothes, even in very young children, is a concern for self image in an age when image seems to be everything. The heroes of the present are the celebrities of sport and entertainment who are themselves made possible, and also ruined, by the ever-present media. It has been proved that the happiest people are those whose concerns are outward rather than inward. With such an emphasis upon self there is little wonder that we are said to live in the age of "stress"; the very word is part of the language and expectation of modern society and inbuilt by social pressure into work patterns and domestic life.

Many people of all ages believe that improved discipline in home and school and in wider society must be part of a renaissance in self and public respect. There is a widespread sense that as a society we have lost something important. Many television programmes warn that they might contain "strong language", violence or explicit sexual activity; what ever happened to good manners and modesty? Is it inevitable that a more affluent society has to pollute its streets with litter and chewing gum, its walls with graffiti and its hedgerows with household rubbish? Perhaps it was the particular circumstances of my upbringing, but I felt there was a sense then that the values of my home were reflected in what was taught in school, in church and in the wider community. We were all on the same side and the freedom we had was won, as Churchill remarked, by blood, sweat and tears. We were a community who had to work together. What has been termed The Protestant Work Ethic or the Nonconformist Conscience certainly operated in my upbringing giving me an attitude that work was worthwhile and necessary for the betterment of all. One's life work should not only benefit oneself but society at large and each day was to be valued for its own sake; as one wit put it: "today is a gift because it is the present".

Yet social life never has been perfect; the perceived social unanimity of my young years was clouded by an immutable pecking order. Social and academic snobbery was rife. However appealing it is to think we can return to the apparent certainties of the past the world moves on. The fact is that a massive paradigm shift in the way we think has been going on since the dropping of the atomic bombs on Japan in 1945. Throughout the lifetime of most of us the technological changes that have produced the nuclear age have also produced the information age with the dominance of television and the computer.

Academics have tried to give useful labels to the period in which we live. One is "post modernism" which posits the idea that "modern" ways of thinking started sometime in the 18th Century *Enlightenment* when the three universal values of reason, order and science were seen as the fundamentals of human progress. Since the 1970s modernism has been questioned as it had led to a distinct lack of progress, indeed a return to appalling events such as the Holocaust, and issues like the nuclear threat and Third World Poverty. Science itself has lost its one-time ascendancy as the engine of progress and hope for the future. Hence we have entered a "post modern" era characterised by consumerism and urbanisation, the collapse of a sense of community, and a lack of any decisive goals for the world to aim for. Truth itself has become relative so there is no overarching view of the world or where it is going. Shopping in our culture has become the new leisure pursuit, the world has become a kind of theme park due to the ease of travel, history has become heritage and the images from television, computer and cinema, enhanced by stunning special effects, distort reality. It was so easy for us as a family driving over to Disneyworld in Paris to become absorbed in its happy unreality. We had breakfast with Goofy and Micky Mouse and for us that was temporarily "real". Post modernism, or simple escapist pleasure, has touched us all.

Vance Packard in a seminal book, *The Hidden Persuaders*, way back in the fifties asked the universal question of advertising: "Who is saying what to whom and with what effect"? Packard pointed out that there was a skill and craftiness in the advertiser's trade; a shop wanting to sell certain products put them at eye level or packaged them in a particular way. We see the phenomenon in our contemporary supermarkets that put small items like confectionery and magazines at the checkouts, just to catch us as we go to pay. Packard's question of who is influencing us is highly relevant in this age of the communication revolution. If the world is open to us sitting at our computer at home likewise, the world can access us. We are at the mercy of the "spammers" and "hackers", the hidden "spyware", "worms" and "viruses" that can infect our computers. As a result not only has a new language of computer-speak emerged, a whole new sense of distrust has grown to counteract unwanted intrusion; thus I have a "firewall", virus scanning software and other devices on my computer that attempt to give me some privacy.

The world is not only watching it is telephoning. The advent of the mobile telephone means that everyone can be in touch at any moment of the day and in every place. It can be very useful, but there is no respite unless one turns the instrument off, and few do: the business executive may be sitting in the bath fixing a deal, Auntie Gladys may be in the supermarket ringing home to see which tea bags she ought to buy, and youngsters are in constant touch sending each other text messages and images. It is considered vital to be able to keep in touch and with youngsters out and about in what is regarded as a more dangerous society it is comforting to know that they can be in communication.

One aspect of the traditional British reserve has changed forever; by mobile phone people tell their most intimate secrets in public and at the top of their voices. Internet chat rooms have become the new confessionals as total strangers can be apprised of one's innermost secrets. The mobile phone can be an intrusion or a danger so that churches, theatres, hospitals, even aircraft now have signs asking people to switch off as they enter. There is a strange irony in that modern communication devices like the mobile phone, the computer and television have an isolating effect, as people may speak to one another yet never meet or become simply voyeurs of life watching events on screen.

In the early days of television most people in the nation listened to the limited choice of programmes available. Everyone knew and would discuss the latest doings in *Coronation Street,* and when *Steptoe & Son* was at its height twenty million people tuned in. Such vast numbers even worried the government who asked for the day of the programme to be moved when it coincided with a particular General Election Day. Some church leaders even blamed television on the decline in attendance at Sunday evening services, and saw a kind of salvation in the invention of the video recorder as, they argued, the faithful could record their programmes whilst they attended church. If television at that time reduced the family circle to the family semi-circle by the nineties the multi-room TV phenomenon, where everyone in a house had their own television or computer in their rooms, profoundly effected family life; one person's privacy had become another's isolation. In a similarly curious way many people out and about in the midst of others now converse on their "mobiles" with unseen voices, somehow detached from their immediate surroundings and unaware of the simple reality of dealing with the people they are currently with. Many have become quasi-prisoners of their phones as if life and limb depended upon them.

Wariness has become another facet of our behaviour and thought. The general public, hyped by the media, is sceptical of the value of genetically modified crops, is unconvinced that the thin blue line of the police is adequate to stem the tide of criminality, and cynical about the ability of any government to fulfil its promises. The pattern of crime itself is changing. Much is fuelled by drug and alcohol abuse and has a violent edge. The housebreaker of earlier times relied on being able to sell off his spoils, but increasingly where the public demands brand-new items few want anything second-hand, thus theft from lorries and warehouses has increased and housebreaking decreased. Technology gives the criminal mind wider scope; the theft of personal identities through scams with credit cards at ATM cash dispensers is a new area of criminality.

Distrust does not apply just to politicians and journalists; all professionals such as lawyers, scientists, teachers, priests and doctors have a different status than in previous generations. Trust has largely gone; in medical matters diagnoses are questioned, second opinions sought and alternatives taken. The same applies to all professions, yet honest questioning is one thing, aggressive behaviour towards those who would serve us is another. I saw the gradual erosion of respect whilst I was in the teaching profession, and experiences in Accident & Emergency departments of hospitals when I did chaplaincy work for a time convinced me that simple tolerance for one another has diminished.

One aspect of life as it is lived at the turn of the 21st century is the growth of the compensation culture. When in Dublin during 2004 we heard of an Irish school which had banned running and skipping in the playground for fear of accidents which might end up in costly damages. One Dublin GP slated the legal profession for what it was doing to society in aiding and abetting prospective claimants. Members of other professions like teaching and medicine are becoming fearful of doing anything that might result in litigation against them. This phenomenon of always seeking someone to blame and to make money out of it is widely seen as immoral and cynical. The ambulance chasing lawyer with the "no win, no fee" motto slowly destroys social trust. Of course there should have been compensation for my Uncle Bill who lost the ends of all his fingers in the shoe factory presses where he worked forty years ago. Justice for all who suffer industrial injuries or the result of gross negligence is not in question, but the trivialisation of compensation is clearly a destructive phenomenon.

A frenetic rush seems to characterise modern living; the world seems to be in a headlong race and everyone is in a hurry with no time to stop and stare. The emphasis is upon speed whether it is in an instant coffee or the fastest broadband internet connection. Vehicles race along our roads making everywhere unsafe for both pedestrian and cyclist. Once the public highway was open and accessible but now the traffic "calming" measures such as "sleeping policemen" and "speed cameras" attempt to restrict and curb. What a contrast to the relatively empty roads of my young years when my friends and I could cycle for miles without fear of accident.

With the rush and bustle of contemporary life when one is never out of earshot of the mobile phone the times and places where one is able to find quietness and peace are now at a premium. During the nineties as a minister in Northampton I met folk who found their way to the chapel at Castle Hill; they expressed their amazement that within a bustling town such a place of peace and tranquillity could be found. Church buildings, once considered sacrosanct by even the most hardened criminal, could at one time be left unlocked for people to enter for prayer; now no longer, because opportunist thieves as well as organised criminals make no differentiation in what they steal. It became necessary to list and photograph all the church's items of furniture and mark them with invisible ink in case of theft. Modern life has thus increasingly lost its sacred places and sacred moments, especially with the decline of the traditional Sunday. The age-old rhythm of the week has altered with few mourning or even noticing its passing.

If all these issues are part of the "post modern" era then a cheerful piece of news is that academics have declared that post modernism is over and we are entering into a "post post-modern" world. In other words things are changing as they always have done, and, hopefully, changing for the better. In 2005 the huge need following the Asian tsunami and the human catastrophe in the Dafur region of the Sudan remind the world that there are widely held values such as justice, human rights and freedom from hunger and homelessness which must be fought for. With the passing of post modernism, however, have come new emphases upon demons and spirits and reliance upon astrology and spiritualism. Such ideas serve a continuing demand in human experience in giving some meaning, however shallow, for the perplexities of life. It is significant that the *Harry Potter* stories by J.K.Rowling and the *Lord of the Rings* trilogy by J.R.R.Tolkien find an almost universal readership and audience at this period of uncertainty.

When in 1976 Alex Haley produced his study of his African-American ancestry, aptly entitled *Roots,* it produced international interest in human origins. Haley had carefully researched his family's oral tradition that maintained they had originated seven generations earlier in the Gambia. His ancestor Kunta Kinte had been abducted whilst collecting firewood in the forest in 1769 and had survived the terrible slave-ship journey to the New World. *Roots* triggered a huge fascination in racial and personal identity. Genealogical research has become a major preoccupation in a period when the individual feels anonymous, subsumed and insignificant in the world's burgeoning population. Many people, especially the retired, who have some time to spend researching, enjoy exploring the intricacies of their "family trees". Finding our human origins has become a vital part in understanding who we are. It is, in itself, part of a quasi-spiritual quest in an age of doubt.

In late November 2000 two well-known fictional characters who had dominated British television for years were "killed off". One was the aggressive, embittered Victor Meldrew who clumsily fell into the most bizarre of circumstances; the humour rested on the pathos of an unfulfilled life. The series *One Foot in the Grave* was an apt title for a man whose life went one step at a time into a meaningless finality. The other character was Chief Inspector Morse, a man obsessed with the all absorbing job of being a detective. Morse was clever but miserable; except for his love of classical music his own personal life away from his job was empty and meaningless. In a real sense both Meldrew and Morse represented something of the culture of the time, an emptiness and lack of direction.

Yet there were voices of optimism beginning to be heard particularly in the cinema which itself had begun to make a remarkable transformation in its fortunes. Over recent years new multi-screen cinemas had been springing up in most towns. To add

217

to the upbeat feeling new British films, tinged with humour, began to appear based on issues concerning the industrial decline and social turmoil of the eighties. *The Full Monty (1997)* set the trend with a tale of men rising out of their depression following the closure of the Sheffield steelworks and the spectre of mass unemployment. They decide to do a full strip-tease act in order to earn a much needed crust, and in so doing learn to laugh in the face of adversity. It is a story of men coming back to a sense of self-worth. By the standards of vulgarity and strong language which has become the daily diet of so much television *The Full Monty* is quite mild. The film had an appealing vibrancy and sounded a clear note that marked an optimistic shift in British cultural thought. In 2000 another film, *Billy Elliot*, appeared, the story of a poor boy growing up in County Durham at the height of the miners' strike in 1984. Billy is put to developing manly pursuits such as boxing but is more interested in ballet dancing. His father and brother are initially outraged, but Billy's persistence and the encouragement of his dancing teacher result in him travelling to London to star in the Royal Ballet. *Billy Elliot* was another voice of hope and humour.

Steff and I have gladly made a regular return to the cinema in recent years. In 2003 we found the local cinema packed with women of all ages, mostly members of the Women's Institute. The film was *Calendar Girls* which tells the true story of a group of WI members who devise an unprecedented way of raising money for a cancer charity; the husband of one member had died from leukaemia. They decide to produce a calendar with members appearing in the nude, although in reality they are all strategically covered up by pot plants and other domestic items. Contemporary voyeurism would ensure the film's success like *The Full Monty*. It marked a massive shift in the image of the WI which for too long had laboured under the "jam and Jerusalem" label. This had been shattered in June 2000 when Prime Minister Tony Blair attempted to deliver a keynote speech instead of addressing WI concerns at their National Conference; he was jeered, booed and slow handclapped by an organisation that has transformed itself into a modern, powerful pressure group for social change.

What is particularly encouraging to me is the way in which the Christian Gospel remains a fundamental challenge in the market place of ideas; it holds out a positive teaching on building community both local and global, of caring for one another across all human boundaries and gives a hope for this life as well as the life beyond. It gives a sensible and convincing rationale of why we should care for one another. There has been a great growth of ecumenical co-operation within the Christian Church. Forty years ago different denominations kept their distance from one another and the Protestant-Roman Catholic divide was acute. One of the most satisfying duties I performed in my last year (2002) as the minister of Castle Hill was to preach at the Roman Catholic Cathedral in Northampton on the occasion of the Golden Jubilee of the Queen's accession to the throne. I began the address by pointing out the significance of a Protestant minister from the Reformed Tradition preaching on behalf of the Supreme Governor of the Church of England in a Roman Catholic Cathedral. There was spontaneous applause. The very fact that it happened is an indication of how far the Christian church has come in healing its own divided state; as I have often said "We all work for the same firm"!

It is my belief that a resurgence of the Christian perspective on the value of human life is long overdue. In all the disasters of the contemporary world what emerges loud and clear is the need for the world to grasp at its commonality, to embrace all people as belonging to one God-given world with the same rights and responsibilities and facing together the challenges of the future. It is this global appeal, summarised so well in the Parable of the Good Samaritan, which gives hope to the world family. It is one that embraces with respect differing cultures and faiths for, at a basic level, there is a universal cause for peace and goodwill. In all the outward changes these truths remain solid.

It is assumed that the contemporary world is dominated by a sense of fear; the terrorist may be lurking around the next corner. On the other hand the chances are that he is not there at all, although it pays to keep one's eyes peeled and to take seriously potential threats from the world's lunatics. In 2005 bio-terrorism or the release of a "dirty bomb" are the current fears. There is an uneasy tension that only half believes the warnings by government on the seriousness of the threat. Across the country multi agency exercises involving emergency services, local authorities, voluntary organisations, utility companies and other organisations have combined to rehearse their strategies in case of terrorist attack. New civil contingencies legislation enacted in the wake of 9/11 have sharpened preparedness for CBRN (Chemical, Biological, Radiological and Nuclear) dangers. There are also threats from conventional explosions or major accidents and natural disasters like flooding so that the overall effect of preparedness is most useful in that authorities are better able to deal with all incidents when they happen. I have been much impressed with the work being done by colleagues in the county's Emergency Planning team. Their emphasis is upon assessing risk and the impact upon society and how best to deal with it. In this we may all take comfort.

Yet what can we do apart from be prepared for the unexpected? In spite of the horrors perpetrated by the few the world must shrug its shoulders and get on with the task of living. Perhaps, then, we are not all helpless in the face of a seemingly changing world and have a role to play in shaping that world. It was a remarkable announcement in February 2005 by the Disasters Emergency Committee, which draws together major British charities, less than two months after the *tsunami* that £300,000,000 had been donated by the British public and that it was sufficient to meet immediate and longer term needs. Such a fact speaks volumes about the level of compassion that most people share for others in the global family and the power of the media to motivate the public in generating practical good.

There is no doubt that the tone of this final chapter has changed; it squarely addresses serious contemporary issues and seeks to make some analysis of where we are at present. Yet keeping a sense of humour is vital! Having the name Deacon has often been a source of amusement to me as well as others; when I was a Baptist deacon I was often introduced to visitors to the church as "Mr Deacon the deacon". The appropriateness of people's names associated with their roles in life has long fascinated me ever since I had a tooth extracted by a Mr Fillingham the dentist. I have come across a much respected orthopaedic surgeon Dr Sever, a CID detective named Chris Cross, a borough treasurer who signed his name "B. Quick" and a head teacher colleague Mr Canem. There is a police officer who rejoices in the surname of Grabhem, a horticulturalist by the name of Root, soldiers Captain Trench and Private Foot and undertakers named Mr Berry, Mr Coffin and Mr Mould. Clerical colleagues include the Rev Angell, the Rev Pagan and the Rev Tabernacle not forgetting in the Philippines the one-time ecclesiastic Cardinal Sin. When I was a head teacher in the eighties I let out a roar of laughter when the Local Authority appointed an official to deal with complaints relating to sexual harassment at work; his name was, appropriately, Mr Lusty!

I write this on 8 April 2005, a cut-off date in order to finalise this book for publication, and the eve of my 65th birthday. What a momentous day this has been with the funeral of Pope John Paul II having a global impact and even forcing a day's postponement of the civil marriage of the Prince of Wales to Mrs Camilla Parker-Bowles. That a Papal event should impact so decisively upon "Protestant England" in general, and the heir to the throne in particular, would have been inconceivable only a few years ago. Even the speed of change seems to be accelerating. In the past five weeks the ban on fox hunting has come into force, a vote in the General Synod of the Church of England has made it possible to debate the introduction of women bishops, and there has been the first ever announcement in *The Times* of the engagement of a gay couple. From the sublime to the ridiculous, from the tragic to the farcical the world's life moves on. Even in compiling the illustrations for this book the transition from black and white to colour and digital photography is striking; being able to download images from a digital camera straight into this text is amazing.

In this concluding chapter I have posed the question "How have we changed"? I have attempted to provide a few indications of the width and depth of developments as I see them over my lifetime so far. Readers will supply further examples from their own experiences and may agree or differ as to my interpretation of the plusses and minuses. I believe that we all need to see change as inevitable and to go along with it whilst keeping our own sense of proportion. Change needs to be used for the benefit of us all and must not be allowed to diminish our own values and sense of community. It is therefore of supreme importance that we nurture the young in a social environment that has strong humane and spiritual values.

Pertinently, I should ask myself "How have I changed as a person"? In answer I would say that through all the material changes and the hugely increased opportunities that life has given me I hope I have learned wisdom, yet feel essentially the same individual as I was in my youth. In those days there were wholesome influences which helped me become the person I am today, warts and all. I was given a purpose and a framework for life by kindly people: family, friends, teachers, youth leaders and ministers who cared about a ginger-haired boy with knobbly knees who when tipped into a swimming pool and told to swim eventually did just that. The purpose of this book is to celebrate and record my gratitude to them.

Spring 2005. Keeping busy in "retirement". The newly redesigned top garden.

"Thanks Grandpa for writing your book for us.
Love from Hannah and Natasha".